# TELLING GLANCES

# TELLING GLANCES

*Voyeurism in the French Novel*

*Dorothy Kelly*

*Rutgers University Press*
*New Brunswick, New Jersey*

Library of Congress Cataloging-in-Publication Data

Kelly, Dorothy, 1952–
    Telling glances : voyeurism in the French novel / Dorothy Kelly.
    p.  cm.
    Includes bibliographical references (p.    ) and index.
    ISBN 0-8135-1845-8 (cloth)—ISBN 0-8135-1846-6 (pbk.)
    1. French fiction—History and criticism.   2. Voyeurism in
literature.   3. Sex (Psychology) in literature.   4. Psychoanalysis
and literature.   5. Point-of-view (Literature)   I. Title.
PQ637.V73K45   1992
843.009'353—dc20                                        91-48336
                                                            CIP

British Cataloging-in-Publication information available

TO MY FAMILY

# Contents

**PART 2. TEXTUALITY AND THE PROBLEMATIZATION OF VOYEURIST TRUTH**

# Acknowledgments

I EXPRESS MY APPRECIATION to all my colleagues who participated in the Nineteenth-Century French Studies Colloquia in the past few years, both for the inspiration their talks provided and for the evaluations of my work that they gave me there. Also to be thanked are my colleagues in the Department of Modern Foreign Languages and Literatures at Boston University, in particular Susan Jackson for her comments on my analysis of *La Religieuse* and Jeff Kline for his on *L'Immoraliste*. Jonathan Ribner, in the Department of Art History, provided me with valuable information. Leslie Mitchner, at Rutgers University Press, has been an incisive reader, an efficient organizer, and a pleasure to work with. Finally, I thank my husband, Paul Blanchard, and my son, Eric, for their equally important help and understanding.

A portion of chapter 7 appeared previously in copyrighted form as "Seeing Albertine Seeing: Barbey and Proust through Balzac," in *Studies in Twentieth Century Literature* 14, no. 2 (Summer 1990): 139–157. A portion of chapter 5 appeared as "Realism as Voyeurism: Balzac's *La Peau du chagrin*" in volume 2 of the *Yearbook of Interdisciplinary Studies in the Fine Arts*. My thanks to the original publishers for permission to reprint those essays in revised and expanded form here. All translations from the French are my own unless otherwise indicated.

I gratefully acknowledge the Boston University Humanities Foundation research grant that paid for the permissions to use the Magritte image on the paperback cover.

# TELLING GLANCES

# INTRODUCTION

## The Voyeurist Gaze: Psychoanalysis and Literature

*The "subject" sidles up to the truth, squints at it, obliquely, in an attempt to gain possession of what truth can no longer say. Dispersing, piercing those metaphors . . . which have constituted truth by the premises of Western philosophy: virgin, dumb, and veiled in her nakedness, her vision still naively "natural," her viewpoint still resolutely blind and unsuspecting of what may lie beneath the blindness.*

—Luce Irigaray,
Speculum of the Other Woman

IMAGINE THE FOLLOWING PLOT SUMMARY: a man desires a woman who is enigmatic and unattainable. He not only desires to possess her; he also experiences an irresistible need to see her and to understand her, to know exactly what she is, or what she desires. But since this information remains hidden, the man resorts to spying on her in order to obtain the information he so desperately seeks; he resorts to an act of voyeurism.

To which novel does this summary belong? In various transformations, it belongs to *La Princesse de Clèves*, often labeled the "first" French novel in the canon; to *La Fille aux yeux d'or*, to *L'Oeuvre*, to *La Chartreuse de Parme*, to *La Peau de chagrin*, to *La Prisonnière*, to *Le Ravissement de Lol V. Stein*, to name some of the texts to be analyzed in the following pages. The pervasiveness of this structure in the French novel cries out for interpretation. Why is this plot used so frequently? What role does it play in each particular novel? What are the variations in these roles in different incarnations of the novel, such as the Enlightenment, the Romantic, the realist, and the New Novel? Why is the woman the object of investigation? Do women perpetrate acts of voyeurism in novels? What exactly do the voyeurs attempt to learn? What do they actually learn? Are the voyeurist acts presented ironically?

These are some of the questions to be answered in the following analyses of French novels from *La Princesse de Clèves* in the seventeenth century to *Le Voyeur* and *Le Ravissement de Lol V. Stein* in the twentieth. Clearly, in the choice of the term *voyeurism* psychoanalysis will provide a structural and theoretical underpinning for the analysis, and the psychoanalytic definition of voyeurism will be analyzed in chapter 1 of this study, "Voyeurism and the Primal Scene in Psychoanalysis." While defining the psychoanalytic concept of voyeurism, I will emphasize those aspects that are of particular interest in literary and cultural studies.

However, it is in chapters 2 through 4 that my own stance in relation to psychoanalysis, and along with it, my understanding of the relation between psychoanalysis and literature, become clear. There, psychoanalysis and literature are both analyzed as discourses that reflect and create constructions of knowledge, identity, and reality. Thus psychoanalysis and literature are seen to be two parallel discourses that attempt to explain why things are the way they are. Viewed in this way, it is not so surprising that both psychoanalysis and literature should be interested in the same questions about truth, knowledge, and desire, and that the discoveries that they make should be illustrated by plots of similar structure. It is not so surprising that ideological structures should mold in similar ways psychoanalysis and literature, the human beings that create them, and their manipulation of fantasy. In the cases of literature that we will study from the late nineteenth century through the twentieth century, literature and psychoanalysis both grow out of a communal soil of European ideology. And in the cases of the texts of the seventeenth, eighteenth, and nineteenth centuries, the literature of these earlier epochs is part of the soil from which psychoanalysis grows. (Think of Freud's familiarity with Balzac, for instance.)

In this study, I take what might be called a neo-Freudian perspective; I attempt to understand the ideological implications of the psychic structures described by psychoanalysis in the light of works by feminist theorists such as Luce Irigaray, Sarah Kofman, Juliet Mitchell, and Jacqueline Rose. Thus psychoanalysis is not taken as the "truth," but rather as a particular description by individuals at a particular time in history of the way the individual is constructed and understood, a description of how a society views that individual, a description that itself perpetuates certain ideological structures and that employs certain strategies in order to achieve coherence. I analyze psychoanalysis and literature in tandem in the final three chapters of part I; I combine the analysis of the three most important themes of voyeurism in psychoanalysis (seduction, castration, and the primal scene) with an analysis of three literary texts which each manifest one (or more) of those aspects. In so doing, I attempt to show how both psychoanalysis and literature construct similar scenarios, and just what the ideological implications of these scenarios are. The literary manifestations of voyeurism in these first three texts are relatively free from irony and questioning; that is why they remain in part I. They present a somewhat simplistic scenario of voyeurism, in which the strategies at work in that scenario are easy to detect; they afford a simple way to observe structures of voyeurism at work and will enable us to perceive these structures in somewhat less evident incarnations in other novels.

In part II of the book, this simplistic scenario of voyeurism becomes more complicated. In the analyses there, I continue to locate typical scenes of voyeurism, but I also show how certain literary texts both repeat the typical scenario of voyeurism and question it. Other texts rewrite the voyeurist scenario in such a way as to reveal the questionable strategies at work in voyeurism itself. Chapter 5, "Romanticism, Voyeurism, and the Unveiling of Woman," shows how in Balzac's La Peau de chagrin woman's body is first represented as the possible locus of the inscription of the truth of gender identity and of scientific truth, but then this belief in truth is undermined. The analysis of Stendhal's La Chartreuse de Parme goes on to show how this text undermines in an even more radical way the search for truth in the visibility of the woman's body, and how Stendhal illustrates the attempt to pass beyond this to another way of seeing.

Chapter 6, "Realism, Voyeurism, and Representation: The Artist's Gaze at the Woman," takes up a theme gleaned from feminist analyses of art: the gaze at the female nude model serves to construct feminine gender identity, and it situates the living female model in a social hierarchy in her relation to the male artist. Here two literary texts, the Goncourt brothers' Manette Salomon and

Zola's *L'Oeuvre*, take up as a part of their narratives the relation of art and the artist both to the representation of the female nude and to the real woman who is the model. The analysis of these texts shows how the naked woman as the embodiment of difference, of the other, is linked to a complicated network of stereotypical representations of the other in general. Zola's text, in fact, tells the story of an artist who attempts to get beyond this ideology but cannot see his own blind spot.

Chapter 7, "Voyeurism and the Elimination of Difference: Male 'I's/Eyes in First Person Narrative," looks at two twentieth-century authors, Gide and Proust, who continue many of the traditions of the nineteenth-century novel, including the symbolization involved in voyeurism. In these two texts narrated in the first person, it is a question of the construction of the identity of the male self in its relation to the other, and in both of these texts the self is shown to make a serious mistake in its constructions. Gide's text cannot see its way beyond the mistake, but Proust's text gives us an understanding of just what went wrong.

Chapter 8, "Voyeurism and the Recognition of Difference: Woman's Writing and the Space of Identity," examines two texts written by women at "opposite" ends of the novel's time line, Madame de Lafayette and Marguerite Duras. In these two texts it is not simply a question of male voyeurism, the pattern we have seen so often repeated, but of female voyeurism also. However, the outcome of female voyeurism is remarkably different from that of male voyeurism, and the concept of identity as constructed in these texts is also radically different. It is the difference of this identity that becomes the subject of the conclusion, "The Comic Gaze: A View Beyond Voyeurism."

What these readings will show is that literature perpetuates the repressive structures of voyeurism, but that at the same time literature contains moments of the questioning, doubting, and undermining of its voyeurist structures, of its own attempts to construct a coherent explanation of the way things are. Literature acts as if it were profoundly suspicious of the ideological foundations upon which its search for truth is based. This literary questioning of the repressive structure of voyeurism, has, I hope, enormous implications, implications that go beyond the boundaries of literature and psychoanalysis.

# Part 1

# VOYEURISM AS CONTAINMENT IN THE FRENCH NOVEL

# 1

# Voyeurism and the Primal
# Scene in Psychoanalysis

VOYEURISM IS DEFINED in the *Psychiatric Dictionary* as "obtaining sexual pleasure from watching an unsuspecting person who is nude, in the act of disrobing, or engaging in sexual intercourse" (Campbell 684). Here, the secretive nature of the gaze is important, as well as the erotic nature of the seeing: the voyeur takes pleasure not just in a generalized seeing but in secretly seeing a particular object or scene (the object is an object of desire). This is the most general definition of voyeurism, and it constitutes, in the main, the definition we will use as we study its literary manifestations.

For Freud, voyeurism has its origins in one of the component instincts, the scopophilic instinct (component instincts are the most fundamental elements of sexuality). The source of the instinct is the organ, the eye; the aim is to eliminate the tension produced by the instinct through the act of seeing; the object of that aim, the object to be viewed, is variable ("Instincts" 122). The scopophilic instinct is one of several component instincts that "function independently to begin with, tending to fuse together in the various libidinal organisations." The component instinct generally "becomes subordinate to the genital zone . . . at the end of a complex evolution" (Laplanche and Pontalis 74, 215). Sometimes, however, it will itself take over the primary libidinal role whose aim seeks fulfillment, such as in the "perversion" of voyeurism in which seeing is the principal means of obtaining sexual pleasure. Voyeurism, then, as a perversion, is the "persistence or re-emergence of a component part of sexuality," the scopophilic instinct; it is a "regression to an earlier fixation of libido" (Laplanche and Pontalis 307). In voyeurism, according to psychoanalysis, a universal human desire becomes excessively important; it becomes the chief means of obtaining sexual satisfaction, instead of remaining merely a component of genital sexual relations. This would be one of the differences—other, more technical differences will come up later—between "normal" pleasure taken in seeing the erotic object, a pleasure that aids in achieving the primary genital satisfaction, and the "perverse" scenario in which the ultimate object of desire is the seeing itself. However, one of Freud's points about normal and abnormal is that they are not separated by any clear-cut lines: "Some perverse trait or other is seldom absent from the sexual life of normal people" (Introductory Lectures 322). Thus the study of the nature of voyeurism and exhibitionism has implications beyond pathology because it may bring out certain constructions that inform more "normal" functions of seeing and being seen. Certainly, voyeurism functions in various ways in the everyday life of our contemporary world, as recent studies on film and pornography show. Likewise, in my analyses of voyeurist structures in texts, I am not claiming that these texts are perverse or that their authors were so; the point is rather that these texts manifest certain "perverse" or pathological structures which are a part of "normal" life.

In literature, the deflection of libidinal energy away from genital sexuality is, of course, necessary for reasons of censorship, but that explanation of the deflection cannot account completely for the persistence of voyeurism in literary texts, nor for the central role it plays in so many plot structures. Voyeurism in literature fulfills more than one simple role in the negotiation and attempted resolution of conflicts. One of the reasons for its prevalence is, perhaps, its link to another instinct that has an obvious importance in literature. In psychoanalytic writing, voyeurism and the scopophilic instinct go hand in hand with this other instinct and another malady: the instinct for knowledge, and the malady Freud labels "epistemophilia" ("Obsessional Neurosis" 245). This instinct to know is not, according to Freud, one of the basic component instincts, nor can it be classed as exclusively belonging to sexuality (Three Essays 194). It is rather a product of later development and Freud describes it as follows: "Its activity corresponds on the one hand to a sublimated manner of obtaining mastery, while on the other hand it makes use of the energy of scopophilia. . . . The instinct for knowledge in children is attracted unexpectedly early and intensively to sexual problems and is in fact possibly first aroused by them" (ibid.).

There are three points made in Freud's description here that will be important in our discussion of voyeurism in literature. First, the instinct for knowledge combines with the instinct to see by using the energy and aims of seeing. Second, the instinct for knowledge is related to a need to solve sexual problems. Third, the instinct for knowledge is a sublimation of the instinct for mastery. These three elements will be discussed in order.

First, the combination of the instinct for knowledge and the scopophilic instinct will be evident in all of the scenes of literary voyeurism to be discussed. The desire to see the erotic object aims not simply at seeing the object but also at learning what is considered to be important information about that object; knowledge is as much a goal as the vision itself. Second, this combination of the instinct to see and the instinct to know aims at a particular kind of knowledge: sexual knowledge. In Karl Abraham's extensive articles on scopophilia, he begins by discussing the normal childhood desire to see where people come from, how people are made, the processes of fecundation and birth. The child comes up with sexual theories and is confronted with the fact or fantasy of parental intercourse (Abraham). (Given the controversial nature of the status of the primal scene and of the scene of seduction as fiction or reality, we will simply skirt that problem for now by allowing for either possibility. Whether these experiences are psychical realities or historic events will concern us only later. Seduction will be regarded for the present as being possibly either or in some cases both.) The child wants to see intercourse, wants to see sexual organs, particularly the mother's; the voyeur continues in this vein, and needs to see the sexual act or object in order to construct a representation of the scene that might resolve problems involved in a previous conception or perception of this scene. This representation involves the repetition of the scene or the fantasy of what was seen (and this will be a link to the re-presentation of literature): "The voyeur tries to repeat the scene in an attempt to master it and deny what he saw. As no sight can bring about complete reassurance, voyeurs have to look again and again and attempt to see more and more" (Lane 56).

It is here that voyeurism and the instinct for knowledge join up with Freud's concepts of primal scenes and primal fantasies. Primal fantasies—the primal scene can be in some cases a fantasy; in some cases, a real observed scene; in some cases a combination of fantasy and reality—are, according to Laplanche and Pontalis, like collective myths: "They claim to provide a representation of and a 'solution' to whatever constitutes a major enigma for the child" (332). Fantasies are usually articulated in a visual, scenario-like form, creating a kind of "mise-en-scène" of desire—thus linking fantasy with the scopophilic instinct. The major themes of primal fantasies are those described by Abraham above as the enigmas of childhood: seduction (what is the origin of sexuality?), castration (what is the origin of gender?), and the primal scene of parental intercourse (what is the origin of the subject?). The scenarios of voyeurism in literature involve these three major scenarios, which will structure three analyses of literary voyeurism in chapters 2 through 4.

Thus, to the initial definition of voyeurism as the secret gaze at the erotic object or scene, we will add that an important part of the aim of the voyeur is to gain sexual knowledge from his gaze. It is a gaze that aims to learn truth, the truth about sexual origins. One must include psychoanalysis in those disciplines linked to the desire to know about origins, and one wonders if Freud, in discussing the role of the eye in sexual excitement, used the phrase "to cast a glance" in the following passage with that inclusion in mind:

> Let us begin by *casting a glance* [*Werfen wir zunächst einen Blick;* emphasis mine] at the way in which the erotogenic zones fit themselves into the new arrangement. They have to play an important part in introducing sexual excitation. *The eye* is perhaps the zone most remote from the sexual object, but it is the one which, in the situation of wooing an object, is liable to be the most frequently stimulated by the particular quality of excitation whose cause, when it occurs in a sexual object, we describe as beauty"
>
> (*Three Essays* 209; *Gesammelte Werke* 111).

Here Luce Irigaray's claim that Freud's theory has overcathected both the eye and the importance of seeing gender identity gains new force (Irigaray 48). In any case, the search for the truth that we will investigate in the fictional texts links up with voyeurism in both fiction and psychoanalytic theory.

Our third and final point in the discussion of Freud's remarks on the instinct to know is its development from the instinct for mastery. The instinct for mastery is nonsexual, and can fuse with sexuality secondarily to become sadism. Freud discusses the instinct for knowledge and the instinct for mastery in terms of the opposites activity/passivity; the aim of the instinct for mastery is actively to dominate or to destroy the object (or in another context, to master certain excitations in the subject). In relation to voyeurism, Otto Fenichel's analysis of the viewing of intercourse emphasizes that the person looking on may do so with a desire to destroy the object (Fenichel 377). What will be of importance to us in our analyses of literary texts is the sadistic violence sometimes attached to the instincts to know and see, and how this violence is represented in many scenes of voyeurism in literature.

Each of the three literary texts to be analyzed next illustrates one of these three themes of voyeurism: the theme of seduction in Diderot's *La Religieuse*, the theme of castration in Balzac's *La Fille aux yeux d'or*, and the canonical primal scene in Robbe-Grillet's *Le Voyeur*. These texts were chosen both because they use these three particular themes and because they span three centuries of French literature. The analysis of the ideological roles these three themes play in the texts (and in psychoanalysis) will be carried out through a close reading of each novel. The prevalence of voyeurism in these texts from different time periods and schools will begin to reveal the extent to which the scene of voyeurism is an important element of the novel form; the textual analyses in the main chapters of the book should continue that revelation.

# 2

# The Primal Scene of Seduction,
# Voyeurism, and La Religieuse

*We exit from life as if from an enchanting spectacle; the blind exit as if from a prison cell.*

—Diderot,
*Lettre sur les aveugles*

IN THE PRIMAL FANTASY of seduction, the enigma posed is the origin of sexuality itself: how does one become a sexualized individual? In an analysis of the primal scene in its relation to seduction, several points need to be emphasized. First, the "scene of seduction" is situated at a point in time of childhood when the experience is not "understood." Only later, at a period of higher development, will the event be interpreted. Thus, at the moment of experiencing the scene, the child passively submits to an unmasterable and incomprehensible event. The passivity is the "seductive" nature of this scene; it is the child's excitation and passivity in the face of an unmasterable experience. (Seduction in the psychoanalytic context here means passive submission to the sexual advances of another.) In the case of the Wolf Man, his early seduction by his sister was an unmasterable and unacceptable primal scene. The Wolf Man's case shows how voyeurism links up with this original scene of seduction: the Wolf Man developed an active "voyeurist" desire to undress his sister as a way of mastering and rewriting what was originally his role in a passive, helpless position of seduction by her ("Infantile Neurosis" 19). In the active repetition of the scene, we have the combination of the desire to master with the desire to see, all included in the act of voyeurism. We also have the need on the part of the male child to overcome the feminizing passivity of the original scene by reversing it in a masculine active viewing, while at the same time being able to repeat and experience through the rewriting of the original scene its original, passive pleasure.

Indeed, in the literature on voyeurism, this structure of reversal is emphasized. In the fantasy of the primal scene (whether it be the memory of a real event or a fiction), the child, who is witness to parental intercourse, is "helpless yet fascinated in the face of strong excitation, terrified of castration," and "the child identifies with what was seen and both wishes and is tempted to repeat the experience" (Lane 56). The voyeur does go on to repeat the experience in a more active way by seeking out and setting up these scenes, in the main to grapple with the passivity experienced in his subjection to that seduction scene.

We can not continue here, however, without discussing the radical revision and reversal that the theory of seduction underwent in the evolution of Freud's thought, and this very revision will help us pinpoint critical areas in the problem of seduction that will be echoed in Diderot's *La Religieuse*. The main revision Freud made in his understanding of seduction is that he ceased to believe that all of his patients' tales of seduction were based in fact, and he decided instead that they were fantasies of seduction created by the patient.[1] This shift in emphasis from the traumatic and abnormal origin of hysteria in a real event to the fantasized construction of the event in the subject has been considered a major founding point in the development of psychoanalysis itself. It is at this point that Freud discovers the sexuality of the child (in the seduction theory, the adult forced sexuality on the uninitiated child); from seduction as abnormal, he can move to Oedipus and infantile sexuality as universal (McGrath 197).

This is a very interesting shift in many ways, and it should be viewed from the two different directions it took in Freud's thought. On the one hand, it involves for Freud the recognition that the self needs to blame the other for the seduction when in fact it is the self that is at fault (it was only a fantasy); on the other hand, in Freud's

text, the very removal of the blame from the other to the self entails
a more radical accusation of another "other" that goes unseen. An
analysis of these two views of the shift in Freud's thought is necessary, because an understanding of the strategy of this shift will be
important for the parallel between psychoanalytic scenes of voyeurist seduction and literary ones.

The need to see seduction, or the origin of one's own sexuality, as
an experience coming from an outside perpetrator who intrudes
upon internal subjectivity is a need Freud recognized in himself
through his own self-analysis. Just as his patients posit the initiation
into sexuality in an external agent, so Freud recognized in himself
the need to blame his father for his neurosis: "If the collapse of the
seduction theory cleared fathers in general of responsibility for the
neuroses of their children, it also removed his suspicions that his
own father was to blame for his neurosis" (McGrath 212). Freud's
discovery was that seduction is a scenario that comes from within,
not from without, and "his search for the sexual basis of hysteria
revealed not fact but phantasy, not history but myth, and as in the
case of Oedipus, his unexpected discovery implied that he himself
was the guilty party" (McGrath 217). Seduction and neurosis come
from within (even though it may be in the final sense, the way the
self deals with a familial situation that comes from without). Thus it
would seem that Freud became "unblinded" and saw that he had
been blaming an innocent victim (fathers and his father) when in
fact he and the hysterics were to blame.

However, Martha Noel Evans adds another twist to this victimization. She shows that in fact the blame was rarely placed on fathers
in Freud's writings on hysteria and that fathers are mentioned
mainly when Freud *abandons* the seduction theory. It seems that
fathers are protected both in the writings on hysteria and then in
Freud's recognition of his own, rather than his father's, guilt. In
fact, the word *seduction* is itself rather a strange choice in the early
work on hysteria, because what was really at stake was rape, incest,
and the victimization of women (by fathers), not "seduction." Furthermore, although it would seem that the blame was turned away
from fathers onto all human beings, in the practical world of the
analyses of Freud's patients, another scenario unfolds. The (mainly)
female hysteric is blamed for the invention of the false accusation:
she really wanted to be seduced by the father and she invented the
scene. Thus Freud's theory "enacts and conceals the abuse of

women" (Evans 76). In the very act of seeing his own guilt in relation to his father, he is blind to his new guilty position in which he ignores what is possibly real abuse of girls by their fathers (especially in Dora's case) and puts the blame on them for "seduction."

This need to foist the blame from oneself onto an external object, or, conversely, to recognize that the self is the guilty party, is one that will come up again and again in the literary texts. The problem of seduction is one that plays itself out on the borders between self and other, between active seduction and the passive submission to it. (Similarly, we saw how, in cases of voyeurism, the passive experience needs to be mastered through an active viewing.) As Jane Gallop points out, the participation by two subjectivities, rather than the forced imposition of the will of one subject on the other, is what differentiates seduction from rape (Gallop 56). Thus, on the one hand, seduction entails the recognition of the other's subjectivity (the other is not viewed as pure object), but on the other hand, it can also be involved in the subjugation and blame of the other.

These problematic borders of guilt seem to call up the need to establish borders either by the self's denying any role in seduction and by its placing the blame outside onto the other, or by admitting responsibility for seduction by recognizing that it originates inside the self. Seduction needs to be inside or outside, actively perpetrated or passively submitted to, and not in-between. What is unseen by Freud in this shift from "seduction" to oedipal configuration is that *he* takes the place of the hysterical woman in his own relation to his father (the hysteric invented seduction, Freud invented his neurosis) just as he rids the structure in question of femininity (from the girl's relation to the father it becomes the boy's relation to the father). In a sense, Freud takes the structural place of the woman as he eliminates her from the scenario. This gender switching, which could be considered a kind of ambiguity of gender and which is specifically related to activity and passivity, will return as a problem later in Part I.

The final element to be mentioned in the discussion of seduction and its role in Freud's thought, before we turn to *La Religieuse*, entails a different kind of ambiguity, which Jane Gallop identifies in *The Daughter's Seduction*. She notes, as she retraces Cixous's analysis of Freud, the various evolutions in Freud's positioning of the blame for seduction in hysteria: from fathers, children, mothers, blame moves in the final instance to the maid (143–145). The maid is a "threshold figure," inside and outside the family, in the same house but in another class, mother and not-mother. Her marginal status is threatening and gives rise to the conflicting needs to seduce her (assimilate her) and to abandon her (expel her). Here her marginality relates not just to subject/other but to economics, class, and politics. The conflicting need to keep her in and send her out, to expel her from the realm in which her ambiguity can contaminate and trouble, and to retain her there where her contamination can homogenize the family, will be seen in what I call the centripetal and centrifugal forces at work in La Religieuse.

To summarize, the elements to be investigated in the scenarios of seduction in the voyeurist scenes in La Religieuse are the contamination of borders between self and other, inside and outside, desirer and desired, and the strategies employed in the text to contain and eliminate those ambiguities. The scenes of seduction and the scenes of voyeurism in Diderot's text work together to define dangerous elements in society and to relegate them to their "proper" spheres. Finally, just as Evans studies the repression of women in Freud's text, I will show how the strategies of seduction in La Religieuse also work to "enact and conceal the abuse of women."

In general terms, the entire text of La Religieuse is a peephole into the secrets of convent life. It allows the reader to feel he or she has gained access to that closed space, which is the secret of female sexuality. The hidden knowledge we gain is supposedly knowledge about what happens in convents, what happens when women group together, what women do when they are by themselves (questions often posed and answered by pornography).[2] We gain access to what Suzanne labels "the spectacle of my pain and humiliation" (124). The novel is proffered as a text written by a woman, but of course, it is really a man's representation of that woman's text.

There are, nevertheless, two main acts of voyeurism that are more specific than this generalized peek at woman. One takes place in a specific scene of seduction in which Suzanne, the innocent "childlike" nun, is seduced by the more knowledgeable abbess—this scene parallels Freud's original notion of the innocent child being unknowingly initiated into sexuality, specifically by the mother. Freud states that the mother, in the normal activities of hygiene, is the child's first seducer (New Introductory Lectures 120). Suzanne, like the hysterics who recount their seductions to Freud, reveals to us the primal scene of her seduction. (Let us not forget that many of the nuns, including Suzanne, display hysterical symptoms.) However the assignment of guilt to the adult other is, as in Freud, much more complicated than this, and, in our analysis to follow, we will see that the blame placed for the seduction is subtly assigned by the text to Suzanne in many cases; to the woman in almost all cases.

The second scene of voyeurism occurs earlier in the novel, when the nuns in the convent strip Suzanne bare in order to learn her secrets: they steal parts of her clothing, they strip her while looking for her documents, they make of her a spectacle in the church for all to see. Here we have the erotic spectacle of the woman's naked body (the desire to see the erotic object) conjoined with the desire to learn the truth (just what Suzanne's documents contain, just what her intentions are). This is our classic scene of voyeurism. In order to understand the function of these scenes of voyeurism and their relation to seduction in this text, let us turn to a detailed analysis of the ambiguity of seduction and the hiding and revealing of women's secrets.

The first element of Suzanne's life in the convent that must be emphasized is that she does not wish to be there: it is a prison for her. Her imprisonment in the convent displays, clearly, the need to master her, and the sadistic actions and voyeurist viewings inflicted on her in the convent are strategies in that attempt to master and imprison. As we saw earlier, the instinct for mastery relates to voyeurism and to the instinct to know and see, as does the sadistic nature of that mastery (a desire to destroy the object).

Why is Suzanne "imprisoned" in the convent: just what is there about her that needs mastering? On one level, readers, such as Roland Desné, see her imprisonment as a critique of the institutions of society that suppress the individual. He reads this novel as a "fable of liberty": "The testimony of Suzanne Simonin accuses a society and a Church that work together to smother in a human being the natural desire for liberty" (22–23). But, on another level, there is a different reason for her imprisonment. Suzanne is forced to enter the convent because she does not "fit" in her world. She figures as a transgressive element in seemingly every sphere.[3] She is the "maid" in the scenario of seduction because of her ambiguous place.

Suzanne manifests numerous ambiguities and transgressions, which need to be confined by voyeurism and imprisonment. First, in the world, she is not an appropriate and proper member of her family because she is illegitimate. She personifies the end product of her mother's transgressive sexuality, because her mother had an affair outside her marriage, outside the confines of society's limits. Thus Suzanne from "before her birth" figures transgression, and most explicitly the transgression of female sexuality.

Indeed, if we take a look at her other "mothers," which she finds in the convent—Mme de Moni, Sister Sainte-Christine, the abbess d'Arpajon—we see that they represent various aspects of transgressive sexuality, aspects which society deems transgressive and which "normal" sexuality represses: homosexuality (the abbess), sadism (Sister Sainte-Christine), and female pleasure (Mme de Moni's ecstatic transports). All of these aspects of sexuality are those which society prefers not to acknowledge, and since they all involve women, they link transgressive sexuality to female sexuality.

Thus the confinement of these three substitute mothers enacts the confinement of certain types of sexuality by the institutions of society; and since these three women stand in for Suzanne's mother and her transgressive sexuality, they also represent the need to confine "free" female sexuality itself, or, more generally, the need developing in the eighteenth century to confine women to the enclosed, "domestic" sphere. This confinement has as its object Suzanne, the female product of illicit female desire. Thus rather than looking at the transgressive nature of the substitute mothers as being simply the *result* of convent life, we might see through that fictional causality to a hidden image of the containment, imprisonment, and surveillance of female and transgressive sexuality itself, of the sexuality manifested and represented by these women, Suzanne and her different mothers.

Tacked onto this figural confinement of female sexuality is also the policing of certain other transgressive behaviors, and one thinks constantly of Foucault's analysis of the transformation of punishment in the eighteenth century, the move, as he calls it, toward surveillance, confinement, and the reshaping of the criminal.[4] One of these transgressive behaviors that must be confined is difference. Suzanne is "different" in her appearance, for she is unusually attractive (she is *seductive*), pleasing to look at, so much so that she actually wishes to be mediocre: "Oh, how many times I wept because I was not born ugly, stupid, dumb, proud, in a word, with all the faults that made them succeed with our parents!" (40). And as her mother tells her, "Your striking beauty has been your downfall" (59). Suzanne's beauty is too seductive, and it must be hidden.

Her difference in one instance relates to a kind of taboo that adheres to her nature when she is punished, for no one may speak to, help, approach, or touch her or the things she uses (99). She, like a taboo object, is at once special in a good, remarkable way (her beauty, intelligence, and talent) and in a bad, unclean way (one must not touch her, she seems demonic): "The meaning of 'taboo,' as we see it, diverges in two contrary directions. To us it means, on the one hand, 'sacred,' 'consecrated,' and on the other 'uncanny,' 'dangerous,' 'forbidden,' 'unclean' . . . Thus 'taboo' has about it a sense of something unapproachable, and it is principally expressed in prohibitions and restrictions" (Freud, *Totem* 18). She is the product of illicit sexuality, and thus she represents the transgression of one of the objects of the taboo: "guarding the chief acts of life— birth, initiation, marriage and sexual functions, etc., against interference" (Freud, *Totem* 19). In her positive and negative qualities we have another instance of her maidlike, ambiguous nature.

One of the most important functions of the policing action of cloistering seems to be that of holding in another often "uncanny" transgressive situation, insanity, and of eliminating it in many cases, for the insane seem to die an early death in the convent. One of the first and most important things Suzanne sees in the convent is the mad nun, and she sees in the fate of that poor soul her own: "It happened that one day one of these nuns escaped from the cell in which she was kept. I saw her . . . I saw my own fate in that of this unfortunate woman" (45).

Indeed there seems to be a sort of contagion of this madness, which may explain the necessity for its isolation and enclosure. And this contagion comes perilously close to the notion of seduction: one is contaminated by sexuality or by insanity through visual contact with the scene of the other. Just after Suzanne sees this mad nun and imagines their common fate, Suzanne succumbs to a kind of attack: "A general weakness came over me in which my knees were knocking together and my teeth were chattering . . . I remember neither having undressed myself, nor having left my cell; even so, I was found in my underclothes, stretched out on the ground at the door of the mother superior, motionless and almost lifeless" (50). A similar attack occurs on the day of her vows, when she loses her memory of that day and of her stripping of her worldly clothes, a loss which she describes as being "insane" ("physiquement aliénée," 70). The loss of memory and consciousness, of "knowledge" in a certain way, and the exposing of one's body are two of the recurring symptoms of madness in the text, symptoms which in the convent are seemingly contagious. Mme Moni succumbs to similar blackouts in her transports, and Suzanne also experiences such transports: "They did not dare interrupt me; they were waiting for me to come out of the state of transport and of fervor in which they saw me" (89). "I have been told that certain melodies, certain inflections changed my face entirely; at those times I was completely beside myself, I almost did not know what was happening to me" (182). Another aspect is the loss of power over one's body, when one is subjected to convulsive movements: "I heard nothing of what was being said around me; I was reduced almost to the state of an automaton; I noticed nothing; I made only now and then some small convulsive movements" (69).

Indeed, the loss of conscious control and the exposing of one's body are exemplified in a single symbol used for both of the women who most visibly transgress sexual mores: Suzanne and the abbess. Suzanne, who is "uncanny," who represents the transgression of the boundaries of social regulation, who cannot "fit" into the structure of society of the time, likewise cannot "fit" into the *veil and habit* which represent the policing of sexuality: "I saw that my habit was rumpled, that my veil was turned almost completely around, and it had fallen on my shoulders . . . I soon came to my senses; I felt the indecency of my state and the imprudence of my words" (95). Her inability to fit into the veil is a sign of her ambiguous and transgressive nature, and in this particular case, the loss of control and the exposing of her body in her fallen veil are the *result* of the policing activities of the sadistic Sister Sainte-Christine. Successful policing results in the unveiling of dangerous secrets, so that further efforts of control can be put in place. This is the "goal," in a sense, of Sister Saint-Christine's tactics: either to make Suzanne conform to the rules and become a nun—to *veil* her (contain her)—or make her "mad" and thus perhaps to eliminate her transgression in the usual outcome of madness, death. Suzanne's tenuous position can be seen when she becomes "mad" and exposes herself in that moment of loss. But immediately after, she regains her control: "I gathered up my veil and put it back; then, turning toward her, I said to her: 'Madame, I am neither insane nor possessed; I am ashamed of my frenzy, and I ask your forgiveness for it; but judge from this how poorly convent life suits me' " (96). Here, however, her reveiling is her strategy of survival through masquerade. She returns to her calm struggle to free herself from her constraints by covering herself up, accepting the veil only to fight against it.

The other person who is "between" submission and revolt is the abbess. After Suzanne rejects her advances, the abbess alternates between her desire to continue in her transgressive behavior and her desire to confess and to adhere to order. This quandary is symbolized by her oscillating behavior and, once again, by the veil: "At times she would look for me, at times she would avoid me, she would sometimes treat us all, the others and me, with her usual kindness, sometimes also she switched suddenly to the most outrageous rigor . . . her day consisted of leaving her room and returning there, in taking up her prayer book and putting it down, in going up and then down stairs, in lowering her veil and in raising it" (189). Thus the veil that does not fit, the ambiguous veiling/unveiling, acts as a symbol that identifies those women who figure the transgressive and who occupy the place of in-betweenness. This in-between becomes almost allegorical when it becomes the uncomfortable place of the struggle between two powerful "institutions," the world (juridical law) and the convent: "I will be, so to speak, between the world and the convent" (87).[5]

The need for sequestration and cloistering would seem to show, then, that the danger these women pose is not only that they will not adhere to the rules and regulations of society but that they will spread the infection of their rebellion to others. Indeed, the contagion of madness seems to be spread through the *eyes*, because a short while after Suzanne first sees the mad nun in the first convent, she repeats, imitates, the symptoms of madness herself. If, as we saw, Suzanne sees her fate in that of the mad nun, the important thing is that she *sees* it: "It happened that one day one of these nuns escaped from the cell in which she was kept. I *saw* her" (45, emphasis mine).

This is then the "medical" purpose of the convent: to lock up the dangerous elements of society which threaten to contaminate the healthy elements with their transgressions. Before Suzanne enters the convent, her unpoliced sexuality, her illegitimacy, seems to give rise to the desire in others to transgress laws. Her sister's suitor desires her in an incestuous situation: "My older sister was sought after by a charming young man; I noticed that he preferred me, and that she would always be only the pretext for his frequent visits" (40). And, in a bizarre, suggestive scene, it is Suzanne's "stepfather" who barges into her room in his nightclothes: "One morning, at nine o'clock, my door was opened suddenly: it was M. Simonin who entered in his robe and nightcap. Ever since I had learned that he was not my father, his presence caused me only fear" (61). Suzanne seems to spread to others that desire to "open the door" of illicit sexuality. If one is allowed to open the door and to escape, many others will follow: "One secretly felt that, if they allowed the doors of these prisons (the convents) to be lowered for one unhappy woman, the mob would approach them and seek to force them down" (119).

This threat of the contagion is most remarkably symbolized in Suzanne's understanding of the abbess's sexuality. She believes it is a kind of illness "a sickness which she was prone to get" (158); she thought that "perhaps this illness could be caught, and that Sainte-Thérèse got it, and that I would get it, too" (158). And she does, indeed, "catch" it when she is aroused by the abbess's advances, even though she does not understand what is happening (the primal scene in Freud's seduction theory, in which an unknowing and innocent victim is initiated into a sexuality that cannot be understood at that moment but can be interpreted only later). The danger posed by Suzanne is that of seduction by contagion; if one sees, one is initiated into desire, and the desire to transgress.

Suzanne likewise seems to infect others with her rebellion so that they no longer function harmoniously in the convent. Mme Moni loses her ability to go into trances because of Suzanne: "I felt, however, as my taking of the vows approached, a melancholy so deep that it made my superior undergo terrible trials; her talent abandoned her, she admitted it to me herself" (65). Similarly, after Suzanne's physical illness, her good friend, Sister Ursule, seems to "catch" the same illness, and it turns out that Ursule has also dangerous written material which must be kept from view.

The imperative in this text is then a centripetal one, in the sense that transgressive elements of society must be enclosed, turned in upon themselves, so that they cannot infect others outside, so that they cannot seduce. This turning-in figures most evidently in the image of the abbess, who links together autoerotism and homosexuality when she questions the innocent Suzanne about her sexual practices. Here woman's dangerous sexuality is imprisoned, turned in upon itself and prevented from infecting anyone except those who are already tainted (Suzanne, in the sense of her illegitimacy).

This imprisoning keeps the transgressive elements from communicating their disorder to the outside world because it keeps them in an "invisible" state; for as we saw, the madness of the convent seems to be spread through the eyes. Thus the veil of the convent keeps these women from visibility, it keeps them in the dark, and in more ways than one, for one of Suzanne's main problems in the text is that she does not *know*, she is "in the dark" about the events around her, not knowing the reason for her imprisonment (her illegitimacy) until very late in the game, after she has already served time. As she herself says, the purpose of the convent is to hide its own state, as does the mother of the novitiates: "She attempts to hide from you all the thorns of that life; it is a course of the subtlest and most calculated seduction. It is she who thickens the shadows that surround you" (44). Indeed, when she has recounted the advances of the abbess to her confessor, he does not let her know why these things are bad, and she feels that she is a "blind" traveler who is somehow at fault: "Such would be a traveler who was walking in the shadows, between precipices that he did not see, and who was struck from all sides by subterranean voices that cried out to him: 'It is your fault!' " (181).

The convent resembles Foucault's prison, not only because it locks up the bodies of the transgressors, but also because it is the locus of surveillance, of spying. Like the panopticon, it maximizes surveillance and imprisonment. It is here that surveillance and voyeurism link up. When Suzanne is suspected of communicating with other nuns against the orders of the superior, an act termed "a revolution in my head" (78), she says, "They spied on us: they surprised me, sometimes with one of them, sometimes with another" (75). Later she is shadowed quite overtly by another nun (101). Significantly, one of the tortures inflicted upon her is that they steal parts of her clothing (75); they expose her to an even ruder surveillance by stripping her, then by making her strip before them as they search for the abridged form of her autobiography (79), then again when they strip her in their search for her documents, for the "truth" which only she can provide (82): "In the end the superior thought that it was possible to know the truth only through me" (80). Their search for the truth of her illicit nature is figured in the text by their stripping of her body, as if seeing the woman's body would make the truth evident to them, and the physical exposure seems somehow to lead to "your most secret thoughts" (143). When they accuse her of being possessed, she becomes a spectacle in the church for all to see (110–111), and when her legal plea is defeated, her pain becomes a spectacle for all to see: "The nuns examined me from a distance; they wanted to lose nothing of the spectacle of my pain and humiliation" (124). This attempt to expose the body of woman to learn Truth is, as we have already seen, important in the structure of voyeurism and will be repeated in nearly every text we study.

This unveiling is shown to be an effect of power in the latter part of the text, when the abbess's sexuality and the power she wields are directed toward Suzanne. As the abbess says, "I am the one who recompenses or punishes" (168). Her attempted seduction is really a kind of power play, a seduction and coercion which begin with the unveiling of Suzanne's body: "On the first evening, I received a visit from the mother superior; she came when I was undressing. It was she who removed my veil and my headband, and who readied me for bed; it was she who undressed me" (144). (Curiously, the one being seduced here is the one shown in the alluring act of disrobing: this is, perhaps, another instance of the way in which this text makes the nature of seduction ambiguous—who is seducing, who being seduced?) The abbess needs to watch Suzanne constantly: "She watched every move I made" (187). Later her caresses them-selves become a spectacle for Sister Thérèse (146).

The stripping off of one's clothes figures, in a more general way, dispossession as a means of rendering powerless: "I undressed myself, or rather, they tore off my veil, they stripped me, and I put on this habit" (127). We have already seen how the attempt to keep some-one in the dark is a way of keeping the power of knowledge from them. Similarly, the madness which results from the policing tech-niques is considered a loss of power over one's self and is linked to dispossession: "She was locked up, *deprived* of the practice of the faith: she became *insane* from it" (121, emphasis mine). When Suzanne is about to enter the convent she is dispossessed of her self and the control of her actions (69). Her madness figures her ab-sence from herself and her absence from her control of her own destiny: "They were resolved to dispose of me without my consent"

(48). And when she continues to defy Soeur Sainte-Christine, she is slowly dispossessed of all her physical belongings: "I was without tapestries, without a chair, without a prayer bench, without curtains, without a mattress, without covers, without sheets, without a single dish, without a door that would close, almost without an unbroken pane in my windows" (118).

This dispossession is also the theft of one's ability to speak and to speak out, for if Suzanne would like to object to her entrance into the convent, her words desert her and, as she explains: "I heard nothing, I saw nothing, I was dumb; they led me and I followed; they asked me questions, and they answered for me" (43). At one point she is physically unable to speak, an inability which she links to the ultimate dispossession, death: "At this idea of approaching death, I wanted to cry out; my mouth was open but no sound came out" (108).

This move toward exposure is only toward exposure inside the walls of the convent, however; it is a kind of spy tactic to keep the machinations of power in place. When it comes to the outside world, there is no attempt at exposure through surveillance, but rather a tendency to "sur-veil," to double the veil, in a move toward protecting the secret transgressions within. This "sur-veiling" parallels the turning-in-upon-oneself in a kind of *mise en abime* of veiling. There is first the veil between the public sphere of the church and the nun's sector, a veil significantly lowered when Suzanne makes clear her unwillingness to "take the veil": " 'Sirs, and above all you, my mother and father, I call on you as witnesses . . . . At these words one of the nuns lowered the veil of the grill, and I saw that it was useless to continue" (52). This veil is echoed in the nun's veils, which hide their faces. Significantly, when the abbesse is struggling to expose her behavior to someone from the outside, their new director, this move toward exposure to the outside is counterbalanced by the fact that "that poor mother superior came out only when her veil was lowered" (191). If Suzanne is in prison already in the convent, then when she is suspected of writing things which would expose the convent to the outside world, she is imprisoned in a prison within a prison: "They opened with huge keys the door of a small underground room, where they threw me down onto a mat" (83).

The text sets up a kind of oscillating movement (a striptease?) between covering up and exposing which can be seen in Suzanne's

relation to her own situation. On the one hand, she wants to shed
the veil, to expose herself and to break out into the outside world:
"Oh! when will I arrive at the moment when I will be able to tear
them up (the veil and the habit) and to throw them far from me!"
(95). Her tactic is to send letters from the inside to the outside,
letters which prefigure her "exposure" and release to the outside as
they "expose" her situation. The letters partake of a centrifugal
force which aims toward the outside and which opposes the centripetal force of imprisonment and "normalizing." On the other hand,
when she is inside the convent, she feels the constant need to hide
herself from the surveillance by covering herself up. The ironic
confrontation between hiding and revealing is symbolized in the
following sentence in the metaphoric representation of clothes and
writing: "I had acquired the habit of sleeping fully clothed; I acquired another, it was that of writing my confession" (78). Here at
the same time she covers her body from the prying inside eyes and
sends out her plea for liberation to the outside world. Similarly, if at
the end of her life the abbesse wears a veil most of the time, she also
writes notes to everyone, displaying the double tendency to hide
and to expose (190–191). This contradictory movement of keeping
in and sending out forms a kind of parallel with the ambivalent
nature of seduction itself, which hovers in a state between origination from within and origination from without.

Obviously, Suzanne's writing is a subversive gesture in the text
and a clear threat to the power of the convent to imprison her.
Those in power try to steal her letters in order to expose them *inside*
the convent and thereby control them. This theft of her letters is a
kind of voyeurism, for her written exposure of herself is seen by the
wrong eyes; her letter to her mother, for instance, circulates among
all those who have an interest in keeping her locked up (62). There
is a clear parallel between exposing Suzanne's body and exposing
her letters, a parallel which shows how those in power search for the
truth of her story. What Suzanne must hide from their eyes is her
body and the body of her letters and texts, for it is made clear that it
is the physical nature of the letters and texts that poses a problem
for her. Containing the body of the letter and the body of Suzanne
seem to be the twin goals of the prison.

Suzanne has three solutions to the problem of keeping the body
of the letter from the gaze of her prison guards. On the one hand,
she can *swallow* it, incorporate it, make it *a part of her body* (84).[6]

Or she can burn her letters and texts, or ask others to burn them, so that they will not fall into the wrong hands, fall prey to the wrong gaze: "You must burn these writings, and I promise to burn your answers" (40). Her third solution is to go into league with another, with Sister Ursule, to form a kind of revolutionary band which can hide the body of their texts together (79).

It is, however, the notion of burning that is most interesting and problematic here. Clearly her burning of the body of evidence is a subversive act, for it keeps those in power from doing their job of surveillance. It is tantamount to her radical gesture of burning her hair shirt and discarding her scourge (74). It symbolizes the revolutionary gesture of "burning down the prison," an act which, as she thinks over her life while writing this very text, she wonders why she did not commit: "One question, Sir, that I must ask you, is why, given all the grim ideas that go through the head of a desperate nun, does the idea of setting fire to the convent never cross her mind?" (77). In a sense, her burning of her text is the parallel, reverse gesture of those who were opposed to the Enlightenment ("les lumières"), the book burners, who are, according to Roland Desné, the objects of the satire of this text: "To write this 'satire' was, for the philosopher/novelist, to answer the adversaries of enlightenment, those who burn books and imprison—or threaten to imprison—writers, in the name of morality and religion" (21). Suzanne must burn her text as a symbol of revolt against those who would use her body and her text as a means to control and "surveil" difference. And perhaps, in the interconnection between the body of the text and the body of the woman, we can see her revolt against those who would "burn" those women who are different, those accused of sorcery and possession (as is Suzanne).

Thus, instead of being "burned," Suzanne represents a woman who would burn letters, convents, power formations. And in the sense that she represents illicit female sexuality, she also represents the woman who "burns" in the metaphoric sense of desiring. Suzanne does indeed "desire" her own liberty; she has a will and asserts it, and this is threatening. She also has a desire to know, to be kept in the dark no longer, to have access to the "lumières" that are constantly denied her, both the "name" of her father and the nature of the abbess's sexual act. And ultimately, of course, Suzanne manages to "see the light," to come in from the dark, when she eavesdrops on the conversation between the abbess and her confessor and finally learns the nature of that sexuality. And this acquisition of the truth coincides contextually with her escape from the convent.

There appears to be a problem here, however, for when she escapes from the convent, she does not find "freedom" but rather a repetition of her previous situation. In the carriage that awaits her for her escape, she finds a monk who takes over the sexual dominance and power play of the abbess (203). She finds herself afterward in a kind of prison cell in a bad place from which she can only wish to escape (204). She escapes, falls into the hands of "men" (204), and is taken to another kind of "prison," the "hôpital," where she encounters the sexual power plays of both men and women (204). She finally ends up working for a launderer and living in a kind of hovel as bad as her worst cell in the convent (205). Now she feels that she is the target of the searches of the real police: "My parents, who cannot but suspect that I am in Paris, must surely be conducting all the investigations possible" (205). She finds out that her own story has been "exposed" to the public, and it comes back to her in a perverted form when the laundress recounts it to her. Thus, just when it seems that she has been freed and has escaped the walls of the prison, we find that she has not, in fact, escaped but is still imprisoned in the same structure.

In a certain sense, the escape itself participates in the power structures it would like to leave behind, for it places her once again in a powerless, helpless situation. The attempt to gain freedom paves the way to her continued subjection. This participation of revolt and revolution in the very power system it attempts to explode can be seen sporadically in the convent in certain situations when Suzanne inflicts on herself the very tortures she would like to escape, such as when she whips herself before the other nuns: "They put in my right hand the scourge, which I then switched to my left hand, and they began the *Miserere*. I understood what they expected of me, and I performed it" (128). In the sense that she seems to have internalized the power structures, to have become "normal" in adhering to the convent rules, the very impetus toward liberty is "internalized" in the power structure it struggles to escape.

This inescapability is also present in the problem of the seductive nature of narratives. If the work of the mother of the novitiates is a seduction which Suzanne labels an "art" (44), this seduction parallels the *involuntary* seduction by Moni: "Her plan was not to seduce; but certainly that is what she did" (65). Similarly, in sending her narrative to Croismare, Suzanne does not want to "seduce" him, but she realizes that this is what might happen: "However, if the marquis, who is said to have the most delicate sense of tact, were to begin to believe that it is not to his good will but rather to his vice that I am directing myself, then what would he think of me? This thought worries me. Actually, he would be wrong to accuse me personally of an instinct that is proper to my entire sex. I am a woman, perhaps a bit of a coquette, how do I know? But I am this naturally and without artifice" (208). It seems that seduction is ubiquitous, inevitable, and ambiguous.

This leads to a kind of double bind in relation to the problem of knowledge and ignorance. Suzanne's attempt at liberation is an attempt also to learn the truth, particularly the truth of the abbess's sexuality as well as an attempt to remain "innocent" of the power plays perpetrated by those in the convent, such as their surveillance and their torture, an attempt not to give oneself over to their ways of doing things. The problem is that in order to learn the truth, Suzanne must herself perform the "guilty" acts which will make her lose her innocence: she must spy on the abbess, eavesdropping behind a door to learn the truth. When she becomes the "surveiller" and learns the truth it is not surprising that the text should speak of this ambiguous liberation in terms of unveiling: "I listened; the veil, which until that moment had hidden from me the peril I had confronted, was torn" (198). She loses her innocence in the sense that she perpetrates the very acts she condemns, and the words which her director spoke just before this scene come true: "There is nefarious knowledge that you cannot acquire without perdition" (194).[7]

This eavesdropping represents a significant difference from a previous episode, in which Suzanne had the opportunity to "listen to" another's text and to learn the truth in secret. Just before Sister Ursule dies, she confides to Suzanne that she has some secret written documents which must be destroyed and never read. Suzanne duly burns the papers, presumably never reading them and certainly never revealing to her own reader what these papers were (134). She does not "spy" on Ursule or make her a spectacle for us as she later spies on the abbess.

However we must situate this attempt at learning the truth in its proper context: it is a text written by a man about the possibility of woman's access to the truth. The situation it constructs for her is the following: either learn the truth and participate in the very voyeurist structures that police woman (Suzanne eavesdrops on another woman's secrets, learns the truth, and "violates" that woman), or renounce any attempt to learn the truth (Suzanne burns the letters of another woman, letters that might reveal the truth about her). This text constructs an impossible situation for the woman.

We the reader are in the same position as Suzanne in relation to a secret text. Suzanne asks Croismare to burn this very text, repeating Ursule's act: "So burn these letters." The fact that we read it "against her will" is an act of voyeurism and surveillance similar to that used against Suzanne by those in power in the convent. Our voyeurism also figures a position of superior knowledge, because if Suzanne cannot figure out what is going on with the abbesse, we can: as voyeurist readers, we know the truth, while she does not. It would seem then that this text puts the reader into a double-bind situation: the narration of the text inevitably leads one to search for its truth and the text thereby seduces its reader into being a voyeur, and the attempt to gain knowledge seems to imprison itself more surely in the very web of control and domination it would shun. Is there no way out of this imprisoning structure of surveillance and seduction?

In fact, we must look carefully at the place where Suzanne learns the truth in order to see just what is revealed. This is how the text exposes the truth to its reader and to Suzanne:

> The first word that I heard after a fairly long silence made me tremble; it was: "Father, I am damned . . ."
> I became reassured. I listened, the veil, which until that moment had hidden from me the peril I had confronted, was torn, when I was called. I had to leave, so I left; but, alas! I had heard too much. What a woman, monsieur le marquis, what an abominable woman! . . .
> Here the memoirs of Sister Suzanne are interrupted; what follows are only sketches of what she had apparently promised herself to use in the rest of her tale. It seems that the Mother Superior went mad, and that it is to Suzanne's unhappy state that one must attribute the fragments that I will transcribe. (198)

It is not revealed how much she in fact learns or what she learns, or if she in fact learns anything new whatsoever (see Mylne). This supposed revelation of the "truth" turns out to be an absence of the truth from this text. Thus, in our role as voyeurs we ultimately get to see nothing, just as we never get to see the secret texts of Ursule. However this is not represented as the elimination of the text, as it is in Ursule's case (the scene of revelation is not absent), nor as a revelation of the truth (we do not see the truth), but as rather an ambiguous "tease" in between. The text sets up the existence of the truth but does not let us see it; in much the same way does Alfred Hitchcock tantalize his audience in *Rear Window*:

> Two women on a rooftop, presumably Greenwich Village "bohemians," discard their clothes to sunbathe. A helicopter approaches and hovers overhead. The implication: those aboard the helipcopter are spying on the women. The helicopter provides a perfect "vehicle" for the spectatorial desire to enjoy a fantasy of omniscience, to go everywhere and see everything, and especially for the socially constructed (and largely male) desire to see women in states of undress. . . . Yet Hitchcock withholds the "pay-off" of these resources by denying us the point-of-view shot from the helicopter. We never see the women; we become aware, rather, only of our desire to see them. The desire is not fulfilled but only designated and exposed.

> (Stam and Pearson)

It is in this refusal to reveal the truth, perhaps, that Diderot's text comes the closest to undermining the surveillance and the attempt at exposure of the truth and of the woman's body, for it shows how narrative subverts that very search and that what is unveiled instead is a desire, a problem, and an absence. This recalls the rather strange beginning of the "Lettre sur les aveugles," where Diderot says that we will *not* be able to see the "unblinding" of a blind *girl*. Here also, in *La Religieuse* we do not see just what Suzanne "sees" and learns, just how she is "unblinded."[8] The revelation of this text lies somewhere between truth and ignorance. Just after this ironic "revelation" Suzanne's memoirs become disjointed, fragmentary, as if the revelation of the absent truth became a very part of the narrative, which remains, until the end of the novel, choppy and full of gaps.

However, it must be repeated that here too the male representation of the voyeurist scene of imprisoned female sexuality comes face to face with its own concealment or blindness. What continues to be untold in this male representation is the woman's story, both in the sense that we do not get to "see" the male's representation of that story, and in the sense that it is a man, not a woman, writing. What is especially nefarious about the impossibility of reading the woman's story is that the text sets up the revelations involved in women's writing as a double bind, in the sense that it doubly binds or sur-veils woman. We never read Ursule's letters and are prevented from doing so: this veils the woman's text so that woman's story can never be told; woman is unable to liberate herself from the prison. Furthermore, it constructs the necessity of that veiling in such a way that it makes us read that veiling as the only way a woman's body and text will not be violated. Limiting a woman's freedom (her imprisonment behind convent walls and veils, the hiding and burning of her texts) is shown to be the only way for her to escape violent gazes, a scenario that remains in effect today when women must watch what they wear and where they go, so that they do not appear to "ask for it."

Diderot's text, on the one hand, shows how the structures of voyeurism act to confine, imprison, and control. But, on the other hand, the text itself is a scenario that enacts a fantasy of the confinement and control of women's texts, subjectivities, and bodies. The male author constructs the scene of seduction in which he puts the blame on the female "maid(s)"; after all, the women are the ones responsible for seduction in this text. This text is itself a scenario of seduction viewed by a voyeur: the male writer/spectator observes female seductions and the origin of sexuality in such a way as to condemn and thereby *master* female sexuality, subjectivity, and writing. Thus the text cannot escape the very act of repeating the scene of voyeurism, the scene of seduction, by repeating the policing structures the text seems to criticize. Like Suzanne, like the reader, when this text attempts to escape the prison of voyeurism, it finds itself imprisoned ever more securely in the structure. The fragmented end and the impossibility of a final, satisfactory revelation, reveal the contradictions inherent in a text that aims to expose exposure, but never considers its own role in that seduction, mastery, and exposure.

The revelations of La Religieuse and the questions it raises in relation to voyeurism, mastery, and the scene of seduction will be useful in the remainder of our textual analyses. First, seduction brings with it ambiguity; the ambiguity between active and passive, between self and other, inside and out. This ambiguity proves to be intolerable in this text and gives rise to strategies of "mastery": in order to master, the elements that transgress boundaries must be surveiled, dominated, and contained. The act of voyeurism itself is, in this text and in others, a means to dominate and control by secretly gaining the power of superior knowledge. This leads to fundamental questions relating to voyeurism and the act of reading (whose answers must await full development of the problem of textual voyeurism in the second part of this book). When we read a text, we do so to "view" from our unseen place of the reader a world unfold before the eyes of our imagination. The question is, to what extent is our secret access to worlds and people who do not (generally) see us a participation in the scenario of voyeurism that "masters" a victim? Can this novelistic viewing be done in a way that does not participate in power structures? Can there be a pleasure taken in the gaze that is not related to the desire for mastery, and specifically the mastery of female sexuality? This leads us to our next theme of voyeurism: the primal scene of the origin of gender identity, the scene of castration.

# 3

# The Primal Scene
# of Castration, Voyeurism,
# and La Fille aux yeux d'or

*A scintillating and incandescent concavity, of language also, that threatens to
set fire to fetish-objects and gilded eyes.*
—Luce Irigaray
*Speculum of the Other Woman*

THE SECOND ASPECT of the primal scene involves the desire to know
the origin of gender identity: in the viewing of the primal scene of
parental intercourse, the child desires to satisfy sexual curiosity about
male and female. What makes a man, what makes a woman? In the
scene or fantasy, the child sees the different genital configurations
and the different roles played by the two sexes. The main differences
observed are, according to psychoanalytic studies, the absence of a
penis (interpreted as castration) as opposed to the presence of a
penis, and the passive role (linked to castration) as opposed to the
active role. Indeed, on a much more general level, the importance of
vision in the construction of the gendered individual was emphasized
by Freud: it is the gaze at the little girl that makes the pieces of the
boy's Oedipus complex fall into place. Thus from the beginning
psychoanalysis acknowledged that gender identity is constructed in

large part in the visual field, an "origin" underscored in particular by Irigaray and Rose (*Visions*) in their studies of the ways in which gender is related to the gaze in psychoanalysis.

Castration, considered as a kind of "origin" of gender in the Oedipal situation, is a common element in the many different configurations of voyeurist scenarios. As Otto Fenichel says: "We see that a certain person's scopophilic instinct really signifies 'I want to see how someone is castrated,' or 'I want to see how I could castrate somebody,' but it does seem incredible that this could also signify 'I want to be castrated myself' " (383). Thus what one needs to see, or the reenactment one needs to make, is the way in which subjects come to be gendered as female and male. In the scenarios of voyeurism, this is interpreted as seeing castration or its absence. Likewise, in the literary analyses to follow, the problem of castration and gender identity is almost always at stake in the voyeurist scenes.

Psychoanalytic literature emphasizes the fact that it is in particular the mother who becomes the desired object of the investigative childhood gaze: "Pleasure in looking and the early sexualization of sight is intimately connected with the mother-child relationship" (Lane 51). "A particular avoidance of seeing even unimportant parts of the mother's body proceeds from a repressed pleasure in looking, which was originally directed in an excessive degree towards the mother, and especially towards her genitals" (Abraham 178). If it is castration that is at stake, then clearly the gender deemed to be castrated would be the object of desired viewing. Seeing castration bears a relationship to the importance of the visibility of woman which we saw in *La Religieuse*, and which will continue to be of importance in the main textual analyses to come.

The other common element of voyeurist scenarios that is also linked to gender is the structure of activity and passivity. There are three fundamental points to be made about the active/passive distinction. First, Freud is careful to insist that activity and passivity exist prior to the distinction between the sexes, and that repression is not sexualized: both sexes have masculine and feminine instinctual impulses, and each can undergo repression and become unconscious ("Child" 202). However, Freud goes on to say that activity and passivity do tend to attach themselves in the main to masculinity and femininity respectively: "The antithesis active-passive coalesces later with the antithesis masculine-feminine, which, until this has taken place, has no psychological meaning" ("Instincts"

134). Although he warns against equating passivity with femininity and activity with masculinity, he continues to assign those opposite qualities to the genders.[1]

Second, in the manifestations of the scopophilic instinct, activity and passivity combine with different configurations involving subject and object to form various structures of perversion. The instinct to see is at first autoerotic: it aims to see an object that is the subject's own body. This preliminary stage then undergoes permutations involving activity, passivity, and extraneous objects (or persons). Active scopophilia is voyeurism: one actively looks at an extraneous object. Passive scopophilia is exhibitionism: one is the object being looked at by an extraneous person.

Thus we have another link between gender and voyeurism, for active looking would tend to be a masculine mode, passive exhibiting a feminine one: "The libido for looking and touching is present in everyone in two forms, active and passive, male and female; and, according to the preponderance of the sexual character, one form or the other predominates" (*Jokes* 98). Freud's description of the gendering of voyeurism and exhibitionism in terms of activity and passivity would seem to correspond to the clinical evidence of the lack of female voyeurs, and the existence of some cases of female exhibitionism. (Here we mean genital exhibitionism; of course a more general tendency toward exhibitionism is often attributed to women.)[2]

I would like to emphasize here, however, that this genderization of activity and passivity are products of a process of construction and interpretation and should not be thought of as some kind of innate, anatomical, essential "truth" about the difference between the sexes. Freud's description of these differences is a description of how gender was constructed and the way it functioned in his society, a society continuous with our own. And, as Louise J. Kaplan has pointed out, the gender identities of woman as castrated/man as intact represent an *infantile* understanding of gender that can become very powerful when it is coupled with the law of the social order: "The danger comes when these infantile gender attributions are employed by the social order to enforce its conventions of femininity and masculinity. A subtle two-way collaboration takes place between the unconscious mind, with its store of infantile representations of male-female difference, and the social order, with its primitively conceived prescriptions for normal femininity and masculinity" (48). Kaplan, in fact, argues that it is the insistence of the social order on rigid, polarized, stereotyped gender identities that is one of the causes of perversion: "As these last few decades of the twentieth century are proof enough, the obsession with sexual normality and gender conformity became a breeding ground for perversion . . . What we are seeing, as a last-ditch effort to contain and regulate the gender ambiguities that are the lot of human beings, is a commercialization and standardization of so-called deviant sexuality" (6).

As a matter of fact, if we follow the tortuous path of reversals and transformations taken by Freud's theory of voyeurism, we are hard pressed to determine the borderlines between activity and passivity. Defined in terms of activity and passivity, the preliminary stage of the scopophilic instinct—the subject looks at the subject's own body—has both an active component, "oneself looking at a sexual organ," and a passive component, "a sexual organ being looked at by oneself" ("Instincts" 130). The addition of an extraneous object or person makes possible a transformation either to active scopophilia, with the emphasis on active, "oneself looking at an extraneous object (active scopophilia)," or to exhibitionism, which has a more passive component, "an object which is oneself or part of oneself being looked at by an extraneous person" ("Instincts" 130). However, given the ambiguous active/passive nature of the preliminary stage of the scopophilic instinct, the division between active and passive cannot be so clear-cut. It is noteworthy that Freud concludes his section on scopophilia and exhibitionism with a discussion of ambivalence, or in linguistic terms, ambiguity. He claims that "the only correct statement to make about the scopophilic instinct would be that all the stages of its development, its auto-erotic, preliminary stage as well as its final active or passive form, co-exist alongside one another. . . . The fact that, at this later period of development of an instinctual impulse, its (passive) opposite may be observed alongside of it deserves to be marked by the very apt term introduced by Bleuler—'ambivalence' " ("Instincts" 130–131).

Thus, the adult voyeur writes his voyeurist script because gender distinctions are not clear: activity as male and passivity as female, having a penis and being castrated, become entangled in a confusion of desires. Ambiguity, the difficulty involved in making the distinction between the sexes, is one of the reasons why voyeurism and exhibitionism develop in a social order that insists on the dichotomy of gender. As David Allen states, there is a faulty gender identity in all cases of perversion; in the case of exhibitionism he describes it as an uncertainty on the part of a male patient about being separate from his mother (64–65). Joyce McDougall too emphasizes the problematic nature of the difference between the sexes in the perversions. She says that the "secret" of perversions is this: "There is no difference between the sexes. For the subject's conscious there are differences between the sexes, but they do not have a symbolic function and they are neither the cause nor the condition of sexual desire" (48, translation mine).

It is precisely because of problems of gender identity that the voyeur needs to construct scenes that negotiate ambiguities and contradictions. Some of the goals of adult voyeurs in their viewings of women show how ambiguity necessitates these scenarios. Some voyeurs have had what Lane calls "seductive mothers" and have undergone a passive sexual relation to her (they have been seduced; they were in the feminine, passive place). Their voyeurist activity "is a repetition of an earlier witnessed experience in the hope of mastering anxiety and excitement" (Lane 55): anxiety at being in the passive place and in the relation with the mother, and excitement because of it. The "mastery" of the scene would put them in the active place while reexperiencing the original passive excitement.

The exhibitionist too constructs scenarios in order to solve a certain problem of gender identity, in order to be reassured about gender identity: "The compulsion to exhibit, for instance, is also closely dependent on the castration complex: it is a means of constantly insisting upon the integrity of the subject's own (male) genitals and it reiterates his infantile satisfaction at the absence of a penis in those of women" (*Three Essays* 156n). It is a "perpetual search for a confirmation of one's being," a confirmation that could contain anxiety when the subject is menaced with the loss of the limits of the self" (McDougall 43).

Like exhibitionists, voyeurs may need to look at female genitals "as a hostile act toward women whom they fear" (Lane 55); here voyeurism becomes linked with hostility and violence against women, and hence with violent pornography. Louise Kaplan describes this hostility as being a necessary ingredient in the voyeurist scenario: the perversion of voyeurism (as distinct from "normal" pleasure in seeing) is dependent on "an unsuspecting or victimized subject" (30). The bulk of Kaplan's study implies that on the literal level of the voyeurist scenario, the woman must be put back in the passive, demeaned position, but Kaplan also seems to suggest that, on a deeper, more hidden level, the repetition of the primal scene reenacts the male's passive and demeaned role. The voyeur's scenario negotiates conflict: it represents both the male desire to be feminine (the pleasure of his femininity is repeated in the voyeurist act) along with his fear of being feminine and his desire not to be feminine (he puts the female victim in her place, and feels the pleasure of reasserting his masculinity in his active viewing and mastering of the unsuspecting female). As Kaplan says of sadistic pornography (which for her involves a voyeurist act that victimizes): "These scenarios are usually invented by men and designed for the sexual arousal of men, who unconsciously identify with the person in the submissive (feminine) position. The unconscious aim, as always, is to express yet disguise, even if barely, the man's wishes to be a submissive, denigrated female" (26-30). Thus the voyeurist scenario can enable the voyeur to suture together contradictory pleasures and cover a profound ambivalence on his part, a kind of ambiguity in his identity.

This ambiguity of gender identity parallels other ambiguities, or "ambivalences" in the voyeurist scenario. There is a copresence of passive and active, or sadistic and masochistic, of pre-oedipal and oedipal (oral/anal and phallic), of identification of the self as distinct and a confusing identification with the other.[3] Thus he who looks at that which has been castrated (the head of the Medusa) himself undergoes castration (petrification) (Fenichel 391). (This "contagion by the eyes" reminds us of the contagion of seduction in *La Religieuse.*) This is, often, a contagion of gender too, a contagion described by Fenichel's analysis of the viewing of intercourse. In that situation, the person looking on does so to share in the experience, and this often entails a cross-gender empathy with one of the protagonists, or a desire to destroy the object. Exhibitionists, too, enter empathetically into their imagined fantasy of the experience of the person looking on (Fenichel 377), and this identification is cross-gender. This ambiguity of gender and selfhood, as well as other ambiguities, will often be at the center of the scenes of voyeurism that we will investigate in the literary texts. They often appear in the narratives, as in clinical cases of voyeurism, as a kind of attempt to resolve basic problems of gender and identity.

Thus, as we turn to Balzac's *La Fille aux yeux d'or,* we will keep in mind the following elements in the voyeurist repetition of the primal fantasy of the origin of gender: the search for the origin of gender, which will take the form in *La Fille aux yeux d'or* of the discovery of the difference between the sexes; gender ambiguity as related to other fundamental ambiguities; the gendered structure of the subject and object of the gaze; and finally, mastery and violence against woman as attempts at containing ambiguities.

In *La Fille aux yeux d'or,* the voyeurist scenario centers on Paquita, a most beautiful, most mysterious woman. It is clear, here, that Henri de Marsay's desire has four different aspects: it is a desire for her, a desire for knowledge about her, a desire to spy on her without her knowledge, and a desire to master her. First, she is not only the object of his desire; she epitomizes the desire of all of Paris. Second, for de Marsay, Paquita seems to hold within her or about her a kind of secret which he desires to learn as soon as he sees her: "For him, this girl became a mystery" (1082). Third, he goes about learning "all her secrets" (1091) by becoming a kind of master spy: he follows Paquita when she does not know he is doing so (1065); he has a cab driver follow her carriage to find out where she is going (1066); he sends a substitute spy, his valet, Laurent, in disguise to find out about her home and her letters from London; he thinks of intercepting one of those letters to read it (an act of stealing her property, her text) and to insert his own in it (1073). In fact, he represents one of Balzac's most privileged character types: the observer so gifted in his talents that they border on the uncanny. He sees everything without appearing to see anything: "The young man examined the strollers, with that quickness of a glance and the ability to hear of the Parisian who appears, at first, to neither see nor hear anything, but who sees and hears everything" (1058). He is one of those superior people in Balzac's world who have the gift of "the apprehension of the result in causes hidden to other eyes, but perceptible to theirs" (1080). He has the gift of vision, and secret vision, which lets one see and reveal what is hidden. And he finally does come to read Paquita's text and understand its hidden meaning: "He could then read this page that had such a brilliant effect, and could guess the hidden meaning" (1096).

Fourth, Henri enacts the ultimate gesture of mastery when he attempts to murder Paquita at the end of the story (he is unable to do so because she has already been murdered by Mariquita). Although there is no one specific scenario of voyeurism in this text, the entire structure is conditioned by all of the elements of the voyeurist scene: the desire to see the erotic object in secret, to know about it, and to dominate it.

The knowledge to be gained in this text is specifically knowledge about the difference between the sexes. On the most obvious level, Paquita had never learned the difference between the sexes because she had been sequestered and imprisoned by her female lover, Mariquita, in a mansion in Paris that offered no way in or out without knowledge of the password, in a soundproofed room which would barely let out the screams of a person being murdered. Paquita escapes from her prison and learns just what a man is when she makes love to Henri. But, as we will see in the detailed analysis of the text which follows, the problematic knowledge in this text is also the feared knowledge of gender ambiguity, which must be nego-tiated by the voyeurist scenario, a negotiation carried out not by Paquita but by the voyeur, Henri de Marsay. In order to learn the nature of this gender ambiguity, we must first study Paquita to understand why she is the object of the gaze, then analyze what is at stake for de Marsay in his attempt to possess her.

Paquita is represented by de Marsay as his ideal of the perfect woman:

> So I examined her. Ah, my dear fellow, physically speaking, the unknown woman [Paquita] is the person who is the most adorably "woman" that I have ever met. . . . Since I have been studying women, my unknown woman is the only one whose virginal breast, whose ardent and voluptuous forms have made real for me the only woman I ever dreamed of! . . . She is all woman, an abyss of pleasures where one tumbles without finding an end, . . . she is an ideal woman seen sometimes in reality in Spain, in Italy, almost never in France.

She is, in addition to being the ideal of the object of individual, erotic desire, the incarnation of social, Parisian desire: money. She is the girl with the golden eyes, and she thus figures the possibility of fulfilling the two fundamental Parisian desires to gain "gold and pleasure" at once (1040).

The literal incarnation (in her body) of this social, Parisian desire gives meaning to the long, seemingly gratuitous description of Paris that precedes the story of Paquita and de Marsay. In analyzing the various levels of Parisian society in an overt reference to Dante, the narrator outlines the various "circles" of financial and social status, from the bottom to the top. From this ascending description emerges a vague image of Paris as a gigantic body: we begin with a description of the "member of the proletariat, the man who moves his feet" (1041); move up to a worker who has managed to start up a small business and who is "all legs" (1044); continue the ascent of this bizarre body which is Paris to reach the "professionals," the "attorneys, doctors, notaries, lawyers, businessmen, bankers, important traders, speculators, magistrates" who form the "Parisian belly," "ventre parisien" (1046); and finally reach the top, a kind of Janus-like head with two faces, that of the "artistic world," whose features one first notices are their "faces marked with the seal of originality," and that of the rich, with their "faces of cardboard" (1051). If this faint, gigantic body is merely sketched in pencil through the text, its lines are made bolder by the mention of that other literary giant, Gargantua (1045).

This giant called Paris is not a man, however, but, as we learn after the introductory description has reached its end, it is rather "a queen" (1051). Thus the figural "embodiment" of Paris in this giant woman becomes, in the second part of the story, a literal embodiment in the hyperbolically perfect Paquita; the money (gold) that circulates as the blood of the giant Paris ("everything stimulated the ascensional movement of money," 1046) becomes the gold of Paquita's eyes and the blood which she spills at the end of the text. The hidden subtitle of this text could well be "La Ville aux yeux d'or" ("The City with the Golden Eyes": *ville* is close in spelling to *fille*). We will return to the inscription of the social hierarchy on the body of Paquita later.

I would like to read the combination of Paquita's perfection and the search for the truth about her through the lens offered by recent neo-Freudian interpretations of film. First, the perfection of Paquita parallels what film theorists have observed in female stars of classic Hollywood cinema. As Rose explains, the beautiful, larger-than-life female stars of film "are meant to *look* perfect, presenting a seamless image to the world so that the man, in that confrontation with difference, can avoid any apprehension of lack" (*Vision* 232). In the fetishist gaze, "the threat of castration is allayed by a process of idealisation and glamourisation: the female image is smooth, fault-

less, without lack" (Neal 127). In cinema, the whole female body
may be "fetishized," it becomes a surface with no interior, frozen
into representation.[4] So too is Paquita's body fetishized in its
seamless image of the unification of all desires fulfilled. Significantly, it is her eyes that are gold, eyes representing the phallus in
Freud's analysis of the Oedipal story. Paquita offers, at first, the
image of the perfect female body that has the phallus, the gold, the
eye, the female body that has not been castrated. She is the fetishized woman whose image continues in that sequel to the
nineteenth-century novel, film. Thus, in the structure of the gaze
in *La Fille aux yeux d'or*, the male gaze of Henri, an avowed narcis-
sist, can look at the fetishized female body and be reassured that
castration has not taken place. Indeed, as Shoshana Felman has
shown, Paquita's golden eyes serve as a kind of mirror which can
reflect back upon the man who could possess her. Henri can look at
her and she can reflect back to him his own plenitude (his phallus).
She initially, in her perfection, represents in perversion the reassurance that there is no difference between the sexes.[5]

However, the fetish both reassures that castration has not taken
place *and* preserves within its own necessity a "memorial to castration," as Freud calls it, the hidden, covered-over threat of castration that gave rise to it. This hidden meaning, Paquita's secretive
nature, makes Henri desire to get beyond the pleasurable surface of
the fetishist's gaze, and he turns to the voyeur's desire to reach the
real, inner, secret woman (Silverman, *Mirror* 82). As analyses of
film have shown, this voyeurist look is aggressive, investigative,
markedly active and sadistic (Neale 127), just like Henri's. This
look aggressively seeks to view the female body so that it will render
up its truth, its difference, the riddle of femininity (Kuhn 30). By
means of detailed analyses of films, film theorists show again and
again how the truth of woman and of her desire are central for the
male protagonist and for his gaze at her; she is the problem or
challenge for him, the problem and possibility of sexual difference
(Bergstrom 178).[6] Susanne Kappeler has linked this gaze to Freud's
own: "Freud's women, subject-patients, are invited to speak in a
controlled, secret, closeted, private place and situation, controlled
by him," seen but not seeing (201).

However, what Henri learns in his investigation of Paquita is
information so intolerable that he feels he must do away with her in
a kind of attempt to do away with what he discovers. When he first

becomes involved with Paquita, he is put in the feminine place in his relationship with her, while she takes the masculine one. As in cases of voyeurs who had seductive mothers, Henri is the non-comprehending male child put in the passive feminine position when Paquita dresses him up, literally, in women's clothes, before they make love for the first time: "Joyous Paquita went to get from one of the two dressers a red velvet dress, in which she dressed Henri, then she put on him a woman's hat and wrapped him up in a shawl." In other, more figural ways, Henri is put in a position in which his gender is ambiguous, both male and female. He is the "chimera," the monster that Paquita caresses; he enters into the woman's space, the space of the boudoir (the narrator's reference to the uncanny spaces of Ann Radcliffe's novels is particularly interesting here [1078]), and he is no longer the same person: "He was no longer himself" (1084). In the Balzacian context, he is feline, lionlike (as well as lionized), as are those other sexually ambiguous characters, Vautrin in *Le Père Goriot*, Mignonne in "Une Passion dans le désert," and, of course, Paquita in this story (she has yellow eyes like a tiger's).

Likewise, Paquita is ambiguous. She is a beautiful woman who has been playing the man's role: she is a woman's lover, and she loves Henri at first when he is in the woman's place. But more importantly, even though she is a prisoner, she performs certain functions that are coded as masculine in the nineteenth century. She is not merely the passive object of the gaze; she is a beautiful woman who looks. "The Spanish woman took advantage of this moment of stupor to give herself over to the ecstasy of that infinite adoration that seizes the heart of a woman when she truly loves and when she finds herself in the presence of an idol she had long hoped for in vain" (1080). Her gaze figures her active desire and her pursuit of Henri (she makes certain bold overtures to him). She wants to look at Henri, to study him and to love him (1099).

The problem is then, as it was in *La Religieuse*, that Paquita desires to learn, desires to go out for her walks in the daytime when she can see what men are rather than in the middle of the night when she can learn nothing. She desires to get out of the confines imposed upon her: "I had the curiosity of a demon, I wanted to break the implacable circle that they had drawn between the rest of creation and me, I wanted to see what young men were, because I knew no men other than the marquis and Christemio" (1100). Like

Suzanne, Paquita longs to break free; in Paquita's case, to break free of the artificial bonds, the gender identity, and the love that confined her. The two women, Suzanne and Paquita, both say "no"; they both assert a subjectivity that differs from the identity prescribed for them.

One of the reasons why Paquita is so intriguing to Henri is because she is ambiguous and enigmatic. As he says to her just before she dresses him up as a girl, "You are, by the faith of an honest man, a living charade whose clue word seems to me to be very difficult to find." If he finds her enigmatic nature and her mirroring of himself desirable, it is not because she mirrors his unambiguous masculinity, but rather because she suggests the reflection of his own bisexual nature. Indeed, Paquita, like Suzanne, is the person who is "in between" different opposing structures. As she says, she is at once slave and queen (1090), master and slave (1066), she is the one who casts a bridge over the abyss which separates opposing things (1090). Her attempt to escape from her feminine confinement and ignorance out into the masculine world of knowledge and desire similarly threatens to blur the borders between the genders.

Most importantly, in her mirroring capacity she causes others to experience this in-between state (again as does Suzanne), for when she meets Henri, it is she who causes in him a crisis compared in the text to one in which the ardor of a clear sky makes "bright light resemble shadows" (1080), and her rendez-vous with Henri brings opposites together: "It was something somber, mysterious, gentle, tender, constrained and expansive, a coupling of the horrible and the celestial, of paradise and hell" (1084). That "in-between" state is unbearable for Henri, for it figures the loss of his secure gender identity.

Paquita's bisexual nature brings out the repressed "other" gender within, and lurking in the rhetoric of this text is a condensation of images that figure the "other within" and that are linked specifically with femininity. In describing Henri's ability to seduce women, the text asks a rather strange question about the way in which his system of seduction might fail. Henri sets up a theory of seduction in which the man who seduces women is vain and pretentious, a man who is occupied with himself. The exception to this rule—the woman who would not fit into Henri's machinery of seduction—is the *pregnant* woman, because she might be seduced by a man who was not primarily concerned with himself: "If this event happened, we would have to attribute it to the whims of a pregnant woman, like those crazy ideas that go through everyone's head" (1072). The pregnant woman is the threatening one who might resist Henri's machine of seduction. Furthermore, the giant body of the woman that is Paris in the introductory section, a body embodied in the second section as Paquita, is a *pregnant* woman: "This crowned city is a queen who, always pregnant, has irresistibly furious whims" (1051).

This caprice of a pregnant woman is also linked to madness, a rather disquieting madness because it threatens the integrity of everyone's sanity ("those crazy ideas that go through everyone's head"—let us remember Suzanne's relation to madness and to contagion). Here a woman's threatening resistance to Henri's seduction machine is the threat of madness within, the "other within" perhaps figured by the other human being developing within the mother's body. Furthermore, what Paquita first finds fascinating about Henri, and what in fact represents her resistance to Henri's seductions (this is what he finds objectionable about her: that she should love him for something that is not manly) is the fact that she sees a woman *in him*. She loves his sister, Mariquita, and when she first talks to Henri, she says, "It is the same voice . . . the same ardor." Henri later learns that what first interested Paquita was the woman, the other, she saw within him; Henri was "pregnant" with his own other ("pregnancy" is yet another feminine image applied to him). If we return to Henri's description of his egoist/seducer, he says to his friend, Paul: "Therefore, to pay excessive attention to oneself, is that not to say that one cares for *in oneself the good of others?*" (emphasis mine). This is to say, perhaps, that one cares for the other in oneself.

The repression of a man's feminine nature as represented by a man's repression of any internal sexual organs has, in fact, been identified by Louise J. Kaplan as an important factor in the establishment of male gender identity: "The body's inner arousals can be immensely disquieting, not only because they give rise to uncontrollable sensations of fullness and loss but also because they resonate with wishes of being a mommy and having babies just like mommy does . . . There is no question at all about the boy child's awareness of his scrotal sac and testicles or the fact that these observable, semi-external inner genital body organs are sometimes associated with femininity and other shameful, frightening fantasies that must be banished from consciousness. So frightening are these fantasies that many grown men continue to think and act as though the penis is their only genital organ" (108–109). To show to Henri that he has inner feminine qualities (organs), to show him that he is a kind of "man pregnant with woman," is the frightening act for which Paquita must be eliminated in order to eliminate the threat of femininity.

Paquita is punished for several reasons, in fact; she is "guilty" several times over. First, she usurps the male role: she loves a woman and she asserts her subjectivity (activity) in the world. Once again, this resembles a filmic scenario: Williams notes that if the female character tries to mimic the male position, if she tries to take over the active position of the gazer, she is punished (83–85). Paquita, then, is punished because her golden eyes do not merely reflect man's wholeness back to him; they seem to seek to take over the "phallic" role of the man and to put him in the place of femininity.

Paquita's punishment for her guilt (gilt) also participates in the active, voyeurist, sadistic gaze of Henri who attempts to get beneath her smooth, golden surface to the secrets beneath. The secret he uncovers is the "primal scene" of the origin of gender, not in the sense that he discovers Paquita's castration, but rather in the sense that he attempts to carry it out (to murder her) in order to return himself to masculinity. Once again this is similar to a filmic scenario: there, the active, sadistic gaze of the male film protagonist reenacts the primal scene of castration by investigating woman and learning about her castration. The following analysis of *Vertigo* by Laura Mulvey highlights some of the ways in which Hitchcock's film parallels the plot of *La Fille aux yeux d'or* and satisfies while exaggerating the voyeurist fantasy:

> The audience follows the growth of his (the male protagonist's) erotic obsession and subsequent despair precisely from his point of view. Scottie's voyeurism is blatant: he falls in love with a woman he follows and spied on without speaking to. Its sadistic side is equally blatant: he has chosen (and freely chosen, for he had been a successful lawyer) to be a policeman, with all the attendant-possibilities of pursuit and investigation. As a result, he follows, watches and falls in love with a perfect image of female beauty and mystery. Once he actually confronts her, his erotic drive is to break her down and force her to tell by persistent cross questioning. (16)

The fact that Scottie is a policeman is important for it reinforces power struggles and the "law," the fact that the male has a "right" to control, survey, possess the woman: "The power to subject another person to the will sadistically or to the gaze voyeuristically is turned on to the woman as the object of both. Power is backed by a certainty of legal right and the established guilt of the woman" (Mulvey 15).

Once these plots ascertain the woman's guilt, they assure she can be controlled and subject her to punishment (or to forgiveness; Mulvey 13). When guilty and punished, her "body in pieces" pleasurably guarantees the totality of the man's intact body (Bergstrom 178).[7] Likewise, Henri's fascination with Paquita and his voyeurist need to discover her truth reenacts the scene of primal fantasy, in which the child, fascinated but confused by gender identity, fantasizes a scene in which the castration (murder) of the female is established.

The "rights" of Henri in this story, the fact that he is never punished for his complicity in the murder of Paquita, relates to several broader issues, outside the realm of gender but related to it. In the notion of "La Ville aux yeux d'or," we see that the equation of Paris with a woman's body suggests that the social hierarchy of Parisian society functions *through the woman's body*, which, because of Paquita's status, is also a slave's body and the body of a foreigner. Paquita's body is imprisoned and harnessed so that she can give pleasure and her golden eyes to the rich Mariquita and Henri, the apogee of Parisian society. Similarly, the introductory description of Paris shows how the workers, business people, and professionals work to satisfy the rich in their desires and to maintain their place at the "head" of the Parisian body.

Indeed, the equation of Paquita's situation with that of a slave becomes more significant if we consider the subjects of some of the paintings done by the artist to whom this text was dedicated, Delacroix, such as *Death of Sardanapalus*, completed before the Balzac text was written. As Linda Nochlin has observed, in such a Romantic vision of the Oriental as Delacroix's, it is not merely "Western man's power over the near East that is at issue, but rather . . . contemporary Frenchmen's power over women, a power controlled and mediated by the ideology of the erotic in Delacroix's time," which she goes on to say includes "the connection between sexual possession and murder as an assertion of absolute enjoyment (Nochlin, "Orient" 123–125). In fact, Orientalist painting "managed to body forth two ideological assumptions about power: one about men's power over women; the other about white men's superiority to, hence justifiable control over, inferior, darker races, precisely those who indulge in this sort of regrettably lascivious commerce (in naked slave women)" (125).

Paquita, then, admirably serves in those two roles, woman and Oriental slave. Paquita's boudoir houses exotic furnishings from India, Persia, the Orient (1088), and indeed, it houses the ultimate furnishing, Paquita, for she has the explicit function in this text of a piece of furniture. As Mariquita says after killing her: "She is from a country where women are not beings but things with which one does what one wants, which one sells, buys, kills, in a word, uses for one's caprices, as you use your furniture here" (1108). And, like Mignonne, the panther/woman/mistress in another Balzac tale with a subtext on colonialism, Paquita is an animal, "a poor animal attached to its stake" (1090), and Christemio has the eyes of "a bird of prey" (1076). Paquita, who represents the Hispanic third world, is accompanied by her "mulâtre," Christemio (who would indeed be her "Christ" by sacrificing himself for her), who is also called, in the slang of the time, a "Chinois", "Chinaman" (1077).

Paquita's death at the end of the story thus continues to promulgate the images of Oriental sensuality and violence that such painters as Delacroix conjured up in their paintings—one can simply imagine the juxtaposition of the painting *Death of Sardanapalus* with the stabbing death of Paquita at the end of the text. And Paquita must be killed because she threatens to upset the power structures of those who control her: she rebels against Mariquita, her master, by loving Henri, and she insults Henri's maculinity by making him literally assume the place and clothes of a woman. Indeed, what she represents is the possibility of the reversal of power structures that always threatens the society of Paris ("one day, those who had nothing, have something; and those who had something, have nothing," 1061), that Balzacian Paris which rests on the fluid foundations of liquid assets, "this floating fortune" (1060). Paquita's destruction seems almost a kind of willful repression of that threat by those who would seek to remain in power (the crème de la crème of Parisian society).

Indeed, if Henri's heterogeneous status figures on the one hand, as Shoshana Felman has demonstrated, his "castration" by Paquita, her suppression of his masculinity and her feminization of him in the symbolic blinding scene in which he must be blindfolded; it also represents the Hegelian ambiguities of the master/slave situation. Henri, the supposed master, is blindfolded by Paquita in this text which equates blindness with the state of slavery. In the very scene in which Henri accepts the blindfold, the narrator recounts his thoughts about Christemio, Paquita's slave (the slave of the slave), as follows: "Besides, he saw the impossibility of laying down arms with a slave whose obedience was as blind as that of an executioner" (1086). Here one of the most powerful men in Paris, the one who is, as we saw, the master spy, is surveiled by this mulâtre, called literally "son surveillant" in the text (1086).

On a larger scale this ambiguity between master and slave is expressed in the introductory description of Paris when, after a long and detailed enumeration of the slavelike existences of all the working people in Paris, the tables are turned and it is the working people, the people who make the luxurious commodities, who seduce and control the rich: "All the inferior classes crouch down before the rich and study their tastes in order to turn them into vices and exploit them. How can one resist the clever seductions that are concocted in this country?" (1050). The fact that the state of the rich and the state of the poor overlap is expressed in the juxtaposition of the statement placed in italics, "*opposite extremes touch,*" with the passage describing how Henri finds himself early in the morning in the streets with all those seducer/workers who are on their way to their tasks: "He found himself on the boulevard Montmartre at dawn, looked stupidly at the carriage that was rushing away; he pulled two cigars out of his pocket, lit one of them from the lantern of a good woman who was selling eau-de-vie and coffee to the workers, to urchins, to vegetable farmers, to all that Parisian population that begins its life before dawn" (1093). Henri's significant cigar literally touches and is lit by the flame of the merchant worker woman (an echo of the scene immediately preceding, in which Paquita lit the flames of Henri's desires). This reversal of roles, when the workers become the masters, also signifies, in the years just after the 1830 revolution when this story was written, the fearful threat of revolutions, when the helpful flame of the merchant woman can become the "ugly and strong nation" of the Parisian workers, "inflammable like gunpowder, and prepared for revolutionary conflagrations by eau-de-vie" (1042), that very "eau-de-vie" sold by Henri's merchant woman.

Thus Paquita, the one who reverses roles and shows their reversibility, is forcefully eliminated in this text, in a kind of attempt to
eliminate many threats: of revolution, of gender ambiguities, of
class interminglings. And it is also a kind of attempt on the part of
Henri to reestablish his masculinity, to destroy the "feminine" doll/
creature that Paquita dressed up in her boudoir. It is an attempt to
eliminate that "other" in Henri himself. This threat of the other
within is also the threat of language itself, a theme treated in the
text through the recurrence of calembours, word-jokes, such as the
one which the postman unwittingly makes. He, acting for Laurent
and Henri as a kind of spy, says that his name is "Moinot" which,
as he claims incorrectly, is written just like the name of the spar-
row, "moineau." Because of the ambiguities of langauge, the spy/
songbird, who "sings" by telling Henri what he wants to know,
later turns into another bird, Paquita, in the rhetoric of the text:
"She laughed convulsively, and resembled a bird fluttering its
wings" (1091). The spy/sparrow becomes, through the play of language, the surveiled, Oriental captive bird (the exotic bird being
a recurring topos of Balzacian Orientalism according to Pierre
Citron).[8]

Paquita's murder thus appears to be an attempt at the destruction
of social and sexual ambiguity, and the restoration of a clear-cut,
preestablished hierarchy. What *La Fille aux yeux d'or* does is to
contruct gender identity for us through its plot. It shows us what a
woman should not be, and why. It shows us what a man is. It writes
for us a scene of voyeurism in which the primal fantasy of the origin
and definition of gender are played out. It also writes into that
primal scene the origin of social inequalities, mapping them onto
the female body just as the introductory section maps its giant Paris
onto Paquita. It is as though the purpose of this text, as some have
analyzed the purpose of pornography, were to define for us in a
"reassuring" way just what the difference between the sexes is: "Pornography tells you what is important in the difference between the
sexes" (Kuhn 32). Pornographic pictures define for the spectator
just what a woman is: she is reduced to those bodily parts exclusively sexual in nature, and then she is put on display for the man's
pleasure (Kuhn 30–35). This is a way of controlling what might be
a difference not so easily recuperable, and it inscribes on the
woman's body the signifier of difference (Rose, "Paranoia" 157).

Thus in the voyeurist scenario, object and subject of the gaze become themselves gendered according to an infantile understanding of gender (castration). The male is intact, he is the voyeur, he looks, he is active; and the "castrated" female is forced, on penalty of death, to be the beautiful, seamless object of contemplation, the passive object of the gaze. The process of idealization covers over her lack, as in the case of female stars of film. This genderization of the gaze plays itself out constantly in many areas of contemporary life where the gaze at the woman continues to mark its place as different from the gaze at the male. In film and photography, to take a very accessible example, female frontal nudity is much more acceptable than male frontal nudity, and thus the visibility of the female differs substantially from that of the male. In film, the person who looks is also often assigned a male gender identity.

The same differentiation holds true in the world of art (which undoubtedly had an effect on the world of film and demonstrably had an effect on this Balzac text): the female nude and its attendant symbolism is very different from that of the male nude. In a discussion of this difference between male and female in pictorial representation, Linda Nochlin shows how the representation of a female nude holding an apple generates a different set of meanings than does a male nude holding a banana (*Women* 141–142). The humor generated by the latter image makes clear the incongruity of the codes involved in such a representation of the male body.

This gendered construction of the gaze that we have found in *La Fille aux yeux d'or* has been both demonstrated and questioned in film, and it will be one of the important questions we ask of the texts in the analyses to follow. To what extent do literary scenes of voyeurism construct a gendered gaze? To what extent do they undermine this gendered structure? Are men ever the object of the gaze? Do women look? How do they look? To what extent are other social hierarchies inscribed in the voyeurist scenario of the construction of a gender hierarchy?

# 4

# The Primal Scene of Parental Intercourse, Voyeurism, and Le Voyeur

*So the seeker after truth builds his hut close to the towering edifice of science in order to collaborate with it and to find protection. And he needs protection. For there are awful powers which continually press upon him, and which hold out against the "truth" of science, "truths" fashioned in quite another way, bearing devices of the most heterogeneous character.*

—Friedrich Nietzsche,
"On Truth and Lying in Their Extra-Moral Sense"

THE THIRD AND FINAL primal fantasy to be analyzed in terms of the voyeurist scenario is the "primal scene" proper: the child perceives parental intercourse and attempts to resolve the problem of its own origin. In the primal scene proper, the other two fantasies are, of course, also operative: the origin of gender and the seduction of the child.

Laplanche and Pontalis have expanded on Freud's writings on the primal scene in an important lengthy article entitled "Fantasy and the Origins of Sexuality." In this article they study the difficulty Freud had in determining the origin of primal fantasies (the origin of the fantasies of origin): Did they originate in a real event? The authors map out the way in which Freud could not give up the belief that the origin of the primal fantasies was somehow a real event.

First it was the real act of seduction. When the seduction theory was rejected, Freud tried to explain the origin by means of phylogenesis: primal fantasies were inherited (they are thus genetic, biological, real). Since primal fantasies are commonly shared, Freud could not accept that they did not have some origin in a real event of some kind. The urgency of this question of the origin of the primal scene as a real event or as a fantasy has not abated today, as can be seen in the intense debate surrounding Masson's contentions about Freud's seduction theory.

Laplanche and Pontalis argue that Freud did not see the importance of the universality of certain structural developments of the human child as a possible explanation of the origin of fantasy, and also that he did not go back before the Oedipal stage to pre-Oedipal erotism, to the origin of the drive, in his search for origins. Laplanche and Pontalis situate the origin of fantasy not in an event per se, but rather in a repeated condition of the loss of a real object. One might view this as an origin in reality, but it is an origin that is multiple (in its repetition) and that is located in "absence" (the missing object). Fantasy is a kind of marginal, supplementary "product" that emerges from repetition and loss: "This is not a pleasure in the fulfillment of function, or the resolution of tension created by needs, but a marginal product, emerging from the world of needs" (15). The two authors stress that Freud was caught up in the familiar structure of dichotomous opposites in his search for origins, when the origin is perhaps not locatable in terms of these oppositions: Freud was "the prisoner of a series of theoretical alternatives, subject-object, constitution-event, internal-external, imaginary-real" (7).

Conscious of the fact that they, too, like Freud, and like the fantasy they are describing, are constructing a "scene" of origins, Laplanche and Pontalis locate the origin of fantasy at the very early stage of the origin of autoerotism: (a "moment" that has repetition inscribed within it): "The origin of fantasy would lie in the hallucinatory satisfaction of desire; in the absence of a real object, the infant reproduces the experience of the original satisfaction in a hallucinated form" ("Fantasy" 15). The authors emphasize that the object here is not the "real" object but the missing object that enters into the "hallucination": the object is a signifier. This is thus the origin of autoerotism (the infant satisfies itself), the origin of the drive (as differentiated from instinct), and the origin of fantasy:

"The 'origin' of autoerotism would therefore be the moment when sexuality, disengaged from any natural object, moves into the field of fantasy and by that very fact becomes sexuality. The moment is more abstract than definable in time, since it is always renewed, and must have been preceded by erotic excitation, otherwise it would be impossible for such excitation to be sought out" (16). This is thus the origin of sexuality, and also a kind of origin of "abstract" signification.

According to Laplanche and Pontalis, the primal scene, in its quest for origins, rewrites (is a repetition of) this infantile scenario of the origin of fantasy and desire, since the primal scene, too, is concerned with the origins of sexuality. In fact, the two authors contend that the primal scene itself stages the scenario of its own origin (it is, after all, about origin). By choosing as an example the female patient in Freud's "A Case of Paranoia," they show how the "click" of a camera reportedly heard by the patient in a state of delirium referred back to the primal scene, to the "noise of the parents who awaken the child" (10). This noise is not the primal scene itself but its *origin,* what happened just before it and what caused it to happen, and its symbolization in the camera click manifests the presence of the origin of the primal scene/fantasy in the fantasy itself: "The origin of the fantasy is integrated in the very structure of the original fantasy" (10).

What is important for us, in terms of voyeurism and literature, is that the primal scene itself raises the question of its own origin. In the fantasy that is literature, primal scenes can be a fitting setting for questions concerning the origin of that very fantasy that is literature: does literature represent an anterior "event"? Written into the primal scene is also the question of the origin of the self: where do I come from? For literature, this becomes the origin of the "subject" of literature itself.

The concept of the origin of the "fantasy"/text comprises one of the central problems of Robbe-Grillet's *Le Voyeur.* Is this novel one that buys into the representational status of literature? In other words, is this novel structured so as to re-present a previous reality, whether an event or an idea in the author's mind (is its origin in reality, not in fiction)? Or is it more "modern" in its relation to representation, in the sense that the combination and interaction of its words create new, previously nonexistent meanings?[1] A study of voyeurism and the primal scenes in this novel (whose title obviously invites this type of study) will give us some answers to this much-debated question.

The structure of the primal scene appears in a number of fragmented scenarios in this novel. There is a present time to the story's main events, and embedded in this "present" are flashbacks to earlier scenes. The first scene in the chronological sense seems to be Mathias's memory of a childhood scene in which he is drawing a picture of a sea gull. This is a visual scene created by the child, Mathias, of a gull, but it is a scene that is significantly missing something: "One has the impression, however, that something is still missing" (22). The "missing element" might also be reflected in the French word for gull, "mouette," which is close to the word "muette," which means mute, silent. The "missing" element relates to the "missing" sound or word, a concept, as we shall see, that is central to this text (in which the crime is absent from, not spoken in, the narrative), for instance to the "hole" in his reconstructed schedule: "A hole still remained in his itinerary" (202).

In the primal scene of the origin of gender, the missing element is, of course, the genitals of the woman. The narrator takes great care to name the specific kind of gull, a "goéland," which perhaps, when put alongside of the "missing" element in the primal scene, might conjure up another word, "gonade" (in a transposition of letters in which one, the *l*, or *elle*, is missing—another important concept), obviously relevant to the "missing element" in the primal scene.[2]

The second scene in the chronology of events would appear to be the first real scene of voyeurism represented in the text. The morning of his trip, as Mathias is walking to the dock to the ship that will take him to the island, he hears a sound, the classic origin of the primal scene represented in the scene:

As he walked down a small street, Mathias thought he heard a whimper, quite faint, but seeming to come from so close to him that he turned his head. There was no one next to him; the alley was empty behind him as well as in front. He was going to continue on his route, when he heard the same moan a second time, very distinct, right next to his ear. At that moment he noticed a window at street level—just within reach of his right hand—in which a light was burning, even though it was already

broad daylight and the light from outdoors could not be shut out
by the simple voile curtain that hung behind the panes. . . . The
folds of the curtain kept him from distinguishing the furniture
inside. One could see only what the electric light lit up with
intensity at the back of the room: the conical shade of the
lamp—a bedside lamp—and the vaguer form of a disheveled bed.
Standing next to the bed, slightly bent over it, a masculine
silhouette raised an arm toward the ceiling.

The entire scene remained immobile. Despite the unfinished
aspect of his gesture, the man did not budge any more than a
statue. . . . From the tone of the voice—an agreeable one, at
that, and without any sadness—the victim must have been a very
young woman or child. (28–29)

Here Mathias observes an erotic bed scene, a scene that is explicitly
sadistic—this is a voyeurism that must punish and castrate the
woman. The importance of the light in the scene might represent
the importance of the knowledge gained (or constructed), knowledge about gender and the difference between the sexes observed in
the parental scene. The street that is "empty behind as well as in
front" represents, perhaps, the interpretation of feminine sexual
organs as missing, in which the front looks like the back. Even
gender ambiguity and the confusion of desires is present, for in the
primal scene the child is the onlooker; here the child is the victim
(in the feminine place) of the scene. (There is another female child
on the boat who stares rather aggressively.) Thus the sadistic violence against woman here could be seen to be constructed so as to
contain femininity and relegate it to the other. Of course, this story
is eventually about the "real" murder of another young woman.
Furthermore, certain vague, sadistic scenes "float" through this
novel like the blue cigarette packs that make their appearance here
and there, scenes like the following one: "At the foot of the pine
tree the dry grass began to blaze, as did the bottom of the cotton
dress. Violette twisted around the other way and threw her head
back, opening her mouth" (86).

One might object, at this point, that Robbe-Grillet, writing in
the fifties, was intentionally controlling and constructing these
scenes of voyeurism through a knowledge of psychoanalysis. I contend that, conscious or not, the strategies of this kind of sadistic
voyeurism have certain effects and involve certain strategies that do

not change. Whether the sadism is deliberate or unconscious, for me, makes no difference: this is still a story about the murder of a woman, of, in fact, several women. And there are scenes of violence against women strewn throughout the novel in more or less muted terms:

> In one angle, at eye level, stood a display mannequin: the body of a young woman with her limbs cut off—her arms just below the shoulder and the thighs twenty centimeters from the torso—and whose head tilted a bit, to the front and to one side, to produce a "gracious" effect; one hip was pushed out a little more than the other, in a supposedly natural pose. She was of small proportions, smaller than normal as far as one could judge because of the mutilations . . . She was dressed only in a bra and a narrow garter belt popular in the city. (71)

This young, small, childlike mannequin/woman reappears in the murdered "real" woman, Jacqueline, whose body is described as "a mannequin thrown from the cliffs" (175).

The third visual scene in the series involves a movie poster that Mathias sees on the island. The poster involves many of the same elements of the earlier, window scene:

> On the poster, done in violent colors, a man of colossal stature, in Renaissance clothes, held next to him a young girl dressed in a kind of long pale nightgown, a girl whose wrists he immobilized behind her back with one of his hands; with his free hand he was strangling her. Her torso and face were bent backward, in her effort to get away from her executioner, and her immense blond hair hung down to the ground. The decor, in the background, represented a vast pillared bed hung with red curtains.

The bed scene, the violence, the man "above" the woman, curtains—all these elements are repeated from the earlier scene. What is introduced here is the relation between fiction and reality: the artistic representation of the movie poster repeats what happened earlier that morning in reality, but of course, in an uncanny way (like a coincidence). However, if we go back to that earlier window scene which takes place "in reality," certain aspects of its "reality" are called into question:

He would not even have sworn that the cries came from that house; he had thought them to be closer, and less muted than they would have been had they come from behind a closed window. In thinking about it, he wondered if he had heard inarticulate whimpers after all: he thought now that they might have been identifiable words, even though it was impossible for him to remember what words they might have been. (29).

To complicate the reality/fantasy problem further, the "fantasy" of the poster becomes reality later when a sailor recounts what must have happened to Jacqueline, the young woman murdered in the novel: "She must have killed herself when she fell—several meters—her thin neck broken" (175). The broken neck, which is real, echoes the stragulation scene in the fictional movie poster, a poster whose scene originates, perhaps, in reality.

In fact, the confusion between fiction and reality, fantasy and reality, is sustained throughout the book, both in the sense that we are never sure what really happened and what was imagined, and we are never sure what is a fictional reconstruction by Mathias or a real memory of a real event. The confusion between present and past, between fiction and reality, between rewritten and purely remembered material, is one of the important elements of the primal scene. The primal scene itself involves a complicated interweaving precisely of fiction, interpretation, symbolization, and reality. The Wolf Man, as a four-year-old child, had a dream that finally made sense of an observation (or fantasy of an observation?) that dated from the time when he was one and a half, the observation of his parents having intercourse: "He understood it at the time of the dream when he was four years old, not at the time of the observation. He received the impressions when he was one and a half; his understanding of them was deferred, but became possible at the time of the dream owing to his development, his sexual excitations, and his sexual researches" ("Infantile Neurosis" 37–38n.6). Only at a later date can the observations, the event, take on meaning because of the development of the mental life.[3] Thus reality would be able to acquire meaning only when it can be integrated into the human's signifying world (or Symbolic world, in Lacan's terms). Here the location of the origin is displaced from the past to the present, for it can take on meaning as origin only in the present, only in its integration into a symbolic system that changes it, because it has meaning only in the secondary moment, not in its moment as origin.

The confusion between the fiction of representational art and reality is condensed in the movie poster, because the next day Mathias finds that the poster has changed from the sadistic strangulation scene to a bizarre, ambiguous, confused landscape image:

> The new poster represented a landscape. Mathias, at least, thought he discerned in the crossed lines a kind of moor strewn with clumps of bushes, but there was surely something else, superimposed over it: certain contours or spots of color appeared here and there, which could not have belonged to the first design. However, one could not say, either, that these colors constituted a second design, because one couldn't perceive any link between them, one couldn't guess at any meaning for them; they succeeded only, in sum, in blurring the undulations of the moor, to the extent that one doubted that it was really a landscape. . . . On the bottom was spread out in large letters what must have been the title of the film: "Monsieur X. on the Double Circuit. (167)

If the origin of the primal scene is an ambiguous combination of past event and present interpretation, of reality and fiction, past and present, and if the primal scenario writes into itself its own origin, then this poster scene aptly figures the problematic origin of this very novel. The "Monsieur X. on the Double Circuit" is Mathias himself going around the island in a figure eight, both in reality and in his reconstruction of the trip. This mise en abîme of the novel and the ambiguous superimposition of images plays out the novel's own problematic origin: which comes first, Mathias's trip or the poster, the event or its representation? Does fiction originate in reality or does it create its own meanings? Let us leave behind, for a time, the question of voyeurism to investigate this literary problematic in Le Voyeur, to see if this novel is representational or more modernly creational. Then we can return to the implications of our findings in the context of voyeurism in literature.

Perhaps one of the most brilliant of Robbe-Grillet's literary talents is his power to perceive the inner workings of the masterpieces of the past and to display them for what they are in his own kind of undermining. It is now a cliché to say that he and the New Novelists took the chronology and continuity of plot, the psychology of characters, and the mechanisms of the reality effect of the novel and stood them on their head, creating action and characters that lack a coherent past on which to base an interpretation of the present, and finally exposing the techniques of the reality effect by making fun of them through such processes as the *mise en abîme* we saw above. And here we must say that Robbe-Grillet also picked up on the recurrent need of narrative prose to dramatize the search for truth by seeing it as the unveiling of woman and by emphasizing the violent nature of that gesture. His work in the cinema multiplies the reliance on the visual, and on the unveiling of the woman in an increasingly pornographic and violent sense. Clearly in *Le Voyeur*, Robbe-Grillet's revelation and "showing" of the "myth" of the revelation of the truth in the novelistic world is evident.

Of course, in this novel, the truth the reader must seek is the truth concerning a death, in order to know whether it was murder or accident, and, if it was murder, to learn the identity of the murderer. The victim is, as we have seen, a woman, and a woman found without parts of her clothing, a woman unveiled. And, for the critics, it is a search for the identity of the voyeur, for it is not clear in the text which character fills that role.

It would seem, then, that Robbe-Grillet's very project seems to be the upending of the tradition that uses the unveiling of woman in the search for truth, because it so evidently shows the clichéd nature of such novelistic techniques. But I will show that the mechanism of this undermining really remains a faithful part of the tradition it wishes to negate. It is interesting to note that the readers of this text seem to fall into two different groups on this issue of tradition and revolution. As Ben Stoltzfus has put it, they belong either to the group of " 'recuperative' critics who see meaning and chronology in Robbe-Grillet's works" or to the group of critics who, like Ricardou, speak for a "linguistic, nonmimetic interplay of verbal signs" in his works (13).

The novel *Le Voyeur* is both radically modern in the sense of the importance of the play of language in the text, and also meaningful in the traditional sense of the nineteenth-century novel. Ricardou's important study shows the modern aspect of Robbe-Grillet, how the very words in Robbe-Grillet's texts generate the text. Applying Ricardou's idea to *Le Voyeur*, we see how each element of the murder is carefully preceded by a similar element in another context. These elements seem to generate the murder itself: the blue cigarette pack, containing the cigarettes which were presumably used to torture the victim, floats in and out of the text as a theme; the cords used to bind her appear so many times in different contexts that the reader may even become irritated by such a heavy-handed clue; emphasis is placed on the curved, bent necks of the young women whom Mathias meets, prefiguring the broken neck of the victim. What appear to be random, descriptive "realist" elements of the text, a cigarette pack floating on the water, generate the center of the text, the murder.

Furthermore, this text plays with language. The letters *v* and *i* appear in one place in the text, and in another the letter *o* (133, 144, 250). In combination, *vio*, they begin to form the name of that enigmatic woman Violette, who seems to be a person whom Mathias knew and possibly tortured in his past life and whom he mixes up constantly with Jacqueline, the girl perhaps tortured and killed in the "present" of the text. But what of the remainder of the name "Violette," the *lette?* We see part of it, again dispersed throughout the text as were the individual letters *v, i, o,* in the oppressively repeated diminutives, in the *ette* of words like "fillette," "vaguelette," "caissettes," "chainette," "gouttelettes," "aveuglette," "mouette," "mallette," "cordelette," "maquette," "maisonettes" . . . . The letters of the name "Violette," missing in one loop of the figure eight, emerge in another way in the diminutive form *ette* of some of the most important words of the text: viol, fille, corde, mal/malle, vague, aveugle (rape, girl, cord, evil/trunk, wave, blind).[4] There remains one missing letter, the *l*, which matches nicely the missing "elle" (already noted above in another context), the almost absent woman, Violette, and the missing Jacqueline. Thus, rather than being a simple narrative which purports to re-present a preexisting story, this text makes evident the narrative generation which comes, not from reality, but from the very words of the text.

Yet most readers also say that there is a skeleton of a plot which permits one to make one's way through the textual play. After all, it is a text whose temporal enclosure is a sea trip to an off-coast village, and the "present" action takes place within that limit. There is a central character in the text, Mathias, even though the point of view of the narrative is fractured and divided among several different perspectives. There is a "plot" which has a neat correlative in the geography of Mathias's trip around the island: time and space try to fit together in a one-to-one mapping, even if sometimes that mapping is called into question. Thus in certain ways this text manifests quite standard elements of nineteenth-century plot construction, but in other ways it seems to be quite radically new. It is the interaction between the traditional and the innovative that I want to investigate here, and this interaction will show how *Le Voyeur* is essentially a continuation of the nineteenth-century realist novel.

Most critics who wish to speak to the innovative nature of this text point to the absent center, the absent crime, of the text which "takes place" between part 1 and part 2 on the blank page between. Thus, they say, the nonrepresentational void of literature becomes the very center of this story. Yet why is it that so many readers (almost all) definitely see and interpret that crime, believe it is Mathias who commits it, and watch him as he tries to come up with alibis for it? Indeed, the crime is never described in the text; it is missing (thematized in the "something missing" of the primal scene). The only descriptions of the actual scene of the torture of Jacqueline/Violette are frozen in that famous immobility which has been frequently observed in Robbe-Grillet's works.[5] The violent act is never shown, only the situation just before and the consequences. It is indeed the hole burned out of the text.

This is, perhaps, where Robbe-Grillet's real genius lies. He never supplies the event; he only supplies the "clues" to the solution of the murder, and he thereby forces the reader to interpret the events, to "invent" the crime, to write the crime: he forces the *reader* to murder Jacqueline/Violette. This is accomplished when the narrator filters several different violent scenes through Mathias's world and links them, as we said before, by common elements. Thus in the "frozen" scene of the movie poster, we see the man strangling a woman (the neck theme); in a newspaper clipping we read of the violent death of a woman; in the morning as he is going to catch the boat, he—evidently the "voyeur" in the scene—looks through that window and sees the man with hand raised against the young woman; in a photograph he sees a girl who seems to be tied up: all these scenes of violence toward women, filtered through Mathias's point of view, prepare the reader to link his point of view, his being, to the death of the girl. Innumerable clues point to his criminality, but the crime is never there and never attributed to anyone. The closest we come to seeing the violence is in a few "frozen" scenes in which there is no action: for example, when he sees her with her shirt in her mouth (179; no noise and no action) and when he assures himself that he threw all of her clothes off the cliff (205; he remembers a previous event).

I would like to argue that indeed, the text lays the ground for one and only one interpretation of these clues, and that, although it seems that the reader is "writing" the meaning of the text, it is there already, existing prior to the writing of the text. This text manipulates and mocks the reader, who is forced to move along the paths set out on that island. Perhaps the best instance of this manipulation of the reader, who is forced to make a connection even though the crime is not described, appears in the following quotation when Mathias is worried about the cigarettes that he left by the cliff where Jacqueline fell, cigarettes which were bizarrely burned only a little bit. What "no one could imagine" is precisely what the reader is here forced to imagine, particularly because of one of Mathias's previous memory/fantasies of a woman burning in a dress:

> He searched in vain, he could not succeed in discovering the third fragment. This last one should have been, in his view, smaller than the two others; it would then be less incriminating—especially by itself—since it was just about the size of the cigarette butts that any smoker might discard. No one, reasonably, would go so far as to imagine the use to which it had been put.

Thus the reader is forced to do the torturing and murdering in this text, because that interpretation is generated by the text. It is not thus a question of the murder being represented in the text: this is where Robbe-Grillet is innovative. It is rather the reader's itinerary that is mapped out in a predetermined and unique way, the author's predefined plan can be carried out because certain meanings are imperative and are imposed upon a careful reader.

Thus it is my contention that there does exist a previous "meaning" for this text, which Robbe-Grillet proceeds to reflect in the plot. This "meaning" is the path of reading which must be taken by the reader. Is this unilateral meaning self-conscious in the text? Perhaps so, for in the following sentence, if the "plan fictif" (the fictive plan) figures representational fiction, and the "verre" (glass) represents the uncontrollable poetic proliferation of language, then the map of the fiction significantly limits the poetic potential of language: "At the same time that the rotation of his wrist came to a stop, the surface of the liquid that had been poured became immobilized, rigorously at the level of the edges—without the smallest curve—as a fictive plan delimiting the theoretic contents of the glass" (107).

The other overriding reason for seeing this text as a text that represents a previous meaning can be seen ironically in the very examples which most critics see as pointing out the radical nature of the text. Consider the oft-discussed name of the text, *Le Voyeur*, which so many people have seen as a truncated version of *Le Voyageur* (*The Traveler*). Mathias is quite often in the text called "the traveler," which represents his job as a traveling salesman, a "commis voyageur." What the title does is "violently torture" the word *voyageur* by cutting off one of its "limbs" (as we saw, there are numerous references to dismemberment in the text, e.g., the crabs being dismembered and eaten, the mannequin dismembered in the store), that limb being the letters *ag* which suggest *âge*, —age, time, the event and time of the murder itself—just as the subtraction from *commis voyageur* of its first term, which in another context means "committed," represents the subtraction of the commission of the crime. What is normally considered to be a radical innovation of the new novel, the subtraction of events, characters, representation, is controlled, mirrored comfortably, and thematized in the very word plays of the text.

Another example of the controlling use of the mise en abîme is in the newspaper clipping, which again forces itself on the reader as a prototype for the violence of Mathias. In this clipping, what Mathias says is missing in the description is again exactly what is missing in the details of Jacqueline's murder:

It did not really say very much. The length did not surpass that of a crime summary of little importance. Again, a good part of it did nothing but retrace the futile circumstances of the discovery of the body; since the end of the article was devoted to commentaries on the direction that the officers intended to take in the investigation, very little space remained for the description of the body itself, and nothing at all was left for the reconstruction of the order of tortures undergone by the victim . . . *It was necessary to reinvent the scene from one end to the other* beginning with two or three elementary details, such as *the age* or the color of hair. (76, emphasis mine)

Thus just as Mathias reinvents the crime missing from the newspaper so we do the same for his crime, and just as the *ag* is missing from the word *voyageur*, the "âge" of the victim is missing from this article.

Thus one simply cannot say that this is a text in which the play of words generates new and original meanings, because the play of the words simply repeats, represents, returns to one univocal sense.[6] Even Ricardou, who shows how this text is not representational, shows how there is a neat mapping, a one-to-one correspondence, between the plot (representation of everyday life) and the word (radical play of language). It is the one-to-one representation of the one by the other, the univocal nature of this reflection, that returns this text to conventionality. When Mathias burns the hole in the paper and invokes the torture of burning holes in skin with cigarettes, he shows the one-to-one mapping of text (the hole in the paper) onto the reader's experience (reading the hole in the novel, the absent crime, as a cigarette burn)—and it links this process to the active castration of woman (the hole). It is not that the text lacks a center, and that around this lack meaning becomes infinite; but rather, the burned out hole, the lack, *is* ironically the recuperable center of the text. The castrated, nonwhole, holed, murdered woman is, precisely, the point.[7]

Thus what normally would be radical discontinuity, the fearful "hole in the text," a kind of fearful nonplenitude of meaning, a symbolic distance, becomes thematized, controlled, a mirror of control, the hole of the text which constantly mirrors itself. The ambiguous nature of gender identity, the confusion of desires, can be dichotomized and the woman can be punished, mutilated, castrated.[8] Thus this mirroring becomes, as in Lacan's description of the mirror phase, the Imaginary, ludic pleasure of mastery. Its violent nature, the child who is aggressively trying to control his image, can be linked to the violent nature of this text and to the attempt to control the reader's image of the text by mapping out the paths so carefully. Indeed, the image of the burned or dismembered body is one of Lacan's "images du corps morcelé," "images of the body in pieces" (*Ecrits* 104). Thus this text could be seen to partake of the structure of the mirror stage in which the corps morcelé, literally the body of Jacqueline/Violette (significantly divided into two), and the frustration of the individual who is not complete can be dominated and mastered in the mirror reflection and in the belief in the image of completion in the mirror, here the mirror reflection being the circular unity and reflection between plot and text.

What would normally be the "symbolic" space of nonidentity in Lacan gets turned back into a neat "Imaginary" reflection of control and mastery here. Symbolic becomes subordinated to Imaginary reflection and circularity. This turn from Symbolic to Imaginary could well be what differentiates erotic, symbolic literature from violent pornography (which in Robbe-Grillet's later works certainly abounds), where the sadism and violence toward woman could be seen as an attempt at mastery and at the violent imposition of a closed, hierarchical world, or as an attempt to give a mirror image of sexuality and violence without mediation or ambiguity. The necessary participant of the "audience" in the art is also, as Susanne Kappeler has theorized, a component of pornography: "The fantasy of porn is not fully depicted, it is not identical with the 'content' of representation, it is to be completed by the active subject, the viewer-hero of the representation" (59). It is also the structure of the identification between the position of the author, who sets up the structure, and the reader/spectator, who takes up that structure of murder, a neat identification between the subject of writing and its audience (32).

As we have seen, *Le Voyeur* perpetuates the representational illusion of the nineteenth-century novel. It also perpetuates one particular classic theme of literature, which in fact, we have seen repeated in each text of part I: the woman who defies rules, a defiance suggested to be an erotic one, is in danger of being killed. In the novel from the eighteenth-century on, as demonstrated by Nancy Miller, and in films of the twentieth century (in "hacker" movies especially), the woman whose sexuality and independence threaten the established order is killed, or at the least, threatened with death. And just as in these hacker movies, the viewer is forced to assume the point of view of the hacker, so the reader of *Le Voyeur* is forced to "murder" Jacqueline/Violette in this text.

Thus, although the ambiguity and the innovative play of language in this text cannot be dismissed, the imaginary nexus of the text keeps the tradition of the novel going. The violent unveiling of the woman is linked to learning the truth about the killer, even if you are the killer. At the heart of the story, several murdered, tortured women show that the "new realism" of Robbe-Grillet may be closer to the old realism than had previously been thought.

The final topic to be considered in the relation between reality and fiction in this text is the way in which fiction can become reality as well as reflect it. In certain pathological cases, such as in the perversions and in hysteria, constructions of the mind can over-power the force of the perception of reality. By this I mean that there are "blind spots" in which the mind prevents the body from seeing what is in the Real. Joyce McDougall describes what happens in the perversions, in particular in fetishism, as just this kind of faulty vision, which she terms disavowal. When the model of the difference between the sexes and of sexual relations is deformed in perversions, the meaning of the discovery of the mother's absence of a penis simply does not take on meaning (for instance, the subject, although having seen that there is no penis, simply "ig-nores" this fact in a certain way). The fetishist, in order to deny castration, "hallucinates" a penis on the woman by means of a real object (McDougall 54–55), thus "seeing" what is not really there.[9]

A different inability to see can occur in hysterical blindness, when looking as sexual pleasure draws defensive action by the ego, and the subject becomes "blind." Freud describes this as a kind of inner voice that says: "Because you sought to misuse your organ of sight for evil sensual pleasures, it is fitting that you should not see anything at all any more" ("Vision" 216–217). Thus again, like the fetishist, the subject misperceives reality, although there is no physi-cal cause of the blindness. In fact, these "blind spots" make up a large portion of the way we perceive ourselves in the world, for, as Lacan pointed out in his models of the construction of the self, the self is an illusion that is constructed on the basis of a fictional identification, just as a virtual image has no physical reality in the place where it is perceived.[10]

There are two important points to be made about this fiction become reality. First, on a theoretical, feminist level, feminist cri-tiques of the phallocentrism of Freudian psychoanalysis show that the visual construction of gender identity, whether "normal" or "abnormal," is itself a kind of pathology of vision because it always contains a very important blind spot: the gender identity that exists outside the field of vision—in other words, female gender identity, which is not visible. As Irigaray makes clear, gender identity as we know it is constructed in the visual field around woman's lack of penis, and what is "foreclosed" is any gender that might not be visible: "The idea that a 'nothing to be seen,' a something not subject to the rule of visibility or of specula(riza)tion, might yet have some reality, would indeed be intolerable to man" (50). The visual construction of gender identity, which is phallogocentric, needs this blind spot in order to function correctly. Thus, as the converse of the disavowal in perversions that does not see what is in the Real (the absence of a penis in the woman), the "blind spot" of phallocentric construction of gender identity is the inability to account for what is not visible unless it is integrated into the visible presence or absence of a penis.

Second, the notion of the "blind spot" helps us also to keep in mind that we must not think the *perception* of reality remains uncontaminated by psychic structures. Hysterical blindness and foreclosure, although extreme cases of the effect of the mind on perception, should make it clear that all instances of perception are already governed by our symbolic world. When the male child looks at the female genitals, this perception can have no meaning unless it can be integrated into an already existing system. The image is not secondary to reality in any simple way: rather, as Rose points out, "It is clear that the perception of an absence can have meaning only in relation to a presence or oppositional term, to a structure—that of sexual difference—within which the instance of perception *already finds its place*" (*Vision* 202). What precedes perception of reality is a differential structure that is already in place and serves to interpret the perception.

What is troubling is that the kind of sadistic violence against women that we see in a text like *Le Voyeur* is not merely, say, a representation of the effects of the primal scene but a text that may have performative effects on reality. The punishment of the woman may serve not only to reflect a fantasy shared by all but also to perpetuate and realize that fantasy in reality, to construct a way of determining the difference between the sexes. The very similarity of certain aspects of the three texts we have studied, the repetition of the theme of the punishment of women, may help to make that punishment seem "real" and natural.

This troubling similarity of the three texts lies in the nature of the female protagonists: in all three of these texts, the women to be exposed are exceptional women. Suzanne is exceptional in her beauty and her illegitimacy, Paquita in her beauty and mystery, and Jacqueline in her supposedly transgressive sexuality. These texts show the need to expose the secret of the woman's exceptional nature, an exceptional nature which in each case has something to do with the transgression of the norm: Suzanne does not conform to the monastic life, Paquita does not fall completely for the irresistible Henri, and Jacqueline defies the social mores of the time to "run around," literally and figuratively. And in two of the cases, the exceptional nature of these women is the nature of their bodies: Suzanne's attractiveness is one of the reasons for her troubles, and Paquita's remarkable beauty attracts everyone's eyes. The need to see the body of the woman and to see the truth of her altogether exceptional nature is at the center of these texts. The exposure of the woman is linked to violence and to a desire to repress that difference through death.

In the three texts, the desire to see the body of the woman is also linked to the bodies of letters, of texts. In *La Religieuse,* it is the body of her writing that Suzanne and Ursule must cover up, and writing is incorporated by eating the text. In *La Fille aux yeux d'or,* Paquita's correspondence with Mariquita is a corpus of letters, which Henri tries to expose and eventually sees, that have a strange, nonsymbolic corporality (strange drawings like hieroglyphs in blood). And in *Le Voyeur,* it is the body of the newspaper article that has cigarette burns like the body of Jacqueline. Transgression and women, in two of the cases, relate to women's writing, to the fact that women write, that women "know," thus that women "see," even though they may be handicapped in that seeing, like Suzanne. The transgressive nature of these women relates to the physicality of writing, and the desire to see and know her difference is perhaps a kind of desire to know the unknowable, the arbitrary physical nature of the sign, a desire to capture what escapes understanding. Thus in these three texts, which span three centuries, we see the relatively unproblematized persistence of the theme of the secret unveiling of the woman and the search for truth in fiction, a persistence that may work to continue the "punishment" of women in reality.

The remainder of the book studies the problematization of this structure. Particular attention will be paid to those places in literary texts where the voyeurist gaze that is present in those texts is undermined. Attention will focus also on those places in which the logic of the field of vision is cloudy—often these places involve not the visual field but the textual one. Jacqueline Rose has analyzed certain muddled, ambiguous places in the visual field in her study of

Freud's understanding of Leonardo da Vinci. She points out that in Freud's theory, a failure to depict the primal scene is related explicitly to bisexuality (as we have seen in our discussion of the primal scene and ambiguities of gender identity in voyeurism). In Freud's discussion of Leonardo da Vinci, this bisexuality is also linked to a problem of representational space: "The uncertain sexual identity muddles the plane of the image so that the spectator does not know where she or he stands in relationship to the picture. A confusion at the level of sexuality brings with it a disturbance of the visual field" (226). Thus a visual image that challenges "the power of illusion and the address of the image" can serve to "challenge the fact of sexual difference" (226). Correlatively, I wish to study those places in literary texts where the ambiguity of textuality challenges the power of representational illusion and the fact of gender identity. In order to do this, in each chapter of part II of this study, at least two texts will be studied together in order to make textual difference (the difference between two texts and in a single text) the foundation of the reading act. In doing this I hope to avoid the one-to-one mapping of text onto meaning that appears so dangerous in *Le Voyeur*, that attempts to master the uncontrollable generation of meanings by mutilating, "cutting off," otherness. The problem lies not in the search for truth itself, but rather in the elimination of "differing" elements in texts, elements that may not fit together to make a neat, coherent story, elements that instead question the possibility of such a tidy conclusion. The analysis will now turn away from the technical, psychoanalytic aspects of the primal scene, to literary texts and the way in which voyeurism relates to more purely literary problems. Nevertheless, such themes as the contamination of borders, the elimination of transgressive elements, strategies of mastery, the quest for knowlege, and castration and gender identity, which were revealed in the psychoanalytic aspects of voyeurism, will remain a constant in the literary texts. After identifying the voyeurist scenes in the texts, I will go on to study how literary texts can challenge the validity of those very scenes.

**Part 2**

# TEXTUALITY
# AND THE
# PROBLEMATIZATION
# OF VOYEURIST
# TRUTH

# 5

# Romanticism, Voyeurism, and the Unveiling of Woman

*What is missing in the internal world is sought in an object or in an exterior situation, because a failure of symbolization left a void in the Oedipal structuration. This failure concerns the role of the paternal penis and the signification of the primal scene.*
—Joyce McDougall,
*Plaidoyer pour une certaine anormalité*

*A real occurrence—dating from a very early period—looking—immobility—sexual problems—castration—his father—something terrible.*
—Sigmund Freud,
"From the History of an Infantile Neurosis"

ONE OF THE MOST OUTRAGEOUS scenes of voyeurism in all of French literature is a scene which, in my opinion, has not received the attention that its peculiar nature warrants. In Balzac's *La Peau de chagrin*, the main character, Raphaël de Valentin, decides to hide in the bedroom of the object of his unrequited love, the enigmatic Foedora, in order to see her naked and thus to resolve the enigma of her identity. Here we have the classic scene of voyeurism in literature as defined in the present discussion, a voyeurism aimed at the revelation of the origin of gender identity: the subject aims to see the object of desire in secret (here Foedora's naked body) in order to obtain hidden knowledge (of her gender identity, and then of the object of *her* desires).

The failure on the part of readers to be shocked or surprised by such a scene is perhaps evidence of the extent to which seeing, seeing woman, and seeing truth is taken for granted as a metaphoric network so common as to be unremarkable. What I will investigate here is just how much the "mal du siècle" of the Romantic hero is linked to this type of male voyeurism in Balzac's text, and how voyeurism is entangled in the Oedipal complexities of the family romance in Balzac, Stendhal, and other French Romantic novelists.[1]

As for "mal du siècle," it is a commonplace in literary studies to say that the French Romantic hero suffers from this infamous disease, from a kind of vague existential angst of objectless desire, and from a certain lack of identity, a feeling of no longer fitting into a world whose values have changed. Often the problems of the hero's identity are linked to the impossibility of finding an object to desire—we think of René's attempts to find a purpose in anything, and his failure to desire and love any woman but his sister.

What has not as yet been noticed, however, is that the Romantic hero, in his quest for identity or for an object to desire, quite frequently violates a woman's privacy by somehow stealing information that she supposedly or in reality possesses, or at the very least, by coming into possession of that information without her consent; he steals the information from her in a kind of voyeurist act, or an act of eavesdropping. Take René, for example, and the way he learns of his sister's incestuous desire for him: he is with her at the altar as she is taking her religious vows, and he eavesdrops on her conversation with God. In the case of Adolphe, he explicitly goes against Elénore's wishes when he opens and reads the letter he had agreed never to read, in a sense violating the will of a dead woman. Claude Frollo in *Notre Dame de Paris* resorts to an explicit act of voyeurism when he hides in the room where Esmerelda makes love to Phoebus, and he thus continues his mad search for knowledge in the carnal sphere.

Now these heroes share one other unusual thing in common in addition to their violation of the woman: they are motherless children, who perhaps because of this must seek knowledge about and from the woman. Indeed, in our investigation of the motherless

Raphaël de Valentin, we will see how the theft of knowledge from the woman derives from the Oedipus complex, and we will then see how a very different Romantic hero, Fabrice del Dongo of *La Chartreuse de Parme,* can manage to escape the fate of his confrères.

## Sexual/Textual Ambiguity in
## *La Peau de chagrin*

Raphaël de Valentin, the hero of *La Peau de chagrin,* manifests the uncertain desire linked to "mal du siècle" in an unusual way. He oscillates back and forth in the novel between two different "systems": the system of "savoir" (knowledge), in which he invests all his energy in the life of the mind and lives in poverty; and the system of "pouvoir, vouloir" (power, will) represented by the magical *peau de chagrin* (wild ass's skin), the system by means of which he desires and succeeds in possessing money and love. The problem is that when he finds he has devoted himself to one of the two systems, he would prefer to adhere to the other: when he devotes himself to study, he desires money and women; when he has money and women, he doesn't want them (because when his wishes come true, he dies a little bit). The effect of this oscillation is heightened by the flashback narrative, for this allows us to switch back and forth between the systems in time.

This oscillation is, as is always the case in Balzac, linked to possession and dispossession of money, and it crystallizes the main conflict in the text. Let us begin with an analysis of possession and dispossession in this text, and then turn to study the infamous scene of unveiling. The link between dispossession and the unveiling of woman may give us a clue to the ambiguous object of Romantic desire and to the Romantic need to unveil the woman.

*La Peau de chagrin* begins with a gambling scene that is an explicit image of divestiture. Raphaël de Valentin is down to his last coin; he enters the casino, places his last sous on one number, and loses everything. This divestiture is linked, however, to a more symbolic image of decapitation when the casino employees and the other gamblers, who are so hardened to the drama of loss and gain, feel the same emotions as would an executioner: "But have not executioners sometimes wept over the virgins whose blond heads were to

be cut off at a signal of the Revolution?" (63).[2] If the text employed
this single image of decapitation, it might not appear particularly
extraordinary, but the image is repeated time and again: "These idle
men were there, silent, immobile, attentive as is the populace at
the Grève when the executioner cuts off a head" (62). "He was
walking . . . lost in an engrossing meditation, similar to the one by
which criminals were seized when a cart drove them from the Palace
to the Grève, toward that scaffold, red with all the blood spilled
since 1793" (66). "He was, so to speak, seeking courage and demanding a cordial, like the criminals who test their strength while
going to the scaffold" (70).

In fact, this divestiture as decapitation takes on numerous forms
in this text, the most amusing being the loss of one's hat. As
Raphaël enters the casino, he must, according to the "law," give it
up: "When you enter a gaming house, the law begins by divesting
you of your hat" (59). The narrator gives this divestiture a certain
depth of meaning by saying that it is perhaps a kind of parable, or an
infernal contract, or a way of keeping the gambler respectful, or a
ploy by the police to learn his identity; even, perhaps, an attempt to
gain phrenological knowledge. In the Balzacian world of hypersym-
bolic clothing, the hat is, of course, an extremely important symbol; for Raphaël it becomes a "worthy representative of its master"
(169) when it is ruined by the rain just after Raphaël is rejected by
Foedora. Given this symbolism, it is not surprising that Rastignac
should come back from a successful gambling trip with his hat full of
gold (206), and that the universal object of desire, Foedora, should
have her male visitors place their hats in her bedroom, where they
can come in and pine for her as they look at her bed. (Should we
add that a fedora, in English, later became a kind of hat, named
after a play by Sardou entitled *Fédora?*)

This notion of loss and divestiture relates to other important
themes in the text and in Romanticism. The loss of identity is
figured by Raphaël's anonymity in the opening gambling scene (we
do not learn his name until after the scene with the antiquary). The
loss of money, identity, and life is figured by the act of signing
promissory notes: "In order to continue dying, I signed promissory
notes with an early due date. . . . My imagination pictured for me
my name traveling from city to city in all the squares of Europe. *Our
name, it is our own self*" (211). Finally, the loss of borders is figured
in the fantastic shop of the antiquary, where nothing is complete,

enclosed, defined, where "nothing complete offered itself to the soul" (74).

This divestiture is also represented as a kind of bodily loss in several contexts. When Raphaël enters the gambling casino, the other gamblers there salute "a deep wound that their gaze measured" (64), a symbolic wound that figures his powerlessness and lack of money. In the antique shop, the place where borders are effaced and law does not exist, the eye of an emperor is threatened by a machine: "A pneumatic machine was putting out the eye of the Emperor Augustus" (72). Clearly, divestiture and castration are linked by this notion of loss of power, loss of the eye, a bodily wound, and indeed, in one striking reference in the text, Raphaël is linked to a particular historical figure who was castrated: "In order to fight more effectively with the cruel power whose dare he had accepted, he made himself chaste in the manner of Origen, by emasculating his imagination" (231). Origen, an early church writer who taught the holy scriptures to women and girls, castrated himself to discourage calumny. Thus Raphaël's symbolic divestiture is linked to this very literal castration.[3]

This emphasis on castrative images might suggest an investigation of family structures in the text, and sure enough, Raphaël, like Adolphe, René, Frollo, and Julien Sorel, is a motherless child (Fabrice has a different family configuration); like Adolphe and René, he carries on rather strained relations with his father, who in this text epitomizes the function of the law. Until the age of twentyone, Raphaël lived under "a despotism as cold as that of a monk's rule . . . His paternity hovered over my mischievous and joyful thoughts, and closed them in as under a dome of lead" (128). His father lays down the law, limits the pleasure of his son, and does not permit him to have any money at all—he embodies the patriarchal law which subjugates son to father, and which is enforced with the threat of castration, here seen in the knife blade of his face, a "visage en lame de couteau" (128).

The drama of the text, the oscillation between two systems, is thus set up early in the chronology of the story, in Raphaël's relationship to his father. To adhere to his father's law is to study, to save, to salvage the family's name and fortune, to refrain from gambling, to work constantly—the system of "savoir" (knowledge). The antiquary himself represents the system of "savoir," because he lives by his imagination alone. His link to knowledge is symbolized by the image of his head, which appears to be suspended in mid-air, and by "his green eyes, full of I know not what calm malice, [which] seemed to light up the moral world as his lamp illuminated this mysterious room" (82). To go against the father's law is to waste time and money, to gamble, to seek to fulfill those desires forbidden by the father—the system of "pouvoir, vouloir." It is to risk loss, literally of money, and symbolically, in the Oedipus complex, of life and limb. The opposition between these two systems can be seen in the spatial disposition of two important opposing objects in the antiquary's rooms. On one side we see a portrait of Christ, who figures knowledge (it is a portrait of his head), paternity, and light, and whose link to Raphaël seems almost familial because it was done by the painter, Raphaël; this is the father's and the antiquary's system of "savoir." Facing this portrait of Christ, the "peau de chagrin" hangs on the opposite wall.

Raphaël's choice between these two systems is dramatized in the remarkable scene in which, at a relative's ball, Raphaël's father gives him his purse and his keys to hold—his purse holding the money, symbol of power in Balzac's world, and his keys being the symbol of the means of entering the father's world.[4] Raphaël chooses to go against his father's law and to use the money to gamble, and he calls this act "the crime of having robbed my father" (131). In terms of the Oedipus complex, he breaks the father's law and is at risk of punishment—castration. In fact, when Raphaël speaks of the pleasure he gained from this experience, he describes it in terms of criminality and of a bodily wound: "Oh! when I should be letting you sleep, I want to tell you of one of the most terrible joys of my life, one of those joys armed with claws that dig into our heart like a hot brand on the shoulder of a criminal" (129). When he wins, we get another image of the scaffold, only this time the person to be executed gets a reprieve (Raphaël wins at the gambling table): "I was like a condemned man who, walking to his death, met the king" (131).

Thus this first successful rebellion against the father assumes the form of gambling, and the divestiture of that other gambling scene, which opens the text and in which Raphaël loses his money, gains more symbolic weight. The opening scene of symbolic castration sets the stage for, in a sense makes necessary, the numerous scenes of voyeurism that follow, and the link between the castration complex and voyeurism in this text will become clearer as we investigate the latter.

In the most important scene of voyeurism in this text, Raphaël decides he will hide in the bedroom of Foedora in order to see her naked. On the level of the plot, he does so because she does not desire him, he cannot understand this, and he thinks there must be something wrong with her. Obviously Raphaël at this point is a kind of unheroic hero: we sympathize with him because of his frustrated desires, but we also laugh at him because he feels he can win a woman's favor simply because he wants her (a fantasy fulfilled by Adolphe).

On a more symbolic level, however, Raphaël needs to verify her sex. The more he gets to know her, the more he feels confused by her. Is she a hermaphrodite? Raphaël alludes to this possibility numerous times: she was, for him, "all of woman and none of woman" (189); she is compared to a statue of a hermaphrodite attributed to Polycles. She reminds Raphaël of a recent story published about a person who sometimes in the form of an officer tames a spirited horse; sometimes in the form of a young girl makes her lovers despair; sometimes in the form of a young man makes a sweet, modest maiden despair (189). What he needs to do, then, is to see the woman naked in order to verify her sex, to see if she has been castrated or not, to see the effects of castration. He needs to enact the primal scene in order to understand the difference between the sexes.

He may also need to verify the effects of castration because his own sex, as that of so many other nineteenth-century heroes (such as Henri de Marsay in *La Fille aux yeux d'or*) is ambiguous. He perhaps needs to verify whether or not he himself has had to submit to castration (because of his transgression of his father's hyperbolic law). It seems that in the motherless world of Raphaël, he has been unable to formulate a definition of the difference between the sexes and must do so to establish his own.[5] Let us mention only a few of the places in the rhetoric of the text where Raphaël's gender is confused. He is compared to "a young girl fallen on her knees before a tiger" (174). He has a "gracious brow like that of a young girl" (309), "the assurance of a duchess" (70), hands "pretty like women's hands" (64), "like those of a pretty woman" (230), a kind of "effeminate grace" (23). He calls himself "an effeminate lover"

(147), a "woman like them [the women who misunderstand him]" (138); a "young girl" married to his father, the "skeleton" (129). Thus he needs to see the woman, to play out that scene of which Freud speaks, when the little boy "discovers" the woman's castration; he needs to be able to set up the symbolic divide that separates "Le TalisMAN" (chapter 1) of money, power, and the possession of the phallus from the "FEMME sans coeur" (chapter 2), the "WOMAN without a heart," the woman divested of a part of her body (emphasis mine).

When Raphaël at last sees Foedora, when "the last veil was lifted," she is perfectly beautiful: "Her blouse, covering the chest of a virgin, dazzled me; through her shirt and in the light of the candles, her white and pink body sparkled like a silver statue that shined in its gauze envelope. No, not one imperfection should make her fear the furtive eyes of love" (195). Raphaël's problem is not solved, because he still cannot understand why she does not desire him and because, in spying on her in her room, he has discovered only new questions to be pondered. She begins to sing—why had no one ever heard her sing before? She utters the words "My God"—what is their significance? (He finds out later that she was thinking of some money she had invested.) It would seem that unveiling the woman to see sexual difference merely gives rise to new enigmas.

There are several other minor scenes of voyeurism in this text which share certain traits with this one. First, when Raphaël defies his father and gambles with the money at the ball, he begins by placing himself in a corner of the room where he is not easily seen, and where he can see women easily. The remainder of the scene evolves very quickly: "I went to a corner of the room in order to be able to eat some ice cream and contemplate the pretty women at my leisure. My father saw me. For some reason, a reason that I have never guessed, he gave me his wallet and his keys to keep. Ten feet from me some men were gambling. I heard gold jingling" (130). We note again his desire to see, without himself having to be on display, his desire to see women, and the manifestation of a sound, here the sound, not of Foedora's lament about money, but of money itself. It was on this night that Raphaël learned he had a certain heightened power of perception: despite the fact that there were many people between him and the gambling table, despite the fact that he turned his back to the table, it was as though he could see and hear everything that was going on: "Despite all these obstacles, by means of a privilege accorded to the passions which gives them the power to wipe out space and time, I heard distinctly the words of the two gamblers, I knew their points, I knew which one of the two men turned over the king as if I had seen the cards" (131). Raphaël, the voyeur, possesses the same hyperbolic powers of vision as that other voyeur, Henri de Marsay.

In a previous scene, but one which is chronologically later, Raphaël, who is postponing his suicide until dark so that he will not be seen, strolls along the quais of the Seine and looks into some shops. At one point, a beautiful young woman descends from a carriage and goes in to buy some illustrated books. Raphaël, here still anonymous, looks at her very pointedly, and we remark in this scene, once again, the combination of his gaze at a woman with the sound of gold:

> He delighted in his contemplation of this charming person whose white face was harmoniously framed in the satin of an elegant hat. He was seduced by a slim figure, by pretty little movements. Her dress, slightly raised by the step, allowed him to see a leg whose fine contours were outlined by snug white stockings. The young woman entered the store, asked about some albums, some collections of lithographs; she bought some for several gold coins which sparkled and jingled on the counter.

Just before this scene, when Raphaël thinks he has lost all his money: "He was surprised to hear several coins jingle in a truly fantastic way in the bottom of his pocket" (68). Again, money is not just seen; it is also heard. Inasmuch as Foedora sings and speaks about money in the main scene of voyeurism, it is striking that in a variant of this novel, Balzac describes the anonymous woman in this scene as a siren (*Peau* [1967] 323).

In another minor scene of voyeurism, the same elements are present. Returning home from one of his visits with Foedora, he notices that the door is open: "The door of my building was slightly open. Through the openings shaped like hearts in the shutter, I saw a light shining out into the street. Pauline and her mother were chatting while they waited for me. I heard my name mentioned, I listened" (171). Here Raphaël spies on Pauline and her mother when they do not know he is there and also eavesdrops on their conversation, and then, after drawing back and making some noise on his second approach, he acts as if he neither saw nor heard anything. It is at this moment that Pauline's mother takes out a key, places it over the Bible, and says that they will all be rich—again a discussion of money. Finally, if the risk of loss in gambling figures the risk of castration, then the spectators at the gambling table who watch Raphaël's dispossession with a certain avidity are, perhaps, voyeurs.[6]

For the moment, let us simply attest the presence of two elements in these scenes of voyeurism: a man spies on a woman or women, and money either makes itself heard or is spoken about by the woman. The presence of the sound of money or the words discussing money could also signal the origin of the primal scene, that "click" that brings it about. As we saw in chapter 4, Laplanche and Pontalis analyze this as the origin of the scene of origins. Furthermore, according to Rosolato's reading of Freud: "Indeed, accidental noises play an essential role in voyeurist fantasies that are linked to the parental complex" (*Essais* 201). Noise plays an essential role in the voyeurist fantasy because, according to Rosolato, it relates to the primal scene in two ways: it belongs to the primal scene itself as a part of the love-making, and it also symbolizes the danger of the voyeur, who could possibly make a noise that would betray his presence. Thus, after Raphaël has won his money at the gambling table, a scene linked as we saw to the parental complex and to voyeurism, he says of his sixty francs: "I wrapped them in my handkerchief so that they could not move or make a noise during our return to our house" (131).

Whereas in the system of "savoir," knowledge remains in the realm of the imagination, it would seem that in the system of "pouvoir, vouloir," Raphaël attempts to transpose knowledge to the realm of the real. Instead of merely imagining love affairs with beautiful women, as does the antiquary in the beginning, Raphaël wants to look at, to gain visual and concrete knowledge about, real women. He wants to use his scientific knowledge to verify gender identity in the Real rather than in the Symbolic mode: "I spent all my time, my efforts, and my science of observation in penetrating further the impenetrable character of Foedora" (183). "My fatal science pierced many veils for me" (185).

This brings us to a consideration of another important aspect of this text: the relation of voyeurism to science through the image of the gaze. "To see, is it not to know?" asks the antiquary, equating the two activities. Their link can be seen similarly in Raphaël's scientific desire to see and know Foedora. As he says, "This alliance of the scientist and the lover, of a veritable idolatry and a scientific love, had a bizarre unknown quality" (164). And as he says to Foedora, "Truly you are a valuable subject for medical observation!" (168).

Indeed, a large portion of the text deals with the attempts by the scientists to study various objects from ducks to the "peau de chagrin," and as the statements above make clear, Raphaël's passion for Foedora is similar to a scientist's passion for the truth. Actually, love, gambling, science, and seeing are all passions linked together in the text. Gambling and spectacle are passions like love: "You would see there [in a casino] many honorable people who go there to seek distractions and pay for them as they would pay for the pleasure of a spectacle . . . or as they would go to an attic to buy for a small amount of money enough burning regrets to last for three months" (61). Finally, love and science are two passions that can have the same effects. When Raphaël enters the casino, the others who are there could interpret his "veiled eyes" in two different ways: "Was it *debauchery* that marked with its filthy stamp this noble face? . . . The poets would have claimed to see in these signs the ravages of *science*, the traces of nights passed by the light of a study lamp" (64–65, emphasis mine).

But it is really the experiment of one of the scientists, Lavrille, that shows the close tie between science and voyeurism. Lavrille studies ducks, and he says to Raphaël, who comes to him for help in understanding the skin, that he has witnessed a very unusual spectacle in his duck menagerie: " 'I have just, sir,' he took up once again, 'been witness to a mating over which I had previously despaired. The marriage was accomplished quite well, and I will wait very impatiently for its result' " (254). The scientist has looked in on a "primal scene" in the duck world, and the expression used by the narrator, "beneath the eye of the naturalists," (253) takes on a larger signification. (In ironic juxtaposition with the voyeurist scientist and his menagerie of ducks, Foedora has a "menagerie of scientists" [159].) The quest of the scientist is rendered even more ironic because his search for the truth of the "canard" (duck) conjures up, especially in this Balzac novel in which the press figures as a subtheme, the expression *lancer des canards,* which means to publish a false bit of information in the press in order to dupe the public.

What do Raphaël and the scientists learn from their gazing? Both of their enterprises fail because the objects they view and study are strangely resistant to their control. The objects of their investigation—respectively, Foedora and the skin itself—share certain rather interesting qualities. Let us see just what it is that they have in common, and how they both resist the prying gaze.

As we suggested earlier, the aim of the voyeurist act on the part of Raphaël is to gain knowledge about gender identity and difference, his as well as others. Since Foedora does not desire him, and since he thinks she might be a hermaphrodite, it seems that he hopes to see that she does, in fact, possess the phallus, and that this would explain her lack of desire for him. He hopes to see in her the phallic woman of infantile fantasy, that early mother figure that he never had.

It is almost as if he hopes to be able to "read" a kind of symbolic writing on her body that would enable him then to set up a symbolic structure of difference in the world. Indeed, he says of her: "This was more than a woman, this was a novel" (160), and he discusses "reading" her: "I wanted to read a feeling, a hope, in all these phases of her face" (163).[7] It is she, and her gender identity as different from his, that gives a certain meaning and value to him: "The countess has attached extreme value, excessive pleasures, to the most vulgar accidents of my life" (170).

Raphaël's voyeurist act is, however, significantly unsatisfactory. Instead of resolving a certain problem of identity, things simply get more complicated. Foedora first of all utters those two words, "Mon Dieu," which pose an even greater enigma than her sex:

> This word, insignificant or profound, without substance or full of realities, could be interpreted equally as meaning happiness or suffering, as a pain in the body or as emotional pangs. Was it imprecation or prayer, memory or future, regret or fear? There was an entire life in this utterance, a life of indigence or wealth; there was even a crime! The enigma hidden in this beautiful womanlike creature was reborn, Foedora could be explained in so many ways that she became inexplicable. (196)

We note that these two words can be interpreted in opposite ways—they are insignificant or deep, physical or emotional—an opposition which of course reflects the hermaphroditic aspect of Foedora's gender. It seems that the attempt to see the woman in order to define the difference between the sexes simply reinforces the original ambiguity.

Foedora does, of course, explain later that when she uttered those two enigmatic words, she was thinking of her broker, about her money. If Raphaël could not see Foedora's phallus in the real world, it is there in the scene symbolically in the form of signifiers and money—we recall that scene in which Raphaël's father tests him by giving him his keys and his money to hold, and how this represents the father's power and law (his phallus), which Raphaël steals. Foedora's utterance of the words that signify her money in this scene of a literal search for gender identity thus perhaps figures her possession of the phallus in a symbolic way. However, this remains a symbolic identity, and gender is not established in a literal, real way. Her gender identity remains ambiguous: symbolically male (presence of money) and literally female (her perfect female body).

Even though Raphaël is not able to resolve the enigma here, two pivotal and symbolic events happen after this scene. Having been unsuccessful in winning Foedora, he dissipates the remainder of his fortune, goes into debt, gambles his last money away (which signifies breaking the father's law, being castrated); and then he enters upon the pact with the skin. The second important event is that, when he learns that the skin really does work, he attempts to *blind himself* in order to prevent himself from being exposed to any more temptations to look so that he will have no more desires. He blinds himself precisely so that he will not be able to see women: "He had promised himself never to look attentively at any woman, and in order to spare himself any temptation, he wore an eyeglass whose artistically formed microscopic lens destroyed the harmony of the most beautiful traits, by giving them a hideous aspect" (240). In fact, sexual impotence or frigidity is linked to blindness specifically by the phrase "blind to love" (168). If, when he looks at Foedora, her feminization (her female body) is accompanied by a symbolic masculinization (her money), now Raphaël's masculinization (his access to power and money through the peau) is accompanied by a symbolic feminization (blindness)—"masculine" and "feminine" being here defined by the presence or absence of the phallus. Raphaël and Foedora remain ambiguous in terms of gender; they manifest both masculine and feminine traits.[8]

This impetus toward the discovery of sexual knowledge and the thwarting of this impetus in the revelation of the ambiguity of the affirmation or denial of castration (the absence or presence of the phallus) reminds us of the structure of the fetish: the fetishist simultaneously denies castration by representing the female phallus in the fetish and affirms castration by the very necessity of the fetish. It is not surprising, then, that after Raphaël's discovery of the ambiguous phallic/nonphallic nature of Foedora and his subsequent formulation of the desire never again to see woman, he should enter into a kind of "relation" with a type of relic: the skin itself. The skin is the remains of a dead animal, a relic that preserves that being after its death. In a sense, it simultaneously affirms and denies the death of the animal from which it was taken. It could be seen as a type of fetish that simultaneously affirms castration (it is, after all, a part of the body that has been cut off) and denies castration (it gives power and money to Raphaël). One could see it as the embodiment of the woman's lost but preserved organ.

The relationship that Raphaël has with the skin is called a "contract": "Not one of them wanted to risk making this contract" (88), says the antiquary. Is it not striking that a love relation between a man and a young, unmarried woman (Raphaël and Pauline) should also be called a "contract"? "To love a young girl or to let oneself be loved by her constitutes a real contract whose conditions must be well understood" (15). Raphaël's self-blinding to the sight of women and his "contract" with the skin suggest a fetishistic solution to the problem of castration, a "solution" that simultaneously affirms and denies its possibility.

Indeed, the ambiguities of gender that run through this nineteenth-century novel (and many others, too) suggest a fetishism general throughout the nineteenth century. Let us simply mention the numerous places in this text in which male desire is fetishistic: "Little narrow feet spoke of love" (115); "She showed an adorable foot in ignoble shoes" (149); "Raphaël . . . contemplated . . . his Pauline, her hair dishevelled and showing a little white foot veined with blue in a black velvet slipper" (251); "How many times did I not dress in satin the darling little feet of Pauline" (152). Finally, in this text in which Raphaël's money grows as the skin shrinks, Rastignac's reason for rejecting his current mistress becomes humorously significant: "The Alsatian woman who was proposed as a wife for me has six toes on her left foot; I can not live with a woman who has six toes! People would find out, I would become ridiculous. She only has eighteen thousand francs as income; her fortune diminishes and her toes grow" (204).

In fact, relics, which could be considered a kind of fetish, form a subtheme of this text. The antiquary's rooms preserve fragments of past history, including archeological finds, mummies, bones, and fossils. These offer a kind of condensed language which can be read in order to recover the past. The antiquary's eyes seem to be "preserved" in his body, described as a skeleton: there is a "strange youth that animates the eyes of this ghost" (80). The preservation of the eye, which as Freud has shown is a symbol of the phallus, aptly represents the role of the fetish or relic, and these preserved eyes remind us of another Balzac short story, "L'Elixir de longue vie," in which Don Juan anoints his dead father's eyes with a magic potion and they return to life, the only living parts of a dead man's body. Indeed, this text itself represents, in a way, the preservation of a young man's life who was on the verge of suicide (writing itself as a fetish?).

This fascination with the preserved fragments of a dead past relates to the Romantic fascination with ruins, and may suggest an interpretation of that fascination. In France, the loss of the ancien régime, of the king, and of a certain law of the past might figure as a kind of loss of paternal or patriarchal power, and the psychic investment in ruins may symbolize the desire to deny that loss and to preserve the relic of the past. Certainly in Chateaubriand's *René*, the loss of the ancien régime has been seen as one of the forces behind René's lack of purpose, and in that text, ruins, both of antiquity and of his own father's deserted house, figure prominently.

There are three entities in *La Peau de chagrin* that are related by certain common properties and by their fetishistic nature: the skin, Foedora, and money. As for their fetishistic nature, as we saw, Foedora represents the ambiguity of castration (she is both male and female). The skin is a kind of relic. Money seems to function like the skin as a symbol of the father's power and control, the phallus, that can circulate like a dismembered limb. All three are physical objects in the world, not imaginary symbols: the skin, in particular, has a physicality that comes under scrutiny because it is indestructible and unstretchable by scientific means; the physical nature of money is shown when the covering of the gambling table is described as "worn from the gold"; and it is Foedora's body itself that is the object of investigation.

Indeed, the skin and woman are linked by their "superficial" nature: the skin is, after all, a surface that has lost its depth, as is Foedora, the woman "sans coeur," without a heart and soul, without depth. In a humorous note, woman and the skin are linked by the aging process: as the doctor Maugredie says, "The shrinking of leather is an inexplicable fact, yet one that is natural, which, since the beginning of time, has been the despair of medicine and pretty women" (275). All three have a surface that reflects light: Foedora's face is "flooded with light, there was operating there I know not what phenomenon that made it glow; the imperceptible down that *gilded* her fine, delicate skin [*peau*] softly outlined the contours of her face. . . . It seemed that light caressed her while uniting with her, and that from her radiating face escaped a light stronger than light itself" (163). The skin "projected in the heart of the profound obscurity that reigned in the shop rays so luminous that you might think they were from a small comet. . . . the irregularities of this Oriental leather seemingly formed many small fires that vividly reflected the light" (85–86). And coins, of course, also reflect the light: "I perceived attached to a lateral plank, sneakily hidden, but clean, brilliant, lucid like a rising star, a beautiful and noble coin of one hundred sous" (179). Guy Rosolato states that one of the common properties of a fetish is its ability to shine ("Fétichisme" 34–37).

All three have, either symbolically or literally, writing on their surfaces. As we saw earlier, Raphaël would like to "read" Foedora's body as a kind of novel about gender; the skin, of course, has writing on its surface; and coins and paper money have images and writing on their surfaces. In addition to, and sometimes because of, this writing, all three are tied to the concept of a "voice." The peau works only when its user voices his desire by saying "I wish." Money is often *heard* in this text: "the sound of gold" (60); "The ivory made the coin render a sharp sound" (65); "He was surprised to hear several coins jingle in a truly fantastic way in the bottom of his pocket" (68). Finally, one of Raphaël's major discoveries in Foedora's room is that she has a beautiful singing voice.

As fetishes, Foedora, the skin, and money thus sustain the ambiguity of castration, both affirming and denying its possibility. Raphaël's attempt to see Foedora naked seems almost to be that primal moment when the fetishist sees the woman's body, tries to deny her lack, and creates the fetish. Raphaël's attempt to see the woman aims at a revelation that will fix her identity as either male or female, but he fails to do so. This failure to provide a limit or boundary for each sex can be seen symbolically in the impossibility of keeping frames on portraits of women. In order to continue in his pursuit of Foedora, Raphaël thinks of getting money for the frame of his mother's picture: "In order to be able to take the countess there, I thought of hawking the gold circle that framed the portrait of my mother" (187). In Rastignac's room, Raphaël notices "a portrait of a woman devoid of its mounting of wrought gold" (206). It is as if the woman's identity cannot be framed, limited, controlled; frameless, it spills over into the real world and the man's world. Similarly, Raphaël tries to keep the skin within its frame, a red line which he draws around it: "He promptly suppressed his secret desire by casting a furtive glance at the Wild Ass's Skin, hanging before him and mounted on a piece of white cloth where its fateful contours were carefully drawn with a red line that framed it exactly" (232). This attempt to frame the skin ends also in failure: "He saw a slim white line between the edge of black skin and the red line" (233).

The attempt to see the woman's body in order to fix in place the system of gender fails, perhaps, because it attempts to see a Symbolic structure in the Real, or to limit the Symbolic to the Imaginary. The phallus belongs to the Symbolic, not to the Real or the Imaginary alone, and any attempt to see it is doomed to failure. When Raphaël hopes to see Foedora, he hopes to see the phallus that would explain her lack of desire for him, he hopes to "embody" the phallus in her in order to assure himself that he, in fact, still has and always had it, that he is still desirable to a real woman, which Foedora is not. But, as he himself says at one point to Foedora, it is impossible to see because the "dress" that covers the Symbolic cannot be taken off in the Real: "Women never take off their dress entirely" (167). It is interesting that the skin is impermeable to any physical action on it—it cannot be cut or stretched—and that the reason it changes shape is because of a *symbolic* action, the "antithèse" (antithesis) of desire and life.

Indeed, Raphaël often seems to mix up symbolic and real. He wants to possess women's souls: "I wanted to possess the soul of all women by making their intelligence submit to me" (139). Most significantly, he mixes things in visual terms, for he desires to "see an idea" (145). One could, in fact, see the entire fantastic nature of this text as an illustration of this mix-up, or the mix-up as illustrating a mixture of Romantic and realist elements. It seems that the visual logic of gender definition in this text—and one could speak of Freud's text as well—will never be able to "see" what gender really is: a symbolic relation that is precisely not visible (or aural, for that matter, in the case of René).

This desire to pin down the symbolic circulation of meanings is also the goal of the scientists. In that scene in which the scientist peeks in on a primal duck scene, he says that he hopes that his name will be given to the new species that may result, and he reveals himself to be interested mainly in the names of ducks:

> "I pride myself in having obtained a one hundred and thirty-eighth species to which perhaps my name will be given! Here are the newlyweds," he said as he pointed out two ducks. "It would be half a laughing goose (*anas albifrons*), half a great whistling duck (*anas ruffina*). I hesitated a long time among the whistling duck, the white-browed duck, and the spoonbill duck (*anas clypeata*)." (254)[9]

He shows himself also to be interested as much in the name of the beast from which the skin was taken and in the origin of that name as in the beast itself. Finally, twice in the text it is stated that science is simply naming: "He took away from this visit, without knowing it, all of human science: a nomenclature! . . . A name, is that any kind of solution? There you have, nevertheless, all of science" (258–259). (We should note, in the first sentence above, the ironic structure of a narrator who points out to the reader just what the main character does not understand, does not "see.") The scientists aim to pin down reality with words in a one-to-one correspondence, even inventing new names for new species. In this way they perhaps attempt to make the symbolic and the real coincide, in much the same way that Raphaël would like to see Foedora's phallus, see the symbolic and the real in one glance.

The scientists, of course, fail, first because they have no power over the skin, no power over the symbolic force it wields. Their naming changes nothing, and they simply accept their inability to understand it. But their desire to map language onto reality in a one-to-one correspondence fails for another reason. Words themselves cannot be pinned down, and much of this part of the text abounds in word plays. When the scientists cannot change the skin, they (and the narrator as well) resort to making word jokes about it:

—Bah! pour nous consoler, messieurs les doctrinaires ont créé ce nébuleux axiome: Bête comme un fait. —Ton axiome, répliqua le chimiste, me semble, à moi, fait comme une bête. (268)

"Bah! In order to console ourselves, the honorable doctors created this nebulous axiom: 'As stupid as a fact.' " "Your axiom," retorted the chemist, "Seems to me to be made like a beast."

In French the word *bête* means both "stupid" and "an animal," the word *fait* both "fact" and "made." (The translation cannot reproduce this word play.)

Raphaël était content. —Je vais tenir mon âne en bride, s'écriait-il. Sterne avait dit avant lui: "Ménageons notre âne, si nous voulons vivre vieux." Mais la bête est si fantasque! (258)

Raphaël was satisfied. "I will be able to rein in my ass," he cried. Sterne had said before him: "Spare your ass if you would live to be old." But the beast is so capricious![10]

It would seem that the impossibility of taking real action on the symbolic, of changing the skin, reveals the unlimitable, ambiguous, and multiple nature of the Symbolic itself. Indeed, this entire text bases itself on a kind of word play that represents the fantastic nature of the text: the realist interpretation of the text would claim that Raphaël believes in the skin and goes insane, dying of worry and of his former unhealthy life-style—he dies of "chagrin" in the form of cares and woes. The fantastic interpretation of the text would claim that the skin really does work, and that a supernatural cause brings about his death—that is, the magic or the wild ass's skin kills him. This text itself remains suspended and cannot be pinned down to one simple meaning, one simple word: the complicated meanings of *chagrin* make that impossible. This text reveals, in an ironic way, that the attempt to pin down the truth of the Real in a one-to-one mapping onto the Symbolic is impossible, and it links that attempt to the violation of woman, to the desire to submit her to vision against her will. This text also shows that gender and identity cannot be located in the real, visible world, and it displaces Freud's phallocentric logic of a visual mapping of gender.

## Symbolic Exchanges in
## *La Chartreuse de Parme*

At first, *La Chartreuse de Parme* would seem to belong to the group of Romantic novels epitomized by *La Peau de chagrin*, in which a younger man struggles to define his identity and his gender identity, and does so by spying on women, that is, through a voyeurist gaze. Sometimes for Fabrice the spying is a defensive measure made necessary by the pursuit of the police, as when he gazes out of his clock tower to contemplate "a quantity of young girls dressed in white and divided into different troops occupied in making designs with red, blue, and yellow flowers" (197; we still study Proust's comment on this image in chapter 7). Sometimes it is simply to see the erotic object without being seen, as when he, like Mosca, takes a particular loge "in order not to be seen" (180) while he gazes upon Marietta, and when he disguises himself and goes to the theater to see Clélia (551). Like Nemours in *La Princesse de Clèves*, he rents rooms across from Clélia's home in order to be able to see her when she cannot see him (520).

As in Raphaël's case, Fabrice's gaze at the woman is linked to the primal scene and the family romance: Fabrice seeks a way out of the Oedipus complex, out of the rivalry he experiences with his father. Fabrice's conflict with his father could not be more explicit, and his desire focuses on Gina, his father's sister, who is more like a mother to him than his biological mother. Indeed, he is referred to in several different contexts as Gina's son. As Gina herself says, "Without a doubt I am being led by the mad fears of a mother's soul" (512).

However, Fabrice, unlike the motherless Raphaël, has several mother figures. This difference is extremely important, and after examining Fabrice's struggles with the Oedipus complex, we shall see how he differs radically from Raphaël, who aims to see the woman to learn of her castration. Fabrice's aim develops: it does not remain one that aims to see castration as the origin of gender, it becomes one that seeks to establish a relationship outside of the

Oedipal, patriarchal law that bases itself on castration. He aims to establish a way of seeing not based on voyeurism, even though the possibilities of desire in the text are at first studied in terms of voyeurism. Thus, *La Chartreuse de Parme* will be of interest to us because it sets up desire inside the structures of the power and control belonging to the voyeurist's universe but then attempts to move outside of that oppressive system. In order to understand the role of the gaze and its relation to voyeurism, we will first map out the symbolic gender and Oedipal positions taken by Fabrice. Then we will be in a position to understand the way in which Fabrice rewrites the scene of voyeurism in his gaze at Clélia. In the scene in which Fabrice has the chance to perpetrate voyeurism as Raphaël does (Fabrice can gaze on the object of his desire, Clélia, without being seen by her, and he can learn secret knowledge about her desire), he rejects that possibility and attempts to go beyond it.

The patriarchal law against which Fabrice battles is based, of course, on the symbol of his father, the Marquis del Dongo. Just as Fabrice is figuratively the son of Gina, a woman who is not his biological mother, so he centers his Oedipus complex on a man who, the novel suggests, is not his biological father (because Fabrice was conceived during the time that the French lieutenant Robert was living in his family's house, because Robert's tastes and personality belong much more to the world of the women and Fabrice, and because of other suggestions in the prose, we are led to believe that Robert is Fabrice's biological father). This nonbiological base for the Oedipus complex emphasizes that it is a social structure, not a biological fact, and makes Fabrice's quest for a different social world seem possible since it is a quest for a new symbolic structure, not an attempt to change the unchangeable.

Fabrice's relationship with his father, the marquis, is an explicitly symbolic rebellion because it is political—he goes off to join Napoleon's army, and his father is pitted against all that Napoleon stands for. Like Julien Sorel, Fabrice finds substitute father figures that more adequately suit his political and personal tastes: Blanès, Pietranera, Mosca. He loves his mother in the person of Gina, and the triangle of rivalry is set up. The Oedipal nature of this struggle is further reinforced by its figuration in the historical anecdote of Ernest II, who made love to his stepmother and was confined, like Fabrice, to the Farnese tower. It seems that Fabrice's rebellion against his father and his love for his mother figure are, similarly, the symbolic causes of his imprisonment in the Farnese tower.

The triangular structure of rivalry takes several forms: Fabrice loves Clélia, and Gina is jealous; Fabrice pursues la Fausta, and le comte M*** is jealous; Fabrice looks at Anetta Marini, and Clélia is jealous; Fabrice loves Gina and Clélia is jealous; Fabrice loves Gina, and Mosca (the father figure) is jealous; Fabrice loves Marietta, and Giletti (the possessor of Marietta) is jealous. It is interesting that the initials in the last two triangles are the same, even though Fabrice is the only common member of the two: F(abrice) G(ina) M(osca); F(abrice) G(iletti) M(arietta). Fabrice kills Giletti in their rivalry for the woman: the triangular structure reveals that Fabrice has killed the man who occupies the symbolic place of the father and that this is the crime for which he is punished. Indeed, just as in *La Peau de chagrin*, there are numerous threatening images of amputated body parts and horrible eyes that here figure the punishment of Oedipal crimes: "The French were monsters, obliged, under penalty of death, to burn everything and to cut off the head of everybody" (23); "A bullet, having entered next to the nose, had exited by the opposing temple, and disfigured this corpse in a hideous way; he remained with one eye open. . . . What horrified him above all was that open eye" (60–61); "You would have passed about ten years in that pleasant place; perhaps your legs would swell and become gangrened, then they would have been cut right off" (209); "It seemed that in his presence the prince wanted to cut off Fabrice's head" (322); "They added that the prince, considering [Fabrice's] noble family, had deigned to decide that he would have his head cut off" (344). Fabrice's fear that he cannot love because he "lacks" something clearly represents the fear of castration: "Should I believe that I am arranged differently from other men? If my soul should lack a passion, why? It would be a singular destiny!" (258). Finally, Fabrice seems to display a certain preoccupation with disfiguration, first when he is concerned about his tree, a symbol for his own destiny, and then after his battle with Giletti, when he fears his face has been disfigured and looks in a mirror to find out.

Clélia, similarly, must pass through the Oedipus complex, although she has a more difficult time of it. *She* is the motherless child in this text, and she finds it hard to choose between loving Fabrice and betraying her father. "Could there be a way to get [Fabrice] a message?" she asks herself. "Good God! That would be to betray my father" (314). Clélia, too, differs from others before she meets Fabrice, for like him she seems not to be moved to love anything; she has "that air of being moved by nothing" (309).

For Fabrice, however, who has broken the law and killed a symbolic substitute for his father, the entry into prison and the sight of Clélia set the stage for his birth into that new world of desire outside the oedipal situation. He breaks the law, he rebels against the symbolic system in a symbolic way, and he is able to break through to a new life. This does not mean that he goes out and murders his father literally, but rather that he rejects the oppressive and distasteful patriarchal system of which his father is a part and finds a new society in his tower. His nine-month stay in the prison, his descent by means of the (umbilical) cord figure his entry into a different symbolic system, his departure from his desire for the mother. And when he returns later to his tower prison, he makes love to the new object of his desire, Clélia.

This new society is, significantly, one that grows not from the patriarchal society of men and power in the novel, but from the feminocentric world that fits Fabrice's tastes more adequately. Indeed, the universe of *La Chartreuse de Parme* seems to be divided into two different, symbolic genders, which do not necessarily correspond to one's biological sex. Let us study this split universe to see how the feminocentric differs from the androcentric, and how Fabrice's new social order grows from the former.

The gender split is first seen in Fabrice's family life: his father and his brother are pitted against the mother, Gina, and his sisters. His father's "male" side is aristocratic, royalist; Gina's side is that of the "usurper," Napoleon, and the French way of life: thus the gender split spills over into the overtly political sphere. The "male" side, headed by the prince of Parma, is despotic, powerful, oppressive, and paranoid. Like the character, Rassi, it has no sense of humor, no honor, no pride.

It is the side of unjust law, of games with particular rules that must be followed: "It is a game that interests, but whose rules must be accepted" (131). There is no room for improvisation here, but previous scenarios must be imitated: the prince chooses to imitate Louis XIV (138); his son chooses, quite ironically, Napoleon (517). Giletti is an actor who imitates roles and does not invent them. These roles and rules are followed blindly, and this in turn creates blind spots: "Such is the triumph of jesuitical education: to give the habit of not paying attention to things that are as clear as day" (242). There is, in fact, a symbolic scene in which la Fausta has gone to church and her lover, M***, has hidden himself there to see if she is meeting her new lover, Fabrice. It appears that she has spotted M*** where he is hiding behind the statue of a cardinal, for she is making eyes in his direction. But we find out that Fabrice was actually standing right in front of M***, that la Fausta was making eyes at Fabrice, who was in M***'s blind spot, hidden by the very thing that was hiding M***. Finally, the male side is anything but a normal cliché of masculinity as brave, honorable, courageous: indeed, it is called in one place a society with "effeminate customs" (21).

On the opposite side, the female world headed by Gina is brave, honorable, charming, young, gay, likable, and most of all, has a sense of humor: the word *rire* is one very often associated with Gina, for she laughs and makes others laugh. This side is also associated with the revolt against tyranny, and indeed, the entire Milanese populace changes from the "male" to the "female" side with the arrival of the Napoleonic forces.[11] Money is not important here, as Gina shows when she rejects a rich suitor for the poor Pietranera, and when moneylenders forget to collect interest during the reign of the female political side (27).

Instead of mandating the imitation of previous roles, this side calls for invention, improvisation, difference. Rather than following the rules of the court, Gina acts as she feels at that precise moment: "She had acted at random and to give herself pleasure at that very moment" (291). Fabrice also acts on the spur of the moment: "Fabrice invented his speech as he said it, with a completely peaceful air" (207). In Fabrice's soul there is no room for "the imitation of others" (119). Similarly, the word *singulier* (singular, in the sense of strange and different) most adequately describes Clélia: "The admirable *singularity* of that face from which radiated the naive graces and the celestial imprint of the most noble soul . . . even though she was of the rarest and most *singular* beauty, she *resembled in no way* the heads of Greek statues [L'admirable *singularité* de cette figure dans laquelle éclataient les grâces naïves et l'empreinte céleste de l'âme la plus noble . . . bien que de la plus rare et de la plus *singulière* beauté, elle *ne ressemblait en aucune façon* aux têtes des statues grecques]" (309, emphasis mine).

This quality of inventing one's life spontaneously is associated with the ability to question oneself, to take a distance from what one has done and is doing in order to evaluate it. Since one is not merely imitating, one must evaluate. "Is it possible," Mosca asks himself, "that at forty-five years old I could commit follies that would embarrass a sublieutenant!" (126–127). Gina is "a woman in good faith with herself" (132). Fabrice constantly asks himself questions: Did he really fight in a battle? Should he find astrology ridiculous? Is this the prison predicted for him? Should he have shot the man whose horse he took?

The split between the two genders is, furthermore, figured by a series of opposing symbols. The male side of oppressive law is symbolized, not surprisingly, by enormous walls, structures that can keep someone in or out (like the walls built by M. de Rênal in *Le Rouge et le Noir*), can keep real and symbolic borders intact. Fabrice's father has a chapel built "entirely of enormous blocks of granite" (45), and when Fabrice returns to see Blanès, he suddenly comes upon "the wall of his father's yard," a wall that "rose more than forty feet above the path" (190). Clélia, too, dreams of covering up the horrible wall of the Farnese tower as much as possible: "I have some money; I could buy some orange trees that, placed under the window of my bird cages, would keep me from seeing the huge wall of the Farnese tower" (315).

If the male side erects giant restraining walls, the female side triumphs either by rising above those walls or finding a way "under" them. The elevation, as in *Le Rouge et le Noir,* can be symbolic and/ or literal. Clélia's "apartment so elevated in the air" (311) befits her "elevated soul" (308). Fabrice loves his stay in the tower prison where he is "a thousand leagues above the pettiness and mean doings that occupy us below" (358). Blanès spends his time atop his belltower studying the stars, and Gina too becomes impassioned by this study: "Almost every evening, with her nieces and Fabrice, she installed herself on the platform of one of the Gothic towers of the castle" (46),

The way "under" the wall, in a sense, the way to undermine walls, is by means of water. Gina is, as has been noted before, associated with water: she takes outings on the lake in boats, where she entertains her family and friends, reads her love letters, and gives secret orders to her servants; her residences are nearly always situated near water (significantly, Fabrice's father's castle has moats "actually without water" [28]). Clélia sends Fabrice water to save him from poison while he is in prison. The undermining of the oppressive order by means of water is clear when Gina has the prince killed, and when, as a signal of the assassination, she has the restraining wall of her reservoir opened and water inundates the city of Parma. Significantly, as Gina chants over and over "And water for the people of Parma!" she stares at the wall in front of her: "She looked fixedly at the bare wall six feet from her, and, it must be said, her look was atrocious" (449). What better symbol of the undermining of oppressive authority by means of water than the following, typically Stendhalian episode?

> Everyone was saying in Parma that the duchess had had a thousand sequins distributed to her peasants; thus was explained the rather cold welcome given to thirty or so policemen that the authorities had the stupidity to dispatch to this small village thirty-six hours after the sublime party and the general intoxication that followed it. The policemen, welcomed by stonings, had taken flight, and two of them, fallen from their horses, had been thrown into the Pô. (459)

Water is the enemy of another symbol of the oppressive, "male" side: powder. As Gina puts it, powdered hair is the "symbol of all that is slow and sad" (131), of all that belongs to the rules of the court, to law, to oppression, to imitation, and Gina bursts out laughing at the suitor chosen by her brother because "he used powder" (28). Gina undermines walls with water and symbolically throws water on powder: "Fabrice's older brother, the marchesine Ascagne, wanted to join these ladies' walks; but his aunt threw water on his powdered hair, and each day had a new trick to play on his gravity" (45). This gesture is transposed to the political sphere when the soldiers at the prison refused to kill their own fellow citizens and had "water thrown on their powder" (468), here on military gunpowder rather than on cosmetic powder. A final symbol of the female world is, as has also been noted before, the image of the enclosed, uterine space: the "voiture" (vehicle) belonging to the woman who sells food, where Fabrice can sleep during his military excursion; the rooms where women hide him from the law; Gina's "isolated boulder" in the middle of the lake, which she thinks of as "a little room" (46).

Gina and Mosca represent the attempt to transport the female side to the male side, to keep it intact and functioning within the oppressive rules of the court. Mosca harbors all the values of the female side within himself, but he must display on the outside his adherence and obeisance to the prince's order; he must wear powder: "Mosca . . . had large features, not a single vestige of self-importance, and a simple, gay air that were in his favor; he would have been even better, if a bizarre desire of his prince had not obliged him to wear powder in his hair as a gage of his good political sentiments" (122). He represents the honorable man in post-Napoleonic times, a man who is not independently wealthy and who, ironically because he is honest, must compromise his values in order to live: "The point is I never stole anything in Spain, and I must live" (122). Gina, too, is troubled by money matters (because even though her family is wealthy, she does not benefit from their wealth), and she manages to gain material possessions by playing the court's games: she marries a rich man who wants honors and, with the help of Mosca, she and her husband agree to exchange money for social status. She also enjoys, as does Mosca, her superiority and her success, her "elevated" status, in her court games. They gamble on bringing their "female" values into the opposing "male" social order, and they succeed quite well for a while.

Fabrice and Clélia, on the other hand, prefer to withdraw from that society in their prison aerie and to establish a new order beyond the conflicts between "male" and "female," between the unjust social order and honorable personal values. This social order also contains the female within the male, as can be seen in the tower walls (male) that contain the room (female): Fabrice is not "above" the wall in his happy prison, is not completely in the "feminine" mode of symbolization, but is rather enclosed in an elevated female room in the male wall, almost in an image of a womb in a phallus (an image echoing, perhaps, the images of internal, female sexuality, specifically, pregnancy, in *La Fille aux yeux d'or*). The happiness he feels there emphasizes the success of this combination, and the difference between this mode and that of Gina and Mosca is that Clélia and Fabrice are separated from the "male" social order, a separation figured by the prison walls, whereas Gina and Mosca plunge themselves into the middle of real society and the society of those who make the law.

In this notion of the symbolic that Fabrice and Clélia attempt to reorder, their mode can be seen to differ from Mosca and Gina's. Powder, the symbol of oppression, is used in the male world as a tool of submission that must not be questioned, and it assumes an absolute value. In a sense, the distance of symbolization is lost, and it acts as the thing itself for those who submit unquestioningly to that order; the symbolic takes on the attributes of the real. Gina, who overtly questions that symbol, shows that it is a symbol, and by her mockery and the distance she takes from it, she undermines its power. Mosca assumes this symbol, and must hide his questioning of it in his secret life. In a sense, he must relegate his distance from it to one part of his life. Gina, by joining with Mosca in the intrigues of the court, thus assumes Mosca's stance for a while (before he fails her and she must assassinate the prince).

Gina and Mosca adhere to the established social order without "believing" in it, without losing their ironic distance from its functioning, and attempt, in a way, to take their symbolic feminine mode into reality. Clélia and Fabrice, by contrast, enjoy the real, physical distance of imprisonment that separates them from that social order. The physical distance appears in their physical elevation in the tower and in their desire for solitude. The symbolic distance can be seen in the very symbol of the exclusion of Fabrice from the social order, the tower/room where Fabrice is "in his element." The room, representing the female, is actually already at a distance from itself, so to speak, because it is a room within a room:

> The general had placed in each room huge beams of oak that formed banks three feet high . . . On these banks he had placed a little hut made of boards, very sonorous, ten feet high, that touched the wall only on the side of the windows. On the three other sides there was a small corridor four feet wide, between the original prison wall, made of enormous hewn stones, and the boarded walls of the hut. (355)

The Farnese tower, representing the male, is, similarly, a tower on a tower: "This second tower . . . was built on the platform of the large tower" (353). Thus in the symbolism of the ideal for Fabrice, we see a hyperdistancing, a "mise en abîme." Fabrice and Clélia represent the putting at a distance of the real (the very building in which Fabrice lives and the physical distance of separation), in other words, transporting the real into the symbolic.

It is distance that characterizes the mode of communication between Fabrice and Clélia, and also between Fabrice and Gina: because of Fabrice's internment, he can speak to no one. Since direct, seemingly "immediate" speech is impossible, their communication must take place in other codes. An examination of the nature of these codes will show how they differ from normal conversation, and how their structure suggests a different symbolic order.

The first thing to note about these codes is their physicality. Instead of abstract words, meaning is often generated by things: Fabrice's tree symbolizes to him his destiny; Fabrice sends flower-messages to Clélia; Clélia, Fabrice, and Gina communicate through the body-language of gestures; an eagle reveals Fabrice's future path to him. Even when it comes to standard language, a space is inserted; the physicality of language itself becomes visible. Clélia and Fabrice communicate by means of a series of individual letters of the alphabet shown one by one, sometimes themselves codified to represent different letters. Handwriting becomes itself significant and recognizable, making one notice even more telling signs: "Suddenly Clélia blushed deeply, she had just recognized Fabrice's handwriting. Large, very narrow strips of yellow paper were placed in the guise of markers at various places in the volume" (455). Even envelopes, normally merely things that contain the real signifying elements, are endowed with signification: "The envelope was made of cheap paper, the seal was applied poorly, the address was scarcely legible, and was sometimes endowed with recommendations worthy of a kitchen maid" (459–460). The real becomes a part of the symbolic.

This added physicality of language is not, however, a kind of reversion to a more immediate, direct mode of communication; a return to the Imaginary communication with the mother as Cixous might imagine it. It is rather an exaggeration of the mode of signification itself, a kind of hyperlinguistic activity rather than a prelinguistic state. It is the mode of added distance in communication: the distance between Gina and Fabrice that is traversed in the coded flashes of light; the distance Gina inserts in her communication with the princess of Parma when, instead of conversing directly, she quotes a fable by La Fontaine; the sonnet used to express feeling between Fabrice and Clélia. It is a mode that calls attention to the linguistic nature of communication and that prohibits making the real object, such as powder, cover up the function of the symbol. It is the mode of those readers of reality who use their imagination to foresee, to remember, to interpret: "Italian hearts are, much more than ours, tormented by suspicions and by mad ideas that a burning imagination presents to them" (105). It is the symbolic nature of signification itself that becomes important rather than the goal of direct communication of literal meaning. Fabrice's pleasure in signification and in interpretation can be seen particularly in one important scene, which we will examine in detail.

Fabrice feels the need to consult Blanès and makes a rather dangerous trip to see him. On the way he thinks about just what interests him so much in the science of astrology, and it is precisely that exercising of the imagination in interpretation: " 'I could not understand,' he said to himself, 'even the ridiculous Latin of these astrological treatises that my master perused, and I think that I respected them above all because, only understanding words here and there, my imagination gave itself the task of giving them meaning, and the most romanesque one possible" (188). Again later he acknowledges that the pleasures he felt in his communications with Clélia were due in part to the abstract way in which they talked: "What could be salon conversation compared to what they did with the alphabets?" (395).

As Fabrice continues his thoughts on astrology, he makes what the narrator describes as a kind of false step, a step that resembles Raphaël's attempt to pin down the Symbolic in the Real. Fabrice asks himself whether or not astrology actually has some correspondence with real life: "Could there be something real in this science? Why should it be different from the others?" (188). Fabrice, unlike Raphaël, however, does not pursue this futile path of pinning the Symbolic down to the Real, and instead takes a step in another direction, the direction of his new world removed from the bitter law of reality, his world of joy in interpretation. In the following important paragraph, the narrator shows how what is important for Fabrice is not whether or not astrology is true, but rather the pleasure he takes in his imaginings:

This is how, without lacking wit, Fabrice could not manage to see that his half-belief in presages was for him a religion, a profound impression received at his entrance into life. To think about this belief was to feel, it was happiness. And he insisted on trying to find how it could be a *proven* science, real, like geometry, for

instance. He searched ardently, in his memory, for all the circumstances in which presages observed by him had not been followed
by the happy or unhappy event which they seemed to announce.
But even while believing he was following a line of reason and
marching to the truth, his attention lingered happily at the memory of those cases in which the presage had in large part been
followed by the happy or unhappy accident that it seemed to him
to predict, and his soul was struck with respect and was glad-
dened, and he would have felt an invincible repugnance for the
being who would have negated the presages, especially if he
would have employed irony.

This is an essential reversal of the normal order of things. Usually
we think of reality, events, facts as being the truth, as being the
ground of all signification which comes to us. For Fabrice, however,
what is important is rather the stories we invent about reality, the
way we interpret events, and what is important about this interpretation is not whether or not it is "true," whether or not astrology
actually corresponds to real-life events, but rather our pleasure as
linguistic beings in invention and interpretation. In a sense, the
real is subordinated to the symbolic in terms of importance. This
does not mean that the real ceases to have an effect on Fabrice;
quite the contrary, the real never stops intruding on his newfound
mode of existing. It is rather the acknowledgment that not only
does the symbolic rule our interaction with the real to such an
extent that we perhaps can never know the real, but that also we
should not try to escape the "prisonhouse" of the symbolic, for it is
there that we find our essential happiness.

This is perhaps why Stendhal deliberately makes Fabrice's life
seem more like that of a character in a novel than that of a real
person. Presages are prefigurations: not only does Fabrice continually think he will end up in prison, he even acts in ways that predict
important events in his later life. In his short stay in the clock tower
of the abbé Blanès, during which he thinks of imprisonment, "he
made two holes for his eyes" (199) in the cloth that covers his
window, two holes that of course reappear later in the text when he
makes the holes in the shutters of his Farnese tower prison so that
he can see Clélia. Everyday events seem to be more significant in
Fabrice's life, and coincidences abound: the false names Fabrice
assumes often begin with the letter *b*: Boulot, Bossi, Bombace (and

let us not forget Stendhal's real name). Indeed, it would seem that Stendhal desired to call explicit attention to the fictional nature of Fabrice's life, because he put as an epigraph to one chapter a near-quotation from the text that follows: on page 281 the epigraph reads "By its continuous cries, this republic keeps us from enjoying the best of monarchies"; on page 476 we read "With these republican slogans, madmen will keep us from enjoying the best of monarchies. . . ." An authorial intervention announces the fiction to come and calls attention to the fictional nature of the text. Life in this novel is a kind of novel that Fabrice, like an author, sees from "above": "Everything is simple in his eyes because everything is seen from above" (175); he sees from the height and distance of interpretation. And Fabrice even goes so far as to imagine a kind of reader of his text: "What would an invisible spectator say who saw my preparations?" (377). Fabrice, associated with lawlessness and fictionality, uncannily reminds us of the other literary figure in the novel, Ferrante Palla, who is both a poet and an outlaw.

If Fabrice and Clélia figure a relationship based on a different valorization of the symbolic, then our question must be: How does the gaze function in this text? Is it a voyeurist gaze, or is there a different visual relation? Is seeing important, or does desire take a different route?

The world of the gaze in the novel also splits up between the paranoid, aggressive gaze of the political order and the gaze of the other (usually female) counterposed to that order. The entire world of the Parma court is filled with gazes that desire to gain knowledge in the black intrigue, spying, and stolen secrets of court life. Mosca, who manages to remain in power in that political sphere, uses all the techniques of spying in order to gain the knowledge he needs: he is, after all, the chief of police. His spying also spills over into the personal mode, for when he first meets Gina, he places himself so that he can see her without being seen: "He went back to the theater, and got the idea of renting a loge in the third row; from there his gaze could plunge, without being noticed by anyone, down into the second row loges where he hoped to see the countess arrive" (127).

The objects of these gazes naturally feel the need to protect themselves from it. Fabrice, for example, feels much happiness when, on his way to the dangerous meeting with Blanès, he can relax under the cover of night and enjoy the beauty of the scene around him without fear of being spotted: "Seated on his isolated boulder, no longer needing to keep watch for the police agents, protected by the profound night and the vast silence, he felt soft tears moisten his eyes, and he found there, at very little cost, the happiest moments he had tasted in a long time" (187).

There is even a certain symbolism in the act of extinguishing lights when painful or dangerous things are being considered or discussed. When the canon comes to Gina's loge to discuss Fabrice, she says: "That evening at la Scala, at ten forty-five by the theater clock, we will send everyone out of our loge, we will put out the candles, we will close our door, and, at eleven o'clock, the canon will come himself to tell us what he was able to do" (116). Even though there is sometimes nothing that can really be seen in the light, several characters feel the need to enjoy the protection that darkness affords. Note Mosca's reaction when he receives the anonymous letter suggesting a relationship between Fabrice and Gina: "He cried out in passing that they were not to let a living soul up, he told the *auditor* of the service that he gave him his liberty for the night (to know that a human being was within hearing distance was odious to him) and ran to close himself up in the large art gallery. There at last he could vent his whole fury; there he spent the evening without light by pacing randomly, like a man beside himself" (171). Similarly, when Gina learns that Mosca has been spying on her, "the duchess ran to the lamp, which she extinguished, then said to little Chékina that she forgave her, but only on condition that she never say a word about this strange scene to anyone" (183).

The women in the text, if they are often the objects of the gaze, have also developed strategies to subvert the gaze, just as the female image of water can be seen to subvert the walls of power. The female members of Fabrice's family hide him from the police in their rooms and their carriages. The Flemish woman who helps Fabrice by paying off one of the prison guards describes what she is going to do in visual terms, saying she will keep the guard from seeing: "If you can give me about a hundred francs, I will put a double napoleon on each of the eyes of the corporal who will change the guard during the night. He will not be able to see you leave the prison . . ." (54). And the woman's gaze is extremely powerful in the text. Gina's is "incredibly striking" (114), and one of the main reasons why the prince feels so uncomfortable is because of Gina's way of looking at him: " 'I can neither,' he added, 'send the duchess away nor suffer her presence; her glances defy me and keep me from living" (414).

As we saw in Mosca's case, the gaze is intricately involved with love in this text, and is quite often a voyeurist gaze. It would seem that the loss of power in the self occasioned by the love one feels for the other is the reason why one feels the need to be hidden when one looks. Looking at the loved one's face causes astonishment, as when Fabrice is "dazzled by Clélia's beauty," "dumbfounded by the singular beauty of this young twelve-year-old girl" (110). It makes one lose self-consciousness, as when Robert looks at Fabrice's mother: "God desired that I be so struck by this supernatural beauty that I would forget my attire" (25).

As we saw at the beginning of our analysis of this novel, Fabrice does perpetrate acts of voyeurism. Yet his gaze evolves in the novel; love's gaze does not remain voyeurist. One of the most touching scenes of love takes place when Fabrice's and Clélia's eyes meet for the first time. This is not a scene of a struggle for power, nor of a quest for hidden knowledge, but rather an equal exchange of glances, a sharing, a kind of recognition, and a communion of souls: "Fabrice had not heard this order; the young girl, instead of getting into the carriage, tried to get back down, and as Fabrice continued to support her, she fell into his arms. He smiled, she blushed deeply; they remained for an instant looking at each other after the girl had disengaged herself from his arms" (107–108). And it is the look on Clélia's face that Fabrice remembers and that changes his life: "In spite of myself, I dream of that gaze of gentle pity that Clélia let fall upon me when the guards were leading me from the prison; that gaze erased my entire life up to that moment" (366).

Indeed, it seems that a change in the role of the gaze goes along with Fabrice's newfound love, and is an intricate part of his new symbolic order in the prison tower. The gaze, like the first one he and Clélia share, is not voyeurist, is not a one-sided means to dominate the other, but is a mutual sharing. When Fabrice sees Clélia from his room while she cannot see him, he at first feels the joy in looking that we might expect: "He saw Clélia, and, to make his happiness more than complete, since she did not think she was seen by him, she remained still for a long time with her gaze fixed on that immense shutter; he had plenty of time to read the signs of the tenderest pity in her eyes" (367).

But he becomes quite unhappy with this situation and strives to return to the mode of exchange: "Two or three times, during the course of this visit, Fabrice had the impatience to try to shake the shutter; it seemed to him that he was not happy unless he could show Clélia that he saw her. . . . He wanted to take from the colossal shutter a piece of wood as big as a hand, that could be put back at will and that would permit him to see and be seen, that is to say, to speak, in signs at least" (368). The voyeurist gaze in which one can protect oneself as well as assume a certain power over the other, and which perhaps characterizes the gaze in a patriarchal order, is no longer satisfactory in Fabrice's new symbolic order, and he seeks a truly mutual gaze with the other. This is especially significant given recent studies of certain techniques of pornographic photography. It has been shown that there is a certain coded pose of the female face in these pictures. In most instances, the woman is either not looking at the camera at all—in other words, the viewer is looking at her voyeuristically as if she were unaware of the gaze— or if she looks at the camera, it is obliquely, her face turned slightly away in a seductive but unaggressive pose (see Kuhn 28–43). This code of the woman's gaze is one of submission in the sense that she does not return the gaze directly, she does not share in the visual process. Fabrice's desire for a mutual gaze could thus perhaps figure a relation based not on power but on cooperation and sharing.

Although Fabrice continues to seek this mode of seeing, it is Clélia who prevents it, and, significantly, for Oedipal reasons. She has betrayed her father by helping Fabrice, and even though her father, like Fabrice's, is reprehensible, Clélia cannot reject him as Fabrice rejects his father and all he represents. Clélia must punish herself because she remains within the patriarchal law and considers herself guilty of disobeying the father and almost causing his death. Her punishment is, not surprisingly, blindness: "Penetrated by the most vivid remorse because of what had been done, not, thank heavens, with my consent, but because of an ideal I had had, I made a vow to the most holy Virgin that if, by her saintly intercession, my father is saved, never will I refuse his orders; I will marry the marquis as soon as I am asked by him, and never again will I see you" (434). She refuses to look upon Fabrice ever again, she refuses to share that mutual gaze that represents the overcoming of the repressive patriarchal order, and she resumes the gazeless pose that belongs to the woman in patriarchy. Even though they continue to make love, she now significantly refuses to look at him. Following the rules of the patriarchal symbolic order, she puts up an insurmountable wall of darkness between them: "She had promised the Madonna, and you perhaps remember this, *never again to see* Fabrice; such had been her precise words: consequently she received him only at night, and never were there any lights in the apartment" (569). Curiously, even this refusal to see, this deliberate blinding, is prefigured in the text by Blanès, when he says to Fabrice: "You must not see me again *in the day*, and since the sun is setting tomorrow at seven twenty-seven, I will not come to embrace you until around eight o'clock" (195). The different order of mutual gazes seems too threatening to the symbolic order and must be eliminated. Fabrice is reduced to gazing at his son in whose face he can at least see some of Clélia's traits: "The few times I see him, I think of his mother, of whose celestial beauty he reminds me and whom I may not see" (570).[12]

Thus even though Fabrice's new order cannot survive in this world and is undone by the patriarchy, we can see how such a new order might function. The power struggles between individuals and between the sexes would give way to mutual contemplation and sharing. The new order would grow not from the paranoid, repressive political order but from the feminine mode of invention, laughter, and courage. It is this order whose praises this novel sings, and from which a new order of seeing could arise. It is an order of playful, charming, spontaneous, and unpolitical relations.

But most of all it is a world of humor. Gina is known for her laughter; Clélia finds her joyful moments at the end of the novel in satiric sonnets (560); when Fabrice first enters his prison cell he is doubled over with laughter at the antics of the dog chasing the rats. We can see how this world of laughter is opposed to the paranoid, overly serious world of political intrigue in Mosca's description of a cook he hired: "You know that I have brought in a French cook, who is the gayest of men, and who makes puns; so, the pun is incompatible with assassination" (497). Jokes, word plays, the distance of laughter and satire belong to the world of the recognition of the symbolic, and indeed, numerous word plays grow out of the names in the text. The title itself sets off a play of sounds: *chartreuse, charme, parme, larme, armes.* Gina laughs, is "riant" (smiling, laughing), and lives for a time at Grianta: *Grianta, Grianta.* The name may even suggest Fabrice's humorous scene laughing at the rats: *Grianta Grianta*.

On the literary level this humor becomes irony, and Stendhal's style constantly makes us smile. It comes in the form of sarcasm in relation to the bravery of Fabrice's father: "The Marquis del Dongo came back to his castle at Grianta on the lake of Como, where bravely he had taken refuge at the approach of the army, abandoning to the chances of war his young and beautiful wife and his sister" (26). It is directed against Fabrice himself when he gallops wildly around the battlefield after having too much to drink and when he shoots the enemy and runs up to see him, as if he were hunting. It is present in many small details, as in the episode when Fabrice wears a red wig while pursuing La Fausta, an episode that ends with the narrator's following ironization of the knowledge possessed by those in power: "The prince remained convinced that the rival of Count M*** had a forest of red hair" (277).

Finally, it is an irony directed at our ability to know the truth, to interpret what really happened even after the fact. Fabrice, who has been at the battle of Waterloo, can never be sure that he has in fact been in battle and thinks that if he reads the newspaper, he will be able to learn the truth: "For the first time in his life he found pleasure in reading; he always hoped to find in the newspapers, or in the accounts of the battle, some description that would permit him to recognize the places he had traversed with Marshal Ney's group" (101). But newspapers are shown to be patently wrong, as when a Parisian newspaper reports that Mosca, the nephew of Gina, was going to be made archbishop (298). The distance of humor and irony reflects that of signification itself and separates us from the real and from truth. This novel accepts that distance and sings its praises. The ideal in this novel is no longer to attempt to unveil the truth of the symbolic in the real, but rather to contemplate and enjoy the symbolic itself. In this sense, then, it is a kind of opposite of Robbe-Grillet's *Le Voyeur*.

Raphaël can never cease trying to bring the symbolic to the real. This attempt involves the mutilation of the subtleties of the symbolic (in that novel, of gender) by squeezing them into rigid polarities in the real; it involves a kind of rape of the privacy of the woman; it involves an attempt to dominate nature (the skin) through science. Fabrice shows, on the contrary, that it is better to acknowledge our inevitable immersion in the symbolic, to be aware of the way it affects our dealings with the real, and to be aware of how we may be violating woman and nature when we ignore the importance of the Symbolic. Fabrice shows how we should enjoy our immersion in the symbolic, which is, after all, the essence of human life.

**6**

# Realism, Voyeurism, and Representation: The Artist's Gaze at the Woman

Men act *and* women appear. *Men look at women. Women watch themselves being looked at.* . . . *A woman must continually watch herself. She is almost continually accompanied by her own image of herself. Whilst she is walking across a room or whilst she is weeping at the death of her father, she can scarcely avoid envisaging herself walking or weeping. From earliest childhood she has been taught and persuaded to survey herself continually.* . . . *In the average European oil painting of the nude the principal protagonist is never painted. He is the spectator in front of the picture and he is presumed to be a man.* . . . *This picture is made to appeal to his sexuality. It has nothing to do with her sexuality.*
—John Berger,
*Ways of Seeing*

*Representations of women in art are founded upon and serve to reproduce indisputably accepted assumptions held by society in general, artists in particular, and some artists more than others about men's power over, superiority to, difference from, and necessary control of women, assumptions which are manifested in the visual structures as well as the thematic choices of the pictures in question.* . . . *This complex of beliefs involving male power, naked models, and the creation of art receives its most perfect rationalization in the ever-popular nineteenth-century representation of the Pygmalion myth: stone beauty made flesh by the warming glow of masculine desire.*
—Linda Nochlin,
*Women, Art, and Power and Other Essays*

WHEN WE INVESTIGATE the search for truth in art as linked to the voyeurist unveiling of woman, one of the most important scenarios is, of course, the male artist observing and painting the nude female model. Indeed, this is a favorite scenario for many nineteenth-century writers: Balzac in his "Chef d'oeuvre inconnu," Daudet in his "Les Femmes d'artistes," and many others.[1] The popularity of this theme in the nineteenth century parallels a shift in the nature of the painting of the human form at that time. As Rozsika Parker and Griselda Pollock point out, "Until the late eighteenth century, painting of the nude was based predominantly on the male figure, but after this date the painting of the nude became increasingly the painting of the female nude" (115–116).

It is especially in the second half of the nineteenth century that the figure of the unveiling and representation of truth/woman in art becomes linked to realism and to the representation of everyday reality and modern life in French literature, modern life meaning life in the city (Paris). Two of the novels that treat this scenario, but in very different ways, are the Goncourts' *Manette Salomon*, published in 1867, and Emile Zola's *L'Oeuvre*, published in 1886. In *Manette Salomon*, the artist's right to gaze at the female body is so absolute, the woman's mastery of her own body so absent, that there is no need for secrecy; after all, if the object of the erotic gaze has no subjectivity, it cannot gaze back, and thus secrecy is unnecessary. In *L'Oeuvre*, the woman does possess subjectivity, and Claude, the artist, begins his observation of her nude body in secret. In studying the figure of the female model in these two texts and her relationship to art and the artist, we will discover some of the issues at stake in (her) representation in literature.

## The Cementation of Ideology in
## *Manette Salomon*

In *Manette Salomon*, the voyeurist gaze is represented in one very minor scene, but it is a scene symbolic of the more generalized gaze in this text. Coriolis, a Parisian artist visiting the Orient, becomes a real voyeur in this small, rather confused segment: "There was a woman who made a small hole for me so I could see what there was inside. . . . On my way to Thérapia, I passed by the windows of a harem . . . in the rays of light that traversed the blinds, one could see shadows moving, shadows . . . [which were] the houris of the house, and nothing but them!" (58). If this scene represents the male right to gaze at and to possess women (in the plural) in exotic lands, this right exists also in the heart of Paris, for the painters in Coriolis's group go out in the street to make the neighborhood women (in the plural), who wish to exit the bathhouse, run the gauntlet of their gazes: "After leaving the establishment, the women, charming, shivering, caressed under their dresses by the memory of the water, like a breath of fresh air, had to move through the men lying across their path. They went by quickly, moving close to each other; but they felt all the gazes of the men searching them, touching them, following them; in passing, their ears picked up fragments of frightening stories, words from tales, animal cries, that terrified them" (62). This scene takes place only a few pages after Coriolis's gaze at the harem women.

More significantly, however, the male gaze at the woman in this novel is diffused throughout the entire work in the more general concept of the artist's gaze at the woman and his search for truth in art. Coriolis's gaze at the model, Manette, is not technically "secret," for the model, of course, knows that she is being observed. However, in another sense, as mentioned above, Manette does not, in fact, have a subjectivity that might return the gaze. She has no "consciousness' of being viewed, because she is immersed in her own narcissistic contemplation of herself. In a typical scene, Manette looks at herself in the mirror, admiring herself, and her gaze does not take into account that of the artist. She does not look at him but rather nurtures the body he so avidly observes. Her gaze ratifies that of the artist, it does not defy it: "She was naked, she was now nothing but herself. . . . With her gaze, she caressed herself down to the tips of her toes, and she pursued her image even further, in the mirror at the end of the divan, which sent back to her the full repetition of her radiant length" (214–215). Here, the female gaze is a narcissistic one in which she becomes the image, the passive object to be observed by the active male gaze. Her aim is to be looked at (symbolized by the mirror), not to look. Her gaze circularly encompasses herself and does not move back to the artist.[2] She is, at this moment, another of those seamless, perfect, reassuring, and passive fetish-women, who, in her status as perfect object of desire, does not threaten. Thus the artist can gaze upon the perfect body/object without himself being observed, and by means of his uninterrupted gaze, he can hope to discover the secrets of Beauty itself. The voyeur here gazes upon the object of his desire, Manette as woman and as object to be represented in art, in order to gain the secret knowledge her body harbors.

In *Manette Salomon*, this clichéd link between the unveiling of woman, and the discovery of truth, beauty, and nature could not be clearer:

> What wanders over *her* [woman], and over the most intimate secrets of her flesh, is serene and disinterested contemplation, is the impassioned and absorbed attention of the painter, the artist, the sculptor, faced with this piece of *Truth* that is her body. . . . *Nature* is a great but erratic artist. . . . From time to time, in the midst of this bric-a-brac called humanity, She chooses a being at random, as if to keep the example of *Beauty* from disappearing. She takes a body that She polishes and finishes with love, with pride. And it is a truly divine being of art that leaves the artist's hands of Nature. Manette's body was one of those bodies: in the atelier, her nudity suddenly gave off the radiance of a master-piece. (184–185; emphasis mine)

What Manette, the artist's model, represents for Coriolis, the artist, is the ideal of Beauty: "He loved her because she provided for his eyes that Ideal of nature, that stuff of masterpieces, that real and living presence of Beauty that her beauty showed him" (197).

But it is important for these artists that beauty be of a particular type. It must be the realist ideal of beauty: this means that it must exist in reality to be put on canvas; that it must not be imaginary, mythological, fantastic, but rather contemporary and real. Earlier, Romantic artists had been seduced by "mists of revery, . . . the sun of mythologies in the melancholy of the fantastic" (29). What the new school must try to do is to paint the truth of modern life: "One saw no attempt, no effort, no audacity that tried to tempt truth, that attacked modern life, that revealed to young ambitions on the move the great disdained side of art: contemporaneity" (30).

The essence of contemporary life in this novel is Paris, and the story opens as Anatole, another artist, and some of his friends stroll through the Jardin des Plantes (artificial, man-made nature, like the realist text). Anatole volunteers to show Paris to the other visitors there, assuming the role of a kind of amateur tour guide. This role is one that both the realist artist and the realist writer would like to assume, and this text does play out this role for the reader: it describes in very artistic terms both the people in the Jardin des Plantes and the city that lies at their feet and all around them.

The Paris of the opening pages of this novel is a heterogeneous mix of people of different nationalities, classes, occupations, states of mind, and "races."[3] There are French and English, princes and maids, masons and interns, mourners and tourists, whites and blacks. Paris is described in painterly terms and often colors are stipulated: blue glasses, gray mustaches, white sunbeams, brown veils. The language of the text seems to attempt to paint the picture these artists see. The artists who observe Paris are incarnations of Baudelaire's "flâneur" (stroller), such as Anatole: "He departed, going ahead, strolling" (95). The "flâneur" is associated here with the bohemian life-style: free and easy, rootless, wandering, a style epitomized by Chassagnol, a third artist, who is "accustomed to climbing the stairs of any friend with whom he had dined once, to taking off his coat, which bothered him, in order to talk . . . , always talking, until Anatole offered him half his bed in order to obtain silence. . . . For two days and two nights, Chassagnol did not leave Anatole. . . . On the third night, Chassagnol abandoned Anatole to go off with some other friend" (74).

The artist-flâneur strolls around Paris as an anonymous voyeur, searching for scenes to paint:

He trod the pavement of the farthest and most varied quarters; he rubbed elbows with the most diverse of populations. He went, pressing forward, delving, with a searching eye, into the grey multitudes, into the mixtures of vague crowds; suddenly, stopping as if struck with immobility before an aspect, an attitude, a gesture, the apparition of a drawing arising from a group. Then, hooked by a bizarre individual, he would pursue the originality of an eccentric silhouette for hours. Those who passed him were troubled, were in a way worried by this ardent inquisition, by the penetrating fixity of this gaze that disturbed them, that lingered over them, having the effect of digging into them and penetrating them to their depths. (307)

But most of all, this artist's gaze is one that follows and investigates women: "He studied this singular, spiritual beauty, the beauty of the

Parisian woman. He followed unexpected apparitions, scrubbed and radiant faces, those strange women, flowering between two paving stones. . . . One day, he carried back with him in his memory, for a study he began the day after, the face of a doorman's daughter" (309).

The "wandering," bohemian characters reflect the "wandering" character of the plot of this novel. There is essentially no plot; the narration drifts from one artist to another; Coriolis drifts from Paris to the Orient, to Paris, to the country, and back to Paris. The text seems to make description take over the function of narration, for the vagaries of wandering are essentially descriptions of the artists and their lives. What the text tries to do is to make us see through the artists' eyes, see Paris, Parisian women, as they do. As Anatole says to one female observer of Paris: "Milady, voilà! give me your eye . . . I will not abuse it! Come closer, mesdames et messieurs! I will make you see what you will see!" (20). With very little plot, and so much description of people, what the text does make us see is the underlying ideology of the characterizations of the Parisians observed by these artists.

The first ideological aspect of these characterizations is one we have mentioned already: the male artist asserts the right he has to view the woman's body. Linda Nochlin, in "The Imaginary Orient," has shown further that this right to view the female body is part of a larger right, the male right to possess the female body itself. Indeed, Manette, who begins by posing for many artists, one of whom is Coriolis, is slowly coerced into posing only for Coriolis, then into moving in with him, then into giving up her own apartment. His right as a male artist to view her is a part of his right to possess her for himself alone: "Coriolis would have liked to have had Manette all to himself" (194). In fact, in part, what attracts Anatole to the artist's life is this right, along with the bohemian lack of responsibilities: "absence of ties and rules, liberty, absence of discipline, the unbuttoning of life's clothes, chance, adventure, . . . the voluptuous unknown of the woman model . . . a kind of eternal carnival: these are the images and temptations that elevated the rigorous and severe career of art" (32). Manette, although she would like to remain independent, has no ability to do so. She is simply a body, a thing, that enables the artist to paint, the artist who is "mind" to her body: "All in all, he felt that wisdom and reason dictated that he ask only sensual satisfactions from woman, in relationships with

no attachments, apart from the seriousness of life, apart from profound affections and thoughts, in order to keep, to reserve, and to
give all of the intimate devotion of his mind, all of the immate-
riality of his heart, the ideal that founded his entire being, to Art,
to Art alone" (146).

This ideological configuration of the male artist's rights and the
female model's lack of rights is, of course, not at all surprising.
What is remarkable, however, is the extent to which this construction ties in with other stereotypes in *Manette Salomon* to create an
intricate rhetorical network that hierarchizes the entire structure of
the hodgepodge that is Paris. This novel in fact presents a catalogue
of many of the stereotypes investigated by Sander Gilman in his
*Difference and Pathology*. Coriolis, as a white, Christian, European,
aristocratic male, is contrasted with all the things that define the
other of his identity.[4] And it is Manette who embodies all the
qualities of that otherness. She is the focal point for the stereotypes
that radiate from her to the pattern of "otherness" set up in this
text.

The first category of the stereotypes that emanate from the central figure of Manette characterizes her as a woman. Women in this
text manifest qualities of animality: "The woman belonging to that
man . . . A beast! An unknown one! A beast!!! who stumps the
naturalists! . . . With the feet and hands of a child! With the teeth
of a mouse! With a velvet paw! And with a cat's claws! . . . Very
easy to tame!" (98–99). When Coriolis wants Manette to move in
and she is reluctant to do so, she is described as "a fine, nervous
animal, with free and flowing instincts, that did not want to enter a
beautiful cage" (195). One of Manette's guardians is described as an
animal that is quite important in this text: a female monkey, "une
singesse" (182). It is not surprising that Coriolis has a pet monkey;
Manette assumes the same position in the household as the monkey: they are there for the pleasure and amusement of Coriolis.

The pet monkey, named Vermillon, furthermore, has the characteristics of a child: "One might have thought one was seeing an
unhappy child that had been left to repent that morning" (295).
In the quotation above in which the woman is linked to an animal, she is also described as having childlike hands, and so another link in the network is established among children, monkeys,
and women. In fact, Manette first meets Coriolis when she is a
child, before he makes his trip to the Orient. This first appearance

of the child Manette, who is later to be the artist's model and mistress, perhaps links up with the specter of child prostitution as discussed by Sander Gilman, when he shows the link that ties childhood sexuality, prostitution, and female sexuality in turn-of-the-century Vienna (40). In any case, Manette is sometimes described as being childlike: she assumes "a little girl's pose"; she asks "questions with the intelligence of a four-year-old" (235); she has "the pure ignorance of the child, of the woman of the streets and of the people" (217).

This last quotation shows that Manette is also linked to the lower classes, as opposed to Coriolis, who is a noble. She is inferior in sex and in class, and that is why Coriolis likes her: "Woman, in general, does not appear to them to be at their level of intelligence. . . . They prefer the silent stupidity [*bêtise*] of an uneducated woman. . . . They have become like that actress, still beautiful, still young, who was asked why she took only the lowest lovers in the theater: 'Because they are my inferiors,' she answered so profoundly" (218). It is certainly not surprising, then, that another woman of the people, a *paysanne*, Madame Crescent, was fed by a goat as an infant, and that she has with animals "secret ties, a kind of chain of relations as if from some other common life . . . those mysterious natural attachments . . . a suffering in communion with the beasts" (269).

This natural, instinctual link between woman and animal, between lower class and animal, becomes a secret link in Manette to her Jewish origins: "Without being conscious of it, without realizing it, the Jewess, going back to the prejudices of her own people, went back to the obscure and confused antipathies of her instincts. . . . There was deep inside her, in a latent, natural, almost animal state, a bit of the feelings expressed by a Jewish king of Money" (404). The woman and the Jew have the same set of values, as incarnated in Manette: "For Manette, being a woman and being a Jew, judged the value and talent of a man only by this base material measure: his clientele and the venal value of his works" (394). Manette's physical type is that of the Oriental, as viewed by Coriolis, because of the difference of her eyes. They are "lengthened at the sides" and resemble those of certain exotic women dreamt of by Coriolis who have eyes "lifted at the sides" (177). Her skin is different: "Beneath the warm pallor of her coloring, appeared that pink color of blood that seems to flower and tinge with carmine the cheeks of Jewesses" (207). Her signs of difference are visible on her body.

This external, physical difference, of course, links up to the most obvious stereotype of physical difference: skin coloring. Child, monkey, female, and black link up in two rather startling images. In one, a certain type of black male physique is linked to femininity; this type is "the negro of the size [or waist] of a woman [le nègre à la taille de femme]" (45). In the second, which occurs at the very beginning of the text, a black child, a woman not of the upper classes, and a monkey combine in an amazing way: "A maid pulled and dragged by the hand a little negro child, encumbered by his pants, who seemed saddened by the sight of the monkeys in cages" (18).

What I would like to emphasize is not just the intricate network of stereotypes linked together here, for this has been shown by Gilman. Rather I would like to point out how this network centers on the visibility of the difference of the other, and on Manette as female object of the male artist's gaze. It seems that the ideology of the visibility of sexual difference is, in this text if not in a more general sense, a kind of nodal point for all other notions of visible difference and otherness—those of class, of species, of race, of age. If this text starts in the zoo, the Jardin des Plantes, and constructs for us the heterogeneous but hierarchized Paris with all its superiors and inferiors, then the ultimate animal on which this text centers is Manette and her body as viewed and possessed by the master, Coriolis.

Although this text does not have much of a plot, there is, however, an evolution, and that is in the character of Manette. She first appears as a child, then a beautiful but mindless body, lazy, unobtrusive, a fixture in Coriolis's house. But she changes, and this change has to do with the emergence of her true nature, one that is covered over by the *Parisienne:* "Over the Oriental, there was, in her countenance, a Parisian" (206). With the birth of her son, the "inner" nature takes over: "By becoming a mother, Manette had become another woman. . . . She had been renewed and had changed her nature, as if in a doubling of her existence that carried ahead of her and of her present life all her heart and all her thoughts. She had finished being the creature lazy of mind and of body, with bohemian instincts, satisfied with the inertia of well-being and with an Oriental happiness. From the womb of her mother, the Jewess had sprung" (319). Manette takes over Coriolis's life, she becomes the powerful one.

What this text constructs as fearsome is the way in which this woman, who at first is so passive and tamed, can allow her true self to emerge and destroy the man and the artist (he burns his paintings and marries her). She is double, with a true depth and a false appearance. Her true depth is the mother, the powerful, controlling figure, the Jew; the surface appearance is the passive mistress, the Parisienne "d'apparence" (181). Madame Crescent has a falling out with Manette because she "sees" this interior: "She began to discover in Manette a kind of inner-self, hidden, enveloped, deep, suspect, almost menacing for Coriolis's future" (286). Indeed, when Coriolis first sees Manette on an omnibus, he describes her to his friend Anatole as typical of woman, as hiding something: "Did you too notice how women seem to be mysteriously pretty in vehicles in the evening? . . . Something of shadows, of ghosts, of costumes, of I know not what—they have all of that . . . a veiled air, a voluptuous wrapping, things that one guesses about them and that one does not see, a vague tinge" (178).

What Coriolis does as an artist is see and paint that secret interior: "Coriolis wanted to paint that head, that physiognomy, with all that he saw there of another country, of another nature, the lazy charm, bizarre and fascinating, of that animal sensuality that baptism seems to kill in the woman" (207). And I would add that this is what this text attempts to do: to construct a way of visibly marking, of "painting," the difference of the two white, male, Christian, nobly born authors, the Goncourt brothers, from any fearsome other. Through their painterly networks, they wish to "paint" the dangers of contamination from "marrying" that other. They wish to warn others like themselves of the danger lurking, not in some far-off place, but in their own Paris:

The Jewess took pleasure in, as in some kind of revenge, the servitude of this man of another faith, of another baptism, of another God; in such a way that one could see—this is the irony of things that end!—the bizarre continuation of the life of ancient human vendettas, of religious conflicts, of the rancor of eighteen centuries, placed like the remains of the mutual devouring between races [*entre-mangeries des races*], of the indo-germanic and the semitic races, there, in the middle of Paris, in an atelier on Rue Notre-Dame-des-Champs, at the heart of this miserable concubinage between a painter and a model. (404)

It is here that we see just why this fear is so strong: it is a fear of the contamination of the self by the other that we saw in *La Religieuse*. The white man must not be feminized, must not associate with "animals," women, other races, other religions; if he does, he will be destroyed. This fear generates the desire of the dominant to distance the weak; to transpose the "other" within him to the other without; to place all blame on that other. This fear of contagion becomes clearest in the most shocking of images, which is not Coriolis, the man, being seduced by Manette, the other; but rather the white woman, the property of all the Coriolises, being raped by the other. This image appears in one of Coriolis's paintings, which is described as "frightening," "revolting," "sacrilegious," "unnatural," "painful," "blasphemous" (337). In this painting, a white, innocent, young girl is violated by a "gorilla," corrupted and old:

In an arrangement that recalled somewhat the *Pâris et Hélène* of David, one could see a life-sized couple: a naked young girl on the edge of a bed, over whom bent, with desiring arms, the passion of an old man. On one side, light: the morning of a body, the first innocence of its form, its first white splendor, a breast half blossomed, knees pink as if they had just knelt on roses, bedazzling like the dawn of a virgin, one of those divine youths of certain women that God seems to make with all the beauty and purity possible, as if to wed them to the love of another youth; on the other side, imagine ugliness, moral ugliness, the ugliness of money, the ugliness of base cupidity and ignoble stigmata, ugliness crooked, crushed, depressed, abject, that which Banking puts on the face of Age, the voracity of Interest in the Millions, that which the physiological caricature of our time seized from life, built to life-size, almost to the point of terror, by the power of the drawn image. . . . Morsels of frightening and grotesque nudities revealed this monster: a minotaur in an old dandy, —the bourgeois satyr. . . . In this contrast of the woman and the monster, of the old man and the young girl, of Beauty and the Beast, the painter had placed that horror felt at the approach of a white woman by a gorilla. (336)

White, celestial/noble, female innocence is threatened by corruption at the hands of the miser (which is associated with the Jew in this text, as we saw in Manette's interest in the monetary success of

Coriolis), the monkey (associated with the "bad" femininity of Manette and with the black), the "bad" class of the bourgeoisie.[5]

It should not be forgotten that this rather incredible list of otherphobias is constructed around the image of the nude female body. Furthermore, perhaps the need of the white man to distance himself from his femininity and otherness is revealed by the fact that in the text it is Coriolis who is in the place of the nude woman corrupted by the other (Manette); this text struggles to show the contaminating dangers of the coincidence of the male with the female position and all its rhetorical baggage.

Upon first reading this text, I was amazed at the incredible "visibility" of the paranoid exclusion of all these others from the self in this story written by two brothers—brotherhood representing the ideal of sameness they would wish to achieve. This text is valuable because it is so enmeshed in its exclusionary ideology that its hyperbolic fears help us to see the illusionary, constructed, rhetorical, and politically motivated foundation of its fears (the desire of the white, male, Christian aristocrat to retain power in a France envisioned as changing).[6] It helps us to see how the construction of difference and inferiority in the visual field is related not only to gender, but also to race, religion, and class. And it shows that this network of visual differences is, in this text, written on the nude body of the woman. What is fearful is that this rhetorical network can function (and in realism, desires to function) as though it were a literal description of reality. In a remarkable passage, as Coriolis is painting an image of Manette, it seems as though, when his brush touches the painted image, it tickles the real Manette's skin (188). The artistic image does indeed have an effect on the real. It is only through self-reflection about ideological structures and stereotypes, a questioning of ideology, that nefarious images can be prevented from becoming reality. It is in Zola's text, *L'Oeuvre*, based most likely in part on *Manette Salomon*, that an attempt to rid art of this and all ideology becomes the subject of literature.

## Inescapable Ideology: Zola's *L'Oeuvre*

Claude Lantier in Zola's *L'Oeuvre* makes a significant step forward in progress on his painting when he plays the role of voyeur and sneaks a look at a young, helpless woman who seeks refuge with him for the night. She has arrived in Paris, has been harassed and abused, and has nowhere to turn. He allows her to stay the night with him in his apartment/studio, and when he wakes in the morning, he directs his voyeurist gaze at her as she sleeps. Her bedclothes have fallen off, and he can study her naked body in secret to learn the truths her body usually hides. Thus Zola's novel replays the scenario of the earlier Goncourt brothers' tale of the artist's dominating gaze at the woman.

However, if the Goncourts' *Manette Salomon* represents in a way so obvious as to be shocking the interrelation between voyeurism, gender, race, and representation, in Zola's novel Claude Lantier attempts to paint a work of art that would simply show the world as it is. He aims to paint the real—the realist and naturalist project: "Life as it happens in the streets, the life of the rich and the poor, at markets, on errands, on the boulevards, at the ends of populous alleys; and all of the occupations in action; and all the passions upright, in the full light of day; and peasants, and animals, and countrysides!" (102). His goal is to paint what is, nature as it appears to the human eye, not the ideal of what nature should be, or a convention of how nature usually appears in a painting. It must be a work that is free from "ideas," from ideology, that has "not even a trace of those tax-collectors of the ideal, that keep nature from coming in" (164). Let us first study this goal of the realist painter, in order to turn later to the role of the nude female body in the quest for that goal.

In order to produce this realist art, the painter must look at nature with different eyes in order to paint the colors really seen there. Normally, one is blinded by conventional modes of looking, conventional modes of seeing. As Claude says, "How many times I have looked without seeing!" (275). When he succeeds, and when the spectator looks at the kind of painting that results from his new way of looking, the following process occurs: "One day when she [Christine] dared to make a criticism, precisely because of the poplar tree washed with a blue color, he made her notice, in nature itself, this delicate bluing of leaves. It was true, indeed, the tree was blue; but deep down, she was not won over, she blamed reality: there could not be blue trees in nature" (213). Christine cannot get beyond the code of just what trees should look like, and Claude's paintings go against all those "habits of the eye" (264) to challenge the way one looks at reality. What seems realistic is conventional, and the real and true have a certain "unrealistic appearance" (81). Claude feels that if one can paint in his way, one can obtain light and truth (238).

Of course, one of the principal objects that Claude paints is woman, the nude Woman, "la Femme nue" with a capital "F" (401). Claude believes that the nude as painted in the conventional way is clothed in that convention: "Golden frames full of shadow followed one after the other, grave and black things, studio nudes yellowing beneath cavelike light, all the old classical clothing, the history, the genre, the landscapes, dipped together in the same blended oil of convention" (188). And Claude discovers the woman who best shows him the unveiled, uncontaminated female body that he wants to paint in Christine, that helpless, homeless woman who wanders onto his doorstep.

Because of his gaze at Christine, Claude can finish his painting. He feels he has stripped the woman of painterly conventions to show her naked to the public. This is why the bourgeois who go to see his painting in the "Salon des Refusés" laugh at it: they do not understand why a woman wearing no clothes would be sitting next to a man in a jacket. The woman is not clothed in the conventions of classical art; she is placed right in the middle of Parisian society. As one of the spectators of the picture says, "That's it, the woman is too hot, while the man has put on his velvet jacket, for fear of catching cold" (184). Since the conventions of classical art do not offer any foundation for the interpretation of this painting, the spectators have lost their means of understanding it. Significantly, Fagerolles, the painter who aims to succeed by remaining in the system of conventions that Claude leaves behind, paints a subject replete with artifice and conventionality: an actress in front of a mirror, à la Manette Salomon (222). Claude, on the other hand, strives to paint a nude woman in a manner free of convention, of ideology.

If Claude is mildly pleased with his portrayal of the woman in this painting, *Plein air,* he is never again happy with the other nude women that he paints. When he is frustrated at not having a model capable of presenting him with the type of body and face that he needs, he puts indirect pressure on Christine, now become his wife, to pose for him, which she does very reluctantly. When she poses for him, she ceases to be a person and becomes a body, a foot or an arm, an object in a still life: "He used her for everything, made her undress every minute, for an arm, for a foot, for the least detail he needed. It was a task in which he lowered her, the job of a living mannequin that he placed there and that he copied, as he would have copied a pitcher or a kettle for a still life" (299). Claude, in his desire to paint without convention, without ideology, ends up reducing the objects in his paintings to mere things which he represents. He is never happy with his image of the woman, and in fact it is in front of the troublesome final painting of this nude woman that he hangs himself.

The reason for his displeasure has its origin in his desire to paint things as they are, to re-present reality. Because he is never satisfied with the results, there is always something wrong or missing in his painting: "What was missing, then, in the creation of living women? A nothing, doubtless" (303).[7] What first intrigues him about Christine is a kind of richness that she affords, because for him she has both surface and depth. On the one hand, Christine is a body, a surface that offers itself to be viewed: she is like all the models. That first morning after Claude has offered her refuge for the night, when her bedclothes fall off her as she sleeps, he, the artist/voyeur, can study her naked, sleeping body. The fact that she is asleep, "inconsciente" (74), signifies her presence as object and absence as subject (like Albertine and the narrator of La Prisonnière, as we shall see later). He draws her, and is surprised at the fact that the woman he met the night before could have hidden such a body under her clothes: "Where the devil did she hide it, the night before, that breast, that he hadn't even guessed it? A real find!" (75). He forgets her subjectivity for a moment: "Already, he had forgotten the young woman, he was engrossed in the enchantment of the snowy breasts" (75).

On the other hand, she is a real flesh-and-blood woman, with whom Claude enters into a friendship. Before he let Christine into his studio that first night, he had never before allowed a woman in. His symbolic act of allowing her into his space opens up the door for her existence as a subject to whom he relates, rather than as a mere object. She is a real person with feelings, thoughts, mysteries in her inner life, a woman with a past and a history, a woman clothed in a social order.

Her inner life, which he cannot know, gives rise to his fantasies about her past: "And he imagined other stories: a young girl starting

out in life who had come to Paris with a lover who then left her; or
perhaps a petty-bourgeois woman debauched by a girlfriend, not
daring to go home to her parents; or yet again, a more complicated
drama, ingenious and extraordinary perversions, frightening things
that he would never know" (75). He wonders about her past sexual
life in a kind of fantasy about her primal scene. And it is precisely
her knowledge of sexual things that he wishes to know, and that she
is unable to reveal to him: "He held her by her waist, tickled her
with his breath, behind her ear, trying to get her to confess. What
did she know about men, when she was young, at home? How did
she talk about them with her friends? What idea had she formed
about all that? . . . But, when he thought he had conquered her
and when he attempted to obtain her confidence, as of a friend who
has nothing to hide, she escaped in fleeing sentences, she ended up
pouting, silent, impenetrable" (206–207). Claude's desire to paint
Christine and his desire to know her desire show that Claude's
painting and his relation with Christine aim to see and learn just
what a woman is and just what a woman wants. He, according to
his philosophy of painting, would like to represent this without
ideology, without the taint of convention and societal codes.

Christine is important because of that double aspect, that richness, because she presents the possibility to Claude, for the first
time, of uniting the two different "women" that she is: the body, the
object on view, the surface to be painted; and the subject, the inner
Christine. She is what he has been looking for in his painting:
"That was it, exactly that, the face he had been unsuccessfully
seeking for his picture" (75).

But this possibility of union never materializes, and instead, the
two "Christines" enter into a kind of battle. Claude finds that he
must choose between Christine, his wife and friend, and Christine,
the body to be painted. At first, soon after they begin to live
together, he chooses his personal relation to her, and he does not
paint her. Indeed, as Christine later states, at this time he does not
*look* at her in the way that turns her into an object of still life: "Her
body, once covered by lover's kisses, he now looked at, he now
adored, only as an artist. A tone of her chest made him enthusias-
tic, a line of her stomach made him kneel down in devotion, when,
before, blinded by desire, he used to crush her against his chest,
*without seeing her,* in embraces in which one and the other wished to
melt" (300, emphasis mine).

Upon their return to Paris, when Claude rejoins the artistic world and his band of male friends, Christine finds that his painting has become her rival; it is a strange sort of rival because at the end of the novel the rival is the painted image of Christine herself. When Claude pulls out the painting *Plein air*, many years after he had used Christine for its model, her painted image becomes the object of Claude's desire: "A veritable love had taken him over, he spoke of her [the painting] as of a person, he had sudden needs to see her that made him leave everything, as if running to a tryst" (311). Christine is well aware of this fact: 'Each day, she understood well that this painting took her lover more and more" (266). Christine is caught in a kind of double bind, for if she does not pose for the painting, she will lose Claude, and if she does pose, she will lose him to her own image. She poses in the hope that he will see *her* once more and love her. She makes a difficult sacrifice: "Ah! to throw off her dress, to throw off the last bit of clothing, and to give herself naked to him for days, for weeks, to live naked beneath his gaze, and to take him back this way, to take him away, until he would fall back into her arms! Did she have anything but herself to offer after all? Was it not legitimate, this last combat in which she paid with her body, ready to be nothing more, nothing but a woman without charms, if she let herself be beaten?" (298). Claude sees Christine as an object, both in reality and as the image in the painting. Thus it is significant that Claude cannot paint the face of his image, the face being what gives an individual subjectivity: "In these moments of mute contemplation, his gaze came back with a religious fervor to the face of the woman, which he no longer touched" (368).

In the final part of the novel, Christine is able to vanquish her rival one last time, and she wins Claude back. But her victory is short-lived, for she finds Claude's body the next morning dangling before the painted woman.

Claude ultimately prefers his painting of the woman to Christine; he prefers his illusion, his image of woman, to the real thing: "He preferred the illusion of his art, that pursuit of beauty never attained, that mad desire that nothing satisfied. Ah! To want them all, to create them according to his dream, those satin breasts, those thighs the color of amber, soft virginal stomachs, and to love them only for their beautiful tones, and to feel them getting away, without being able to embrace them! Christine was reality, the goal his

hand attained, and Claude lost his taste for her in one season"
(302). Claude's preference for his own images over the flesh-and-
blood woman shows that his representation of woman has more to
do with his own desires and needs, with his own sexuality, than
with his purported goal of representing the reality of what stands
before his eyes. Recalling John Berger's description of the European
oil painting, Claude's art fits in perfectly with that theory: "In the
average European oil painting of the nude the principal protagonist
is never painted. He is the spectator in front of the picture and he is
presumed to be a man. . . . This picture is made to appeal to *his*
sexuality. It has nothing to do with her sexuality" (54–55). Or, we
might add, with her subjectivity. What the painter represents in his
painting is a mirror of himself; when another painter, Chambou-
vard, looks at his paintings, the looking is described as a kind of
self-contemplation: "What a big brute, transfigured in the contemplation of his own navel! . . . He imagined nothing other that
would express the adoration he had of himself" (189). Christine is
but a mirror for the man's self-reflection; Claude even describes her
face as "unbroken as a clear mirror" (75).

Claude fails in his project of painting the nude woman, and
painting her without the trappings of ideology, because the very
subject matter of his painting, the nude woman, is loaded with
ideological implications. One of these implications is the male
painter's rights to the female body, especially to the body of his wife:
"His wife was his victim" (211). He fails in his project of representing "reality," because he paints, not what he sees, but himself: his
paintings are the representation of his own desire. Thus this representation of the nude woman cannot be reconciled with woman's
subjectivity (we remember that it was precisely Christine as subject
that was of special interest to Claude); it cannot represent woman
as subject because it has nothing to do with her. Christine is correct
to feel that she has a rival, for Claude loves the image he made of
Christine and not Christine herself. At the end of the novel,
Claude significantly lets Christine's sleeping head drop back—"He
let Christine's head slip down" (409)—goes back to his painting,
and approaches his death.

It is interesting that Claude feels he fails in his project because
there might be something wrong with his eyes: "Was it a lesion in
his eyes that kept him from seeing correctly?" (109). He feels that

this lesion, this wound or space, is a kind of blind spot that prevents him from seeing what is there. Indeed, he does suffer from the blind spot of not being able to see the ideological import of his very project.

And this is what Zola's text shows us: it shows us what Claude cannot see. Claude has indeed represented reality in his painting *Plein air,* the reality of the power and content of ideology, especially when it comes to the image of the woman's body. This novel shows Christine's fate, something that Claude is never quite able to see. She is the victim of the process of representation when her body is shown, when it and she become an object. When Christine goes to see herself in the painting, she feels violated: "That nude tart had her face, and a revolt arose in her, as if the other had her body, as if they had brutally stripped bare there her virginal nudity. She was above all wounded by the intensity of the painting, so primitive that she felt brutalized" (150). This novel shows us what happens when one believes that the representation of woman is linked to the revelation of "truth and light." It is a tragedy that victimizes the woman and kills the man.

This violation is paralleled by the express linking of violence and Claude's painting. First of all, the paintings themselves have a kind of latent violence: from her point of view Christine sees *Plein air* as a "ferocious painting" (149). Claude's goal of representing reality as it is becomes a battle in which Claude must work "fighting relentlessly with nature" (100). Nature is like a woman that must be taken and vanquished: "In those days, he came back home beside himself, threatening heaven with his fist, accusing nature of defending herself so as not to be taken and vanquished" (266). The colors that penetrate like a kind of light into the shadows are described as sabers: "She took, in spite of herself, a look around the studio, at the terrifying sketches that made the walls flame; and, in her clear eyes, a concern reappeared, the uneasy astonishment caused by this brutal painting. From a distance, she saw the back of the study the painter had begun of her, and she was so concerned by the violent tones, the large strokes of pastel slashing through the shadows, that she dared not ask to see it close up" (82). The word *sabrer* (I translate it as "to slash" because a *sabre* is a saber) is used often to express this violence, and in one instance, it is the gaze of the artist itself that "sabers" Christine: "During the first hour, the painter, from the top of his ladder, cast her way gazes that slashed her from her shoulders to her knees, without addressing a single word to her" (299).

The physical act itself of Claude's brush stroke is described in figural terms as being rather violent. The word *attaquer* can mean simply "to take on, to tackle," but it can also mean "to attack": "He attacked the velours jacket, with large brush strokes" (92). Finally, the figural violence of this painting turns into literal violence. Claude, instead of sabering with brush strokes, really cuts and mutilates his painting: "The painter, rubbed raw, weeping with rage, tore the canvas into small strips and burned it in his stove" (293).

What is most remarkable about his violence toward his painting is that it is directed at the image of the woman there. First we find again that figural use of the word *attaquer:* "He attacked the neck, barely sketched in the study" (106). Anyone who has read *La Bête humaine,* Zola's novel about a woman-killer, Jacques Lantier (Claude's brother), will recognize this image of attacking the woman's neck, because Jacques wants to slit the necks of the women he desires. For Claude, this turns into real violence against the neck in the painting: "In his hand, he had picked up a knife with a wide blade; and, in one stroke, slowly, deeply, he scraped away the head and the neck of the woman. It was a real murder, a crushing: everything disappeared in a muddled pulp . . . there was nothing left of this naked woman, without chest or head, but a mutilated torso, but a vague corpselike spot, the evaporated and dead flesh of dreams" (112–113). Again later Claude cuts the neck of a woman in his painting: "Then, blind with rage, with one terrible blow of his fist, he rent the canvas. . . . The point [of the blade] struck in the middle of the neck of the [woman in the painting], a gaping hole was dug there" (304–305).

Thus, in this novel the art that aims to represent the woman is violent. First, the artist can represent only his own desire in his image of the woman, and the real woman can merely stand by, unseen, unrecognized, unknown. She is annihilated metaphorically. Second, this male representation of woman that is the end point of Claude's work is a woman cut, or burned, one that has "a gaping hole" (113); it is the image of woman as castrated that is the final product of Claude's work. In a remarkable passage, the paintings of female body parts (feet and belly) that are the only paintings Claude is happy with are linked to his rare moments of success and are contrasted with his other moments of "impotence." His "potency" thus becomes linked with the images of the woman's body in pieces. To drive this link home, we find here again the word *sabrer* used to describe his painting technique:

> On one side, there were more admirable pieces, the feet of a young girl, exquisite with delicate truth; the belly of a woman was the best, with satin flesh, quivering, alive with the blood flowing under the skin. In these rare hours of contentment, he was proud of these few studies, the only ones he was satisfied with, the ones that bespoke a great painter, admirably gifted, floored by sudden and unexplained impotence.
>     He painted on with violence, slashing with great brush strokes the velvet jacket. (100)

For Claude to paint the woman, he would, and must, kill the woman: "He swept away the world with a gesture, there was nothing left but painting; parents, friends, women most of all! should have their throats slit" (151).

This violence against the woman in painting is not the only kind of violence against women present in the text, however. The first time that we see Christine, she has been the victim of a violence that is only too common for a woman in the city, and thus this text describes the way in which the society of the time is itself violent. Upon arriving very late in Paris, where she was to begin a job working for an older woman, Christine was brutalized and abandoned by a carriage driver. Curiously, her fear of the violence of Claude's painting is compared to her fear of a driver's swearing: "Never had she seen such a terrible painting, rough, startling, with a violence of tones that wounded her like a cart driver swearing" (78). She then accepts Claude's hospitality when he invites her in for the night, but his invitation is not without cost. He expects her to pose for him in payment for her night's stay: "It is not very nice to refuse me this service," he says to her, "because after all, I took you in, you slept in my bed" (76).

In this "modern" text, a text that itself aims to be realist and naturalist, the link between woman, violence, the city, and representation should not be surprising. As Griselda Pollock points out: "It is generally agreed that modernity as a nineteenth-century phenomenon is a product of the city. . . . Modernity stands for a myriad of responses to the vast increase in population leading to the literature of the crowds and masses" (66). This text dramatizes the plight of the woman in the city by showing first the fate of the woman who takes it upon herself to go out alone at night and second the fate that is hers if she limits herself to the domestic sphere prescribed to her. Christine loves to move about and to work; she cannot abide sitting still.

He, stupefied, watched her come and go, turn while singing. Was this that same lazy woman who got intolerable migraines doing the least bit of work? But she laughed: the work of the mind, yes; whereas the work of the feet and the hands, on the contrary, did her good, stood her up straight like a young tree. . . . Even today, if she had been able to fight dust, at Mme Vanzade's, she would have been less bored. Only, what would they have said? Suddenly, she would no longer have been a lady. (157)

Because of her need to remain within the bounds of what a "lady" should do, Christine must "suffocate" in the domestic space of Mme Vanzade's house: "She was so alone, so suffocated in this sleepy house." This is just as she suffocated in her mother's house, and then in the convent before coming to Paris.

Thus the person able to go out into the city is a male—one thinks again of Baudelaire's "flâneur," who can stroll and gaze, anonymously and thus voyeuristically, at the city scenes around him: "The flâneur is an exclusively masculine type which functions within the matrix of bourgeois ideology through which the social spaces of the city were reconstructed by the overlaying of the doctrine of separate spheres on to the division of public and private which became as a result a gendered division" (Pollock 67). We must say, however, that the city has changed from Baudelaire to Zola, for in Zola it is no longer an isolated male who strolls but a gang of men, a group composed first of four and then growing slowly into a fearsome band: "All four, strolling, seemed to take up the width of the Boulevard des Invalides. It was the habitual expansion, the band slowly growing with friends picked up en route, the free march of a horde going off to war. These young men, with their handsome twenty-year-old builds, took possession of the pavement" (129). The pace, too, has picked up for Zola, and the strolling male has been replaced by a galloping horde of young men: "The line galloped, forcing passers-by to squeeze up against the houses, if they did not want to be knocked over" (118). (One thinks of the parallel with gangs today.) In fact, the rivalry is not only between Christine and Claude's art; it is between Christine and Claude's friends. Separate spheres are set up for these two rival groups: Christine and Claude love each other in the country house; when Claude goes back to the city it is to his art and his friends.

For the flâneur, the city and its crowds represent love, and this is represented in L'Oeuvre when Claude's love for Christine vanishes when they return to Paris. Benjamin points out this erotic aspect of the city in Charles Baudelaire, when he says that the crowd in poetry does not deal with the life of the citizen but the life of the erotic person (45). The male who goes out to observe the city as voyeur thus bears a remarkable similarity, through this erotism, to the voyeur as such, who views the woman. In a remarkable passage in "Le Peintre de la vie moderne," Baudelaire speaks in parallel constructions of man as loving woman, loving paintings, and loving crowds:

The observer is a prince who enjoys his incognito above all. The amateur of life makes people his family, just as the amateur of the beautiful sex composes his family from all the beautiful women found, findable, and unfindable; the amateur who appreciates painting sees in an enchanted society dreams painted on canvas. In the same way, the lover of universal life enters a crowd as he would an immense reservoir of electricity. (1160)

City and woman are structurally in the same place (as in La Fille aux yeux d'or) and indeed, in Zola's text, the two are images of each other, at least in the eyes of Claude. In a typical complicated network of metaphors, Zola creates an equation linking painting, the woman, the city, and sculpture. First, statues of women represent cities: "One saw obliquely, under the trees, near one of those fountains whose surface rippled, a tiny bit of the balustrades, and two of the statues, Rouen with giant breasts, Lille putting forward the enormity of her bare foot" (192). The word "énormité" is one of the semes that holds this network of metaphors together, because it is the colossal woman that is emphasized (again, as in Balzac). The statue that Mahoudeau is making is a "colossal" woman who has "the breasts of a Giant and thighs like towers" (123). Women with towering thighs seem to make up the buildings in this fantastic feminine city. In Claude's final painting, the nude woman represents "the flesh of Paris itself, the naked and passionate city, resplendent with the beauty of a woman" (295).

If woman is a building of a city, then the city is like a woman, too: "Evening came, the torrent of passers-by flowed more slowly, it was the tired city waiting for dark, ready to give herself to the first male rigorous enough to paint her" (136). The word "colossal" often, again, links the two together. Paris offers to Claude a subject that fulfills his need for the huge: "When he traversed Paris, he discovered paintings everywhere; the entire city, with its streets, its intersections, its bridges, its living horizons, rolled itself out in immense frescoes that he always thought were too small, taken as he was with the intoxication of colossal works" (261). Buildings are also tenors for this metaphor. Notre Dame, a building with a feminine name, is a giant being: "As they arrived at the Saint-Louis bridge, he had to tell her the name of Notre-Dame because she did not recognize it, seen from the other side, colossal and crouched between its buttresses, like resting paws, topped by the double heads of its towers, above its long monster backbone" (158). The final painting that kills Claude is one of Paris and nude women, and it is immense in size, five by eight meters.

The rivalry that is set up between Christine and the painted woman/city would seem to express a certain conflict in the changing nature of life in the city. It is almost as if the city and the set of new codes it puts into place make Christine fail in her quest for love, in her desire to be recognized as a subject by Claude. The city takes Claude from her just as a rival woman would; it puts him into the group of men who roam about freely, while she is relegated to her domestic sphere. Claude's final painting seems to express this very structure in its content: the activity of the city near the Seine surrounds the central image of nude and semiclothed women.

It is clear, then, why this painting is a failure in Claude's eyes. If he wishes to paint reality pure and simple, in this painting the nude women simply do not fit into his representation of reality: "The boat with the women, in the middle, made a hole in the painting with a blazing of flesh out of place; and the large nude figure above all, painted in a fever, had a brilliance, an aggrandizement of hallucination, with a strange and disconcerting falsity, in the midst of the surrounding realities" (317). The women are figural, they represent the very nature of the city and its relation to the woman. They are representations of ideology and not of "reality."

What Claude's failure shows us through Zola's text is that one cannot paint, cannot see without already being contaminated by ideological meanings. In this text, it is called being tainted by "Romanticism," by a dreamlike state of symbolism rather than attaining the goal of reality they seek: "Ah! We are all immersed in it, in that Romantic sauce. Our youth wallowed in it too much, we are sullied with it up to our chin" (103). Claude is strangled by the "ideal" (418). This is the reality that Claude shows when he paints the nude women in the middle of the city of Paris. It shows, as we saw earlier, what ideological implications the painting of a nude woman carries. It shows also how life in the city functions at the expense of a certain violation of woman. It shows how art is always already tainted by ideology. It shows how society constructs uses of the woman's image, and how it constructs her gender—what she can be and do.

From this perspective, Claude's paintings and the women represented in this text reveal much about constructions of the gender identity of woman. When one collects the disparate metaphors and comparisons that qualify the various women in the text, one comes up with a rather incredible list. Women are first and foremost associated with images of castration, or its equivalent, decapitation. When we first encounter Christine, it is on the "rue de la Femme-sans-Tête," the "Street of the Headless Woman." What Claude wants to paint of Christine is her head, and when she becomes an object for him, losing her subjectivity, she "loses her head" in the sense that Claude is interested merely in his representation of her, which is called in the text "Christine's head" (87). When he is unhappy with his painting of a nude woman, it is the head that he destroys (112). At the end of the text Christine develops a "brain fever" (412), an illness of the head. Thus Claude's artistic voyeurism appears to aim to see the origin of female gender identity, to show on canvas just what it means to be a woman.

In addition to images of decapitation, the text also presents us with images of the woman's body in pieces. In the paintings of studio nudes we see singled out for study legs and bellies of women (110); old statues of women have only stumps left for limbs (279); when Claude looks out on a garden of statues he sees a conglomeration of body parts, "heads, breasts, legs, arms" (357). Women are often blind in this text: Christine's mother goes blind at the end of her life, and after she dies, Christine goes to Paris to read for the blind woman, Mme Vanzade. Sandoz, the writer, has a paralyzed mother. Christine's mouth has lips that are too big and that "bled" (76). Claude wounds his painting so that it has a "gaping wound" (113). The way women appear in the ideology of this text are as sick, wounded, amputated.

There is one peculiar scene in which constructed, fictional images of woman, such as those Claude paints or those that Mahoudeau sculpts, show their power of illusion, show the way in which we come to take them for reality. When Claude goes to visit Mahoudeau and the two of them stand admiring the immensity and beauty of his statue of the colossal woman, something strange begins to happen: "The Bather moved, her stomach quivered in a slight wave, her left hip stretched out more, as if the right leg was about to begin walking. . . . Bit by bit the statue came completely alive. Her back rolled, her breast swelled in a great sigh, between her loosened arms. And suddenly, her head bowed" (281–282). Here we believe that the statue has come to life and is moving, the statue being a male representation of the woman, the constructed image of what a woman is.

But the text goes on to destroy that belief, when it reveals the secret behind this movement: "Her thighs weakened, she fell in a living fall, with a frightened anguish, in the manner of a woman that throws herself down in pain" (282). Mahoudeau did not have enough money to construct an adequate scaffolding for such an immense "fiction," and she falls, breaking into bits, showing that the seeming reality of this image is an illusion. Mahoudeau is so attached to the statue, that he tries to save it and almost dies beneath its weight, prefiguring Claude's self-sacrifice to his image of the woman.

But this remarkable scene introduces us to another aspect of the production of art in this text by conjuring up the myth of Pygmalion. The artist would like to create an image that would become reality, a woman that would become flesh and blood: "And it vibrates, and it takes on a sacred life, as if one could see the blood flowing in her muscles" (299). He wants to breathe life into his work (400).

One of the female body parts that particularly fascinates Claude is the belly: "The belly, for me, that has always exalted me" (300). He is fascinated with this area because it is where human beings are created, the area of the primal scene of the origin of the self. Indeed, his desire to make a living work of art is couched constantly in terms of giving birth metaphorically. Art for Claude is to produce what is in your "ventre" (100). Painting is referred to as a "giving birth," "accouchement" (144), most often a difficult one, even in one place a kind of cesarean section: "A fever stiffened him, he worked with the blind obstinacy of the artist who opens his flesh, in order to pull out the fruit that torments him" (262). He even feels the nausea of pregnancy: "One might have called it the deaf work of a germination, of a creature being born in him, the exaltation and the nausea that women know" (272). Claude, in his wish to give birth, shows the kind of "womb envy" discussed by Irigaray:

> But it seems, all the same, that one might be able to interpret the fact of being deprived of a womb as the most intolerable depriva-tion of man, since his contribution to gestation—his function with regard to the origin of reproduction—is hence asserted as less than evident, as open to doubt. An indecision to be attenu-ated both by man's "active" role in intercourse and by the fact that he will mark the product of copulation with *his own name*. Thereby woman, whose intervention in the work of engendering the child can hardly be questioned, becomes the anonymous worker, the machine in the service of a master-proprietor who will put his trademark upon the finished product. It does not seem exaggerated, incidentally, to understand quite a few prod-ucts, and notable cultural products, as a counter-part or a search for equivalents to woman's function in maternity. (23)

Chodorow mentions in this light the interpretation made by Bettel-heim of certain male initiation rights that involve some kind of cutting as a means of symbolically acquiring a vagina, and with it the means of bearing children (Chodorow 38). Thus, in *L'Oeuvre* and in *La Fille aux yeux d'or*, the question of the male's possible access to femininity is at stake in the image of male pregnancy.

The male artist wishes to give birth to a new Eve (103): thus he would be the original producer of a new humankind and woman-kind. (It is interesting to note that Zola took about nine months to write this novel.) Claude's attempt to give birth is of course a failure, one that he describes sometimes in terms of a forceps birth:

"I give birth with forceps, and the child, even so, seems to me to be a horror" (321). Sometimes the pregnancy does not come to term and is called an abortion: "Sandoz, silent, despaired when faced with this superb abortion" (317).

His last paintings take this failure to give birth to a living being as their very subject. First, Claude paints a picture of his dead son, Jacques, and this death of his progeny figures his inability to produce a living painting. What is particularly curious in his son's death and in Claude's painting of it is the description of Jacques's head, which grows abnormally large. When Claude looks at his own painting of the dead child in an exhibition, he cannot tell whether the image in the painting looks like a head or a *belly*: "Ah, *The Dead Child*, the miserable little corpse, that was at this distance no more than a confusion of flesh, the washed up carcass of some formless beast! Was it a skull, was it a belly, that phenomenal head, swollen and white?" (352). The swollen head that looks like a stomach suggests the swollen belly of pregnancy, of the fetus/art that cannot be born. And the image of the sickness of the head parallels the image of the "headless woman" associated with Christine and the woman-as-object, suggesting perhaps the common victimization of woman and child by Claude's merciless representation.

Second, the impossibility of giving birth is the subject of his last painting, whose themes bring together many of the obsessions attributed to Claude. He is fascinated often by the image of things floating in the Seine, a fascination presented at the very beginning of the text: "Strange masses peopled the water, a sleeping flotilla of skiffs and boats, a laundry boat and a dredger, moored at the quay; then, farther away, on the other shore, barges full of coal, sloops full of the leftovers of mills, and overshadowed by a gigantic iron crane" (68). These craft floating in the water, if viewed in the light of the artist's desire to give birth, appear to be images of the womb in a kind of attempt to picture the primal origin scene.

This image of an object in the water develops next into the image of an object that cannot advance—in the birth metaphor it would be a child that cannot be born. Claude is fascinated by the "île de la Cité" in the Seine, which seems to be a ship that never reaches its destination: "But their treasured find, that day, was the western point of the island, that bow of a ship continually anchored, which, in the flow of the two currents, sees Paris without ever reaching it" (158). In his final painting, this island that appears to be a boat

becomes the image of a boat on the Seine situated in the middle of
his painting. And what should this boat contain but a nude woman,
the "Eve" that Claude would like to create, but cannot. If Claude
would like his new Eve to arise in the Seine in his picture, this
desire is expressed by the metaphor of a different mythological
figure. When one looks at his painting one sees "Venus being born
from the froth of the Seine, triumphant, among the omnibuses of
the quays and the dock workers of the Saint-Nicholas port" (295).
This painting could indeed be said to represent, if I can be permitted a play on words, Claude's "Seine originaire" ("primal Seine"),
his desire to represent the process of birth, or birth from a male.

Thus, the final painting figures the failure of Claude's project, of
his desire to show reality without the ideal, for he continues to
desire the impossible: to create without a womb, to create without
the ideal/ideology. If what he lacks to do this is, as he says (in an
echo from Balzac's "Le Chef d'oeuvre inconnu"), "un rien" (303),
this "nothing" is the empty space of the womb. His final image of
the woman's body is the most metaphorical and ideological of all his
paintings, for the nude woman becomes a mere bringing to light of
certain common metaphors that represent woman, and of the reasons for the position of woman in the city at that time:

> He finally woke up from his dream, and the Woman, seen thus
> from below, from a distance of several feet, filled him with stupor.
> Who, then, had just painted this idol of an unknown religion?
> Who had made her from metal, marble, and gems, as she spread
> out the mystic rose of her sex, between the precious columns of
> her thighs, under the sacred vault of her belly? Was it he who,
> without knowing, was the builder of this symbol of insatiable
> desire, of this superhuman image of flesh turned into gold and
> diamonds by his fingers, in his vain effort to create life? Stunned,
> he was afraid of his work, trembling because of this sudden leap
> into the beyond, understanding well that reality itself was no
> longer possible for him, at the end of his long battle to vanquish
> it and to reshape it more realistically with his man's hands. (405)

Here the woman is a flower, a building, beautiful gems, gold—she is
symbolic not real.

Although Claude fails in his artistic attempts, Zola's text succeeds remarkably well at showing just why he fails. This text shows

the victimization of woman at the hands of a certain kind of representation and her plight in the new "modern" order of urban society. Although the text does not solve the problem of woman in representation and in modernity, it does point out the process of her victimization, and here the word "process" is particularly important. For if we take another look at the theme of the final painting, we see that in the background are workers, and the process of production itself is emphasized. Here is both the work of the dockers *and* the work that goes into a work of art: "To the left was another excellent group, the dockers who unloaded sacks of plaster; these were parts [of the painting] that were carefully worked, with a beautiful power of craft" (316). Thus what this novel shows is the process of production and construction of images, often discussing in lengthy terms the physical work involved in painting and sculpting. What prevents this text from falling into the trap of Claude's project is its recognition of the process of the production of meanings, and of the fact that one cannot "create" a perfect, simple and clear "reality," one cannot overcome the inevitable distance between representation and reality. The distance of language, of ideology, of re-production is always there. Sandoz, who often bears the voice of the "author"—in the early sketches for the book Zola used the first person pronoun when he spoke of Sandoz (Niess 63)— makes the impossibility of pure creation from nothing (without ideology) and the necessity of the distance implied in re-production clear when he says: "We can create nothing . . . we are but weak reproducers" (421).

Another aspect of the production of art taken up by this novel is the commercial one. There is a constant struggle between the "pure" goals of an artist like Claude, who cares not for money, and the "fiscal" goals of an artist like Fagerolles, who makes a great deal of money by painting canvases that please the public. Art is a commodity in this text and partakes of the world of work and production. The art dealer who replaces the one who used to buy Claude's paintings is a speculator who does not love the art works he buys (243).

When Sandoz notices the strangeness of the image of the nude woman amidst the workers of Paris, this "rendering strange" serves to make the ideological constructions visible. As we saw, the society of the city functions at the expense of the construction of the gender identity of the (nude) woman, and this ideological structure could be said to be the very theme of the picture. What Zola's text shows is what reality tries to hide: the reality of ideology, the reproduction of it in art, and the act of production that is art. In one remarkable passage, Sandoz describes the novel he is in the process of writing, and it is this very novel and the series we are reading:

> I am going to take a family, and I will study its members, one by one, from whence they come, where they are going, how they react one upon the other; in other words, humanity in miniature, the way humanity grows and acts . . . Furthermore, I will put my people in a determined historical period, something that will give me the surroundings and the circumstances—a piece of history . . . Eh? You understand, a series of books, fifteen, twenty books, episodes that will continue, while each one has its own place, a suite of novels. (219–220)

Zola cannily presents in this novel a representation of its very production.

As for the woman in the novel, her access to artistic creation is suggested but thwarted. On the one hand, Christine, surprisingly, is herself a painter, as was her mother. Her mother painted fans, and encouraged Christine's artistic leanings also: "She spoiled me, there was nothing too good for me, I had professors for everything. . . . It was always at painting that I was best. . . . Mamma, who had a lot of talent, had me do a little water color work, and I helped her sometimes with the backgrounds of her fans . . . She painted such beautiful ones!" (82). Here, although the women themselves paint, what they paint is relegated to "female" genres: fans and watercolors. As Linda Nochlin points out, women were denied access to the real art world, because they were denied access to the inner world of artistic initiation, that is, the painting of nude female models:

> The very plethora of surviving "Academies"—detailed, painstaking studies from the nude studio model—in the youthful oeuvre of artists down through the time of Seurat and well into the twentieth century, attests to the central importance of this branch of study in the pedagogy and development of the talented beginner. The formal academic program itself normally proceeded, as a matter of course, from copying from drawings and engravings, to drawing from casts of famous works of

sculpture, to drawing from the living model. To be deprived of this ultimate stage of training meant, in effect, to be deprived of the possibility of creating major art works, unless one were a very ingenious lady indeed, or simply, as most of the women aspiring to be painters ultimately did, restricting oneself to the "minor" fields of portraiture, genre, landscape, or still life. It is rather as though a medical student were denied the opportunity to dissect or even examine the naked human body.

(*Women* 159–160)

When Claude looks at the paintings done by Christine, which she does in order to get closer to Claude, he finds them "innocent" (165), lacking the "knowledge" he has gained. The difficulty of becoming a woman painter is shown ingeniously when, in a second attempt to get close to Claude by painting her own pictures, Christine becomes a kind of student of the master. This gives her access to the training necessary for artists. She finds, however, that a student cannot be a woman: "She gave up only when she saw that her attempt was producing the effect that was the opposite of what she wanted, because he [Claude] finally forgot the woman in her, as if fooled by their shared task and by the footing established between them of simple friendship, man to man" (297). A relation between artists is between men and there is no place for a woman.

The second opportunity at feminine artistic creation is represented by Irma Bécot. On the one hand, Christine finds that being an artist's model means becoming a thing, and in this text it means becoming a statue while the artist attempts to turn his painting into living flesh: "Immobile, under the brutality of the way things were, she felt the discomfort of her nudity. On each place where Claude had touched her, there remained an icy feeling, as if the cold that made her shiver was entering now in those places. . . . And, her gaze in the distance, she kept the rigidity of marble, she held back the tears that swelled her heart, reduced to the misery of not even being able to cry" (300). Irma, on the other hand, does not become a thing, a statue, a work of art, at the hands of a male artist. Rather, she turns herself into a work of art: "She pulled her hair back from her forehead, she seemed to erase with her hand the blood in her cheeks, she lengthened the oval shape of her face, she redid her wild courtesan's head, with the intelligent charm of a work of art" (237). She imitates the master, Titian, and turns herself into a real work of art: "In four years, she had become other, her head made up with an actor's art, her forehead shrunk by the curls of her hair, her face pulled out longer; thanks to an effort of the will no doubt, she had now become an ardent redhead from the pale blond that she was, so that a Titian courtesan seemed to have arisen out of the little urchin of the past" (234–235). Irma is extremely successful in her society's terms: she becomes very rich. She creates what Claude would like to create: a living female work of art.

Irma's success comes about because she recognizes and uses the necessity of a kind of "female masquerade." A woman makes herself, as society makes her, and by emphasizing her role in her creation, she points out the artifice of her gender identity. By exaggerating the female masquerade, she undermines its illusion of reality and reveals it as a mode of production—something like what Zola himself does when he represents the production of this very novel.

Although neither Irma nor Christine becomes a "real" artist, a combination of their various attempts to do so suggests an interesting possibility. If a female artist could pursue Christine's "female genre" and thus remain female, and pursue Irma's tactic of emphasizing the necessity of the female masquerade, she could perhaps create a painting whose subject is the representation of representation as masquerade, as imitation and production. We will see in the discussions of *La Princesse de Clèves* and *Le Ravissement de Lol V. Stein* in chapter 8, how two texts written by women seem to pursue this strategy. But before we turn to that production, we must pursue, in the next chapter on male eyes/'I's, the ultimate mutilation of the woman by the male's gaze.

# 7

## Voyeurism and the Elimination of Difference: Male 'I's/Eyes in First Person Narrative

*How many buds we carry in us . . . they will open only in our books! They are like "dormant eyes" . . . as botanists call them. But if, by our will, we suppress them all but one, how it grows immediately, how it gets bigger! How it takes up the sap right away! In order to create a hero, my recipe is very simple: take one of these buds, put it in a pot—all by itself—you end up soon with an admirable individual. Advice: preferably choose (if it is true that we can choose) the bud that bothers you the most. You can get rid of it at the same time. That is perhaps what Aristotle called the purgation of the passions.*
  —André Gide, quoted in Henri Maillet,
  *L'Immoraliste d'André Gide*

*Léa was the actress who was the friend of the two girls, the ones that Albertine, without seeming to see them, had, one afternoon, at the Casino, watched in the mirror.*
  —Marcel Proust,
  *La Prisonnière*

IN THE TWENTIETH-CENTURY novel in France, André Gide and Marcel Proust continue to be concerned with many of the topics developed in the nineteenth-century French novel. In the two texts we will be studying, it is in particular the problem of the male self, its definition, desires, and identity, that relates to the topic of voyeurism. In both of these texts narrated in the first person, the "I" of the male narrator/character attempts to protect or define the self by controlling what the self defines as its other, a controlling effected with the help of the voyeur's gaze. I will not study these two authors in terms of homosexuality, self, and other. Although this might prove to be a valuable way of investigating the construction of gender identity, my purpose here is to show how the visual functions in the construction of truth and identity and how it affects gender, self, and other. As we saw in *La Chartreuse de Parme* and *L'Oeuvre*, the gender of the author is not of primary importance in the ability to question the visual construction of truth; a male author and male character can manifest just as much desire to escape from a coercive and repressive visual policing as do the typically female victims of the system. So too, the gender identity and desire of the author or characters will be of interest to us only in so much as they relate to questions of power and control over the object viewed and desired.

In the epigraph taken from Proust, the scene of voyeurism represented displays the structure that it will assume in both Gide and Proust: the narrator shows himself spying on the object of his desire, Albertine, as she spies on the object of her desire. Albertine, the "voyeuse" here, becomes in turn the object of the narrator's voyeurist gaze. The mirror in this Proustian scene symbolizes the problem of the identity of the self in its relation to the other and to desire: let us not forget that in one scene in *La Prisonnière*, the narrator embraces Albertine while looking at himself in a mirror (76).[1] The symbol of the mirror is also important in Gide's text in the famous scene of voyeurism in which Michel watches Moktir in the mirror as Moktir steals the object of his desire. (All the while, Moktir is secretly observing Michel's voyeurist gaze, and both are metaphorically "observed" later by Ménalque, as he tries to understand Michel by engaging in a kind of espionage in his reconstruction of events.) The mirrors in the scenes represent the reversibility of the structure of voyeurism—the one observing can always assume the position of the observed; active can become passive—and they also represent the importance of the act of voyeurism in the establishment of the subject's identity, his mirror image of himself. It is perhaps here that homosexuality is manifested in the structure: Albertine's and Michel's desired objects, significantly the objects seen in the mirrors, have the same gender as they. (Here gender is taken on its most superficial level; Proust's texts certainly go on to question that superficial definition.) The main difference between these two texts is that in Gide's text, the main goal involved for Michel in this act of voyeurism is to know himself and to define the self in relation to the other; in Proust, the goal is to understand the obscure desires of the other, Albertine. As we shall see, however, the "other" as it is defined in these texts will be the object of painful repression and control by the self.

## Eliminating the Feminine in *L'Immoraliste*

André Gide's *L'Immoraliste* shifts the scene of the gaze away from the typical scenario in which the male gazer eyes a female object; although the gazer remains male, he here turns his sights upon a male object. From this gaze springs a network of themes and structures linking narcissism, voyeurism, theft, and androcentrism, a network that generates a kind of allegory of the primal scene of the origin of gender identity in a patriarchal society. Although the term androcentrism might seem surprising in a text by an author usually discussed in terms of homosexuality, we will see that it is in fact the structure of androcentrism and not that of homosexuality that sets in motion the tragedy of this text, that sets up the definition of femininity in relation to the male, and that then eliminates the feminine.

The narration of Michel's past, and thus the beginning of the crisis of his life, begins with his contact with the feminine. As with the heroes and heroines of much Romantic fiction, Michel lost his mother sometime in the past, and he seems to suffer from both the early influence of his mother and the lack of maternal contact after her death. Unlike the mothers of Romantic fiction, however, Michel's mother represents the law, a function usually reserved for fathers. Much is made by Michel of his mother's austerity, her puritan regulations, and the link of those qualities to his work: "The taste for a kind of austerity, which my mother gave me by inculcating principles in me, I carried over in entirety to my studies (372). In psychoanalytic terms, Michel's mother is apparently not the "castrated" mother whose image results from the Oedipus complex, but the "phallic" mother who wields the law. It seems that Michel's mother dies while retaining her masculine nature, and Michel, like the Romantic heroes, has never been able to come into contact with the oedipal "feminine"; he has not worked out his relation to castration. He remains at a kind of infantile stage in the primal scene.

Michel's work interests—archeological and historical studies of the past, and in particular, studies of the ruins and "relics" of the past—resemble Raphaël's interest in the objects in the antiquary's shop and in the ass's skin; both motherless children are interested in the preserved "fragments," whether organic or inorganic, of the past—their way of preserving the mother's phallus. And for Michel, who speaks of his mother's influence on him as preserved "folds" in his mind, writing, the symbolic, the ruins and books that belong to the rule of Michel's life, are closely linked to the rule of his mother and to her identity. Her rule, the lessons she taught him that he thought had been "erased from his heart" (373), continue to "master" him: "I did not suspect to what extent these first lessons of childhood master us" (373). The unerased writing of this ancient past, his mother's text and law, become the object of his study of himself later on, the study of that older "writing" on his soul: "And I compared myself to a palimpsest; I tasted the joys of the scientist who, under more recent writing, discovers, on the same paper, a very ancient text infinitely more precious. What was it, this hidden text?" (399). This metaphor of the older, effaced text bears an uncanny similarity to the metaphor used by Freud to describe the pre-oedipal mother as the Minoan-Mycenaean civilization that preceded Greek culture. Michel's study of his mother's law as inscribed on him becomes the investigation of his own gender identity when he marries Marceline.

Not surprisingly, Michel's marriage is described by him as a kind of discovery of the feminine. He admits that his notions about women had been foolish clichés in the past: "I had made for myself, to the extent that I could, some ideas about the stupidity of women" (376). And when he goes on his honeymoon, it is curious that he expects to rediscover experiences that he associates with his *father*, with the male, perhaps revealing that his understanding of gender is based on a masculine definition: "I had allowed myself only short vacations up until that time . . . but they were working vacations;

my father was not ever distracted from his precise research . . . That is what we will find again, I thought" (375). He did not know that anything "different" could exist: "Not once did the idea occur to me that I might have led a different life, that one could have lived differently" (374).

When he first looks at Marceline, really looks at her, he is sur-prised by his discovery that she is a human being: "So, then, the woman to whom I had attached my life had her own real life!" (376). He learns that she is an "other," a different subjectivity to be dealt with, and at first this subjectivity is veiled for him: "On a simple black straw hat she had put a large floating veil" (375). It is not until his marriage that he comes into contact with the "other," with woman, and with other possibilities for his own life.

But when he makes these discoveries of other possibilities, they call into question his own identity. As we have seen, he has formed clichéd notions about what women are, about "the stupidity of women" (376), and on this very page Michel talks about his own "stupidity": "Next to her, that evening, it was I who seemed to me to be awkward and stupid. . . . I will confess to you my stupidity" (376). It is almost as if, in his discovery of the female, he now undergoes a kind of castration complex in his attempt to situate his own gender, and he experiences the possibility of his own "stupid-ity," his own femininity, his own castration.

Perhaps the most striking scene symbolic of the assumption of femininity is his first manifestation of tuberculosis. As he discovers femininity, Michel "bleeds," in a kind of imitation of menstruation, particularly in the type of blood he emits: "It was no longer clear blood, as in the first times that I spit blood; it was a large, horrible clot that I spit onto the ground with disgust" (383). As he says, the blood came from his mouth "in regular intervals" (378), and, as Emily Apter points out, he takes Marceline's scarf which is worn as a kind of "belt" and uses that when his handkerchief is saturated (114). The displaced location of femininity to his mouth is again displaced when he makes up the excuse he will use if Marceline discovers the blood: he had a nosebleed. In the midst of this scene he thinks of his puritan upbringing, his "puritan childhood" (378), which, as we have seen, is associated with his mother. Thus this discovery of femininity is threatening for Michel because he himself becomes tainted by femininity and castration. The rules and regulations of his mother become, perhaps, the "règles" of his feminine identity.[2]

Michel's illness could be seen to be a symbolic "plunge" into femininity. When he finally encounters what a woman is, which in Freudian terms is a castrated being, he acts out his own femininity, his own bleeding and castration. He becomes "feminine," in the clichéd sense of being weak and helpless when he is ill, and femininity becomes associated with a threatening sickness—again we have the problematic of contagion. His illness is also a "plunge" into another cliché of feminine identity, that of fluidity. Throughout the text, water is associated with the feminine, particularly in the symbol of the Normandy farm which belonged to his mother. The farm is green and wet; it has a garden with a pond (408). Significantly, when he coughs up blood for the first time, he forgets where he is and says: "I thought I was on the sea again, and the sound of the wheels became the sound of the waves" (378). Finally, when he begins to recover, he describes himself as a lost sailor who finally spies land (380).

Thus Michel's struggle against his "malady" becomes a symbolic struggle against his own femininity. He envisions his disease as an active inner enemy that he must vanquish: "A numerous, active enemy was living in me" (384). Even in Michel's own discourse, this enemy within takes on a larger connotation than that of a simple physical illness, for it becomes an enemy "thought," perhaps the enemy "concept" of femininity: "Who can say how many enemy passions and thoughts can live at the same time in man?" (460). His task becomes the effort to dominate his femininity, and he begins doing so by applying his methods of studying to his illness itself: "For a time, only my cure was to be my study" (384). Since his mother's law is linked to his work and study, he in a sense uses the feminine against itself. This he continues to do in his manipulation of Marceline and her love for him.

Marceline becomes the mannequin on which he can place all the accoutrements and all the blame of femininity. She becomes his scapegoat: "My irritation was so intense that, pushing it off onto Marceline, I burst out with outrageous statements in her presence. I accused her; it seemed, if one were to listen to me, that she should have felt herself responsible for the poor quality of my meals" (385). She is "responsible," not only for the bad quality of his food (a reproach often made to mothers), but also for his illness, in a certain way, and he goes so far as to say that her presence itself is what bothers him: "But what bothered me, if I can admit it, was not the children, it was she" (388). She becomes responsible for the existence of castration, she becomes the denigrated feminine so often seen in Freud's writings.

Michel attempts to foist the blame of femininity and castration onto Marceline and to define himself as different from her: he picks as his favorite children those who are the most different from Marceline's favorites (387). And finally, his "illness," his tuberculosis as a symbol of his femininity, is transferred from him to Marceline. She turns into the one who bleeds. He seems to succeed in symbolically dominating his own femininity by shunting it onto her.

Part of what is unbearable in Michel's confession is that he cannot stop at the blaming of Marceline for her femininity: he must eliminate the externalized feminine, and eliminate the person for whom he blames his own brush with castration. He pursues his own itinerary when Marceline becomes sicker and sicker, forcing her to travel to a climate that aggravates her illness, a climate that is symbolically the opposite of feminine fluidity, the desert. One could say that he murders her through neglect and negligence, a murder figured by his tardy discovery of the dying Marceline covered with blood, almost as if he had literally hurt her (469), in the ultimate image of violence against women.

Indeed, a strange sort of balance is established in the sense that one of the two must be the stronger who is well, the other must be the weaker who is sick; one must be active, the other passive. When Michel is sick, it is Marceline who is strong and robust. His confinement is her liberty: "The freedom that my illness gave her permitted her to take long walks from which she returned in a bedazzled state" (391). This "delicate balance" can be seen in the remarkable passage that follows, in which Michel describes the way in which his becoming well suggests Marceline's illness:

I rose up gently, and tenderly I bent over Marceline. She was sleeping; she seemed to be smiling while sleeping. It seemed to me, now that I was stronger, that I felt her to be more delicate, and that her grace was fragility. . . . The smile left her cheeks; the dawn, despite the golden hue it gave to everything, made me see her suddenly as sad and pale—perhaps the approach of morning was tending to make me feel anguished: "Must I, one day, take my turn and care for you, worry about you, Marceline?" (406)

The scales are set in motion: as Michel gets strong, Marceline weakens.

Once Michel becomes strong, he not only can eliminate the culpable feminine by disposing of Marceline but can also expunge the maternal rule from his life (and here one thinks of Nancy Chodorow's interpretation of the repudiation of femininity as the distancing of the self from the powerful mother). It seems significant that when Michel and Marceline take up their residence at La Morinière, the place Michel associates with his mother, Marceline should announce her impending motherhood. She becomes the substitute for his mother in the walks they take in the garden: "We went to sit near the woods, on the bench where I used to go sit with my mother in the past" (410). La Morinière is constantly associated with bearing fruit and with pregnancy, from "this land, where everything is readying itself for ripening, for the useful harvest" (410) to the "pregnant cows in these opulent pastures" (410). It is here that the memory of his mother is resurrected—"the entire past suddenly rose up" (410)—and it is here that he can begin to eliminate that maternal by eliminating the new "mother," Marceline. Uncannily, "La Morinière" contains within it the sounds of both the words *mort* (death) and *mère* (mother).

Perhaps the most striking symbol of the "draining" of femininity and maternity comes in the image of the "draining" of water on the farm. As we saw, fluidity represents femininity, and here, specifically, Marceline's impending motherhood: "As a breath of wind sometimes ruffles a very tranquil water, so the slightest emotion could be read on her brow; in her, mysteriously, she listened to the stirring of a new life; I bent over her as over a deep, pure water, where, as far as one could see, only love was visible" (420). If water represents femininity, then the two men, Michel and Charles, work together to drain femininity and motherhood when they empty a pond that is already leaking; leaking, perhaps, its femininity into the masculine world: "This large pond was leaking; we knew the place of this leak, and we had to cement it. In order to do that it was necessary to begin by emptying the pond, which we had not done for fifteen years" (412). How significant that the two men,

Charles and Michel, share this experience of emptying, evacuating the feminine, an experience that brings them closer together, and after which Michel admits that he did not miss Marceline's presence (413). They get rid of the feminine and replace it with an andro-centric, in fact a uniquely male, world, and one that differs from Michel's original world only in that it includes the possibility of castration.

One final strange detail in this scene is the arithmetic of time that is sprinkled over the two opening pages. Charles is seventeen years old; the pond hasn't been drained for fifteen years; and Charles was four when Michel's mother died (411–412). This arith-metic invites the calculation of the relation of Michel's mother's death to the draining of the pond: the pond was drained when Charles was two, which means that Michel's mother died two years after the draining of the water. How close this comes to the time of death of Marceline after the second draining of the pond! (In Henri Maillet's calculation of the chronology of the narrative, Michel and Marceline go to La Morinière for the first time in the summer of the first year of the narrative, and she dies in the spring of the third year of the narrative [32–35]. Marceline's life blood drains from her as her "feminine" fluid identity does; just after Marceline is compared to pure water, Michel says, "Ah! if it were still happiness, I know that I wanted from then on to keep it, as one wants to keep in one's joined hands, in vain, the water that leaks out" (420).[3]

The repudiation of femininity takes on even larger connotations and is related to the domination and exclusion of the weak in general (here the avowed relation to Nietzsche is evident). This can be seen in Michel's relation with children, as well as in his relation as a member of the upper class to several lower class workers. As Michel gets stronger and sheds his weak femininity, one of the major symbolic markers of this change comes when Marceline, now becoming the weaker, takes a carriage to Sorrento while Michel walks. As he is on his way, a vehicle approaches him from behind, and he realizes with horror that it is Marceline's and that the driver is drunk. Just then the horse stumbles, Marceline rushes out, and Michel tests his new strength by giving the driver a thrashing. His dominance over this worker (the driver) later becomes his domi-nance over the workers on his farm: "We savored that proud joy of preceding and dominating the workers" (417).

What Michel finds most disgusting about the driver is the symbolic signs of his "weakness," which in this text is his femininity: "He spit, drooled, bled, swore. Ah! that horrible being" (405). The fluids, even the words, that come from the driver are "horrible," and Michel significantly thinks of murdering him just as he will eliminate the feminine through Marceline later. Immediately after this scene, Michel finally consummates his marriage with Marceline, as if now, being the stronger, he can be secure in his dominant relation with the feminine. The erotic chain is extended one link further: Michel thrashes the driver, makes love to Marceline, then near the end of the novel, "makes love to," embraces, a *different driver:* "I stood up in front of the carriage to chat with the driver. . . . and since I was bent over him, I could not hold back, and so, drawing him to me, I embraced him" (462).

If power, then, is power over workers and children, just as it is power over women, then the objects of certain of Michel's attempts at voyeurism are significant. Michel desires to see, to understand, to know the male other that he dominates, this "other" being the male children and workers on his farm. As we saw above, exactly the same type of desire for knowledge motivates a certain mode of pornographic photography: "The existence of each one of them remained mysterious to me. It always seemed to me that a part of their life was hidden. What did they do, when I was no longer there?" (442).[4] The desire to dominate women then takes on the more general connotation of political domination in all its manifestations.

Since Michel blames Marceline for her femininity and for the existence of castration, he attempts to eliminate the feminine from his world, and to reestablish the entirely masculine, pre-Marceline world. He attempts to create a new process of "birth" by which he brings forth his own new self: as he sits alone in the countryside, he asks himself, "Was it finally on this morning that at last I was to be born?" (390). His early identification with children perhaps also suggests the early period of the development of this new being (also, perhaps, a reversal of child and observer in the primal scene). And even as he recounts how he destroys Marceline and the new life that grows in her, he speaks of his own "pregnancy": "But all this that was growing in me and that I am telling you about today, what did I know about it?" (422). He calls his newfound identity a "new being" (399). This transference of the feminine function of giving birth to a masculine one in the primal scene, which we saw in *L'Oeuvre* and in *La Fille aux yeux d'or,* is here symbolized in the preface by the transference of a liquid state to an arid one in the image of the "fruit full of bitter ash," the fruit filled not with feminine pulp and fluidity but with the dry ash from a fire.

A problem remains, however, because even though the person responsible for castration (Marceline, the mother) has been eliminated, castration exists and remains in a new kind of "postlapsarian" world. The struggle for "health" and power continues; it is, however, transferred to a struggle for power between males for the dominant position, and it becomes a struggle to gain control of castration. If, as in Freud's writing (the case of the Wolf Man and the primal scene), the desire of the male child for the male/father entails the threat of the child's castration (to desire the father is to be in the place of the mother, the place of the castrated), certain scenes of *L'Immoraliste* stand out as "primal scenes" in which is symbolically situated the continued possibility of Michel's castration in his relation to other males. The important aspect of the primal scene here is that of its symbolic structure, which both refers to the past and carries out an interpretation, or, as Ned Lukacher says, is situated between memory and invention, between "archival verification" and "interpretive free play." These primal scenes function as an avowal of castration *and* as a means of distancing oneself from castration (24).

The first of the "primal scenes" takes place when Michel is just beginning to recover and can take a walk by himself in the oasis. Here he comes across the brother of one of his recent young acquaintances. In a starkly symbolic scene, the allure of this young man is linked to the revelation of his male body and to the image of the wounded, "castrated" tree he climbs:

> He climbed to the top of a beheaded palm tree; then descended agilely, allowing one to see, under his flowing coat, a golden nudity. He carried back from the tree top, whose summit had been cut off, a small earthen gourd: it had been hung up there, next to the recent wound, in order to collect the palm sap with which to make a mild wine, which the Arabs like very much. (393)

The pleasure in this gaze at the desirable, "golden" male object is linked, then, to the image of castration. Here, however, the potential victim of the castration remains unclear, unresolved; castration remains a mere possibility in its symbolism in the tree.[5] In another early scene, Bachir cuts his thumb with his knife, and his chéchia is described as having a "hole in the place of the tassel," ("trou à la place du gland" [382]). *Gland* in French has a genital meaning in addition to its meaning of "tassel." Again the presence of the desirable, healthy male child is accompanied by an image of castration.

As his health improves, Michel perpetrates more scenes of voyeurism, and they take on more and more the allure of a struggle to dominate, and, paradoxically, to dominate his own castration. In the most remarkable scene of voyeurism in this text, Michel watches the child, Moktir, steal a pair of scissors. Viewed in terms of our definition of voyeurism, the subject, Michel, gazes at the object of his desire, Moktir, a newly found and still nebulous object of desire. The knowledge that Michel seeks to gain is knowledge about his own self. The stolen scissors, of course, can be seen to relate to castration in several ways: they could be the instrument by which one cuts, or, in their very form, they can play the role of the male genitals (here we see both the affirmation and denial of castration in this symbol). The fact that Moktir steals them, takes them away from Michel, would seem to indicate that Moktir possesses power and the phallus, which he steals from Michel. However Michel's role in the scene shifts the power relation because it is he, in reality, who is in control of the scene: he lets Moktir take the scissors, he watches him do it; and thus he seems to win in the game of one-upmanship (although later he finds that this was not, in fact, the case). Thus he is in the role of the one who is dispossessed, but he is in control of his own dispossession: "When I had *given* to Moktir enough time to *rob me*, I turned back to him and spoke to him as if nothing had happened" (395, emphasis mine).[6]

The importance of this scene for Michel, who is just beginning to heal from his bout with tuberculosis and who is attempting to construct a new and powerful self, becomes clear when he says that he has learned something important about *himself* as he watches this theft *in the mirror:* "One morning I had a curious revelation about myself" (394). To repeat, the aim of his act of voyeurism is the acquisition of knowledge about himself and his desires. He feels great joy as he watches his own dispossession because he seems to find a way to relate to the male as desired other, and thus to relate to dispossession and castration, but he has also been able to remain in the position of power, a position that is superior in a symbolic way, one that Freud might term "active" rather than "passive." This gives him a construction of identity in which he accepts his castration (his dispossession) because he is the author of the deed (he lets himself be dispossessed, he is in control), and he can watch the act. He has found a way to play the role of the one who castrates and the one who is castrated; thus he can solve the problem of remaining a male (in power) as he assumes the role of the powerless (the one who desires a male). In a similar scene of cutting, Michel has his beard shaved off, he takes off his mask, as he says, and now he is able to see himself, to master and to see his own dispossession (403).

This structure of controlling one's own dispossession is a primal scene that gets repeated over and over as the narrative progresses. Michel spends more and more money, and the loss of his fortune corresponds to the weakening of Marceline, as if the elimination of the feminine (Marceline) and the continued threat of castration make it necessary for him to master the situation by inflicting on himself his own dispossession. The word *abîmer* ("to ruin"; it implies also *abîme*, "abyss"), which appears several times in the text, describes this attempt at self-dispossession, for instance when Ménalque says that he uses and tarnishes ("ternir") his beautiful wall hangings before he gives them away (426). This structure can be seen even in Michel's dealings with his father: Michel wrote a book and his father "stole" it from him with his consent, that is, took credit for the book (373).

But this attempt to be both active and passive, both the victim and the perpetrator of dispossession, never works for Michel. He discovers, when he thought he was in control of the dispossession (which means that he would be in control of the gaze), that he was in reality the victim of the other, and the object of the other's gaze. The first instance of this is when Michel helps Alcide to steal in the scenes of poaching at La Morinière. Michel goes out at night to "steal from himself" as he helps Alcide poach on his own land, and later he pays Alcide for the traps that they make; Michel is still in control of this theft, this dispossession. However, he later learns that Alcide is stealing from him in a third way: Alcide brings their very snares to Bocage and receives money for turning them in. Thus Alcide has in essence stolen from Michel behind his back, where he could not see what was happening, and thus Michel has lost control of the dispossession.

The clearest instance of Michel's mistake occurs when Ménalque tells him that when Moktir stole the scissors as Michel watched, Moktir knew all along that Michel was watching him steal, and so Moktir was really the one in final control of the situation. Most significantly, these scissors are "something . . . with dulled points [*épointé*]" (427), just as the palm tree in the desert was "beheaded" (*étêté*), and just as Michel is now totally dispossessed, no longer in control of the gaze or of the theft. Indeed, Ménalque has the final gaze, the final control, because it is he who has been watching from the greatest distance; he has followed Michel's trail, spying on him and learning about what he did, and watching him now as he learns of his dispossession. In fact, Michel asks Ménalque not to look at him as he recounts Michel's past: "Tell it without looking at me" (427).

What Michel discovers, then, is that one cannot be in charge of one's own dispossession, one can never have the final gaze. As Ménalque tells him, "You thought you had him [Moktir] and it was he who had you" (428). Dispossession is radical dispossession and cannot be controlled. He also finds that he cannot be in charge of possession either: "You think that you possess and you are possessed" (435). One cannot "have," in any simple way, in a world in which the possibility of castration exists. The solution to the problem of castration put forward by the narration of this text does not work, and we see Michel in a kind of ambiguous paralysis at the end of the text: he asks for help from his friends, needing to find a way to get back to living a life with substance; but this plea for help can still be read as an act of seduction, as we watch him attempting to win over his male friends.

We can trace Michel's mistake back to the desire to eliminate femininity, to remove his contact with dispossession. When he gets rid of the feminine, which is in his terms the dispossessed, the castrated, he attempts to dispossess himself of dispossession—paradoxically reiterating the function (dispossession) he attempts to eliminate. In the same way, when he attempts to dominate in an active way his own passivity and dispossession, as in the scissor scene, he finds that at another level he is actually the passive object of another's gaze. Michel's mistake is to attempt to master dispossession, to choose one state over another, a choice Ménalque also recommends: " 'One must choose,' he murmured. 'The important thing is to know what one wants . . .' " (435). Michel shows that the choice of one over the other is impossible; it is an attempt to separate what is inseparable, to eliminate a part of oneself that is not removable. Gide spoke of Michel as a part of himself that could not be eliminated or, rather, as half of a delicate balance of passions that must remain in equilibrium: "That a bud of Michel is in me goes without saying; but it is with this as it is with those opposing passions of which Pascal so cleverly speaks, because you give in to one of them only to the detriment of the other" (1515). Michel does not recognize the need for the maintenance of opposing elements in equilibrium; he tries to make one dominate or eliminate the other, and instead finds himself doubly dispossessed, having eliminated a part of himself as well as the other who loved him.

Michel's mistake goes back to a kind of belief in presence, as Jameson noted in *The Prisonhouse of Language*, a belief in the possibility of eliminating that delicate balance, that difference in oneself in favor of a "pure" nature, of pure dominance and activity (177–178). The failure to purify resonates with Mallarméan echoes of "Le Pitre châtié," when Michel speaks of the more authentic "old man" that lies under the surface of civilization. He attempts to wash off that layer of artifice, as does the clown in the Mallarmé sonnet, but he finds that once the surface is gone, one he has eliminated femininity in himself, he has destroyed his entire being, his "sacre" or sacredness. It would seem that the feminine, Marceline, as she is being eliminated, tries to tell Michel that his desire for purity is not possible when she says, "You cannot ask everyone to be different from all the rest" (423). Michel cannot expect each person to be a unique, pure, purely different being, because each person always bears the other within.

Michel believes that there is that unique inscription of the true self in his nature, that hidden layer of the palimpsest that he would like to uncover. He believes in the truth of his pure nature; he believes he can dominate and possess that truth; and this novel recounts his attempt to do so. To find this inner inscription he asks himself: "What was this hidden text? In order to read it, was it not necessary to begin by erasing the recent texts?" (399). The recent text, the discovery of femininity and his own femininity, he attempts to erase, in order to get back to the domination of the male, of the one who is in control, to the active voyeur putting his own dispossession in its place: "My only effort was then to blame systematically or to suppress all that I thought was due to my past learning and to my first morals" (399). The narrator "Michel," however, on this very page, in his distance from that Michel who is the subject of the discourse, shows that this past text is recuperable only through the present rewriting of it, and he cannot, at that moment of narration, recover the original text because his telling of it falsifies, interprets, the past: "All these thoughts—I did not have them then, and my painting here falsifies me" (399). The "pure" self that Michel would like to discover in the past does not exist, because the writings that cover over the old text of the palimpsest change irrevocably the "original"; the original exists only in its rewritten form (we again find the structure of the primal scene, a combination of memory and invention).

Once again it is Marceline, the eliminated feminine, who sees the force of interpretation on the formation of the self. As she tells Michel, when he attempts to reveal the vices he suspects in the people who work on his farm, his very gaze, his very attempt to reveal them *changes* them, rewrites their identity: "Do you not understand that our gaze develops, exaggerates in each person the point on which it rests? And that we make that person become what we claim that he is?" (464). If we put this notion in terms of Michel's definition of femininity, the gaze becomes the powerful, detrimental force of patriarchy that sees the woman as the dispossessed, the castrated, and in fact is the instrument of her dispossession and "castration." In Michel's view of the world, gender, as for Freud, is defined in male, visual terms of castration alone, and once he has established the identity of Marceline as that of the castrated and dispossessed, he "rupudiates" it, eliminates her from being, and continues to attempt to eliminate "femininity" from himself by being in control of the gaze, of activity. Since castration "exists," in the post-Marceline world, he attempts to remain in the dominant position by being in charge of dispossession, even if it is his own.

This book reveals the mistakenness of that repudiation, as it points out the paradoxes in Michel's attempt to "possess his dispossession." Marceline, the feminine, has been "suppressed," both in the sense that she is never allowed to be anything but the definition Michel makes of her (she is a castrated male)—she is never allowed to be the real other, the nonmale, the "feminine"—and in the sense that Michel's elimination of dispossession entails an elimination of that equilibrium of which Gide speaks, the elimination of a part of *his own being.* That which he has suppressed comes back to affect him, something he admits he fears to his friends at the end of the text: "I fear that what I have suppressed will revenge itself" (471).

This text tells the tale of the gaze used to suppress the other, the weak, the feminine; it tells the tale of the desire to dominate and possess, to put the androcentric self above all else, to create a pure male world. This text tells also of the tragedy and failure of androcentrism, a tragedy that affects both genders. It tells the tale, not of a unique individual, but of a "type" that can be found all too often. The opening paragraph invites us to regard this book as a mirror in which we see, not the other from a position of dominance, but rather ourselves in our own state of error, which is the same as Michel's: "Ah! what are you going to think of our friend? . . . But there is more than one today, I fear, who will dare to see a mirror image in this story" (369).

And what of Marceline? Let us turn to a text written by a man whose name is inscribed in that of *Marcel*ine: Marcel Proust. Here, the surprising and highly gendered play on proper names begins, for Proust certainly used literary precursors, as well as real people, to form the name of the object of the narrator's gaze in *La Prisonnière*, the name *Albertine*. (We will see, in the section to come, just which literary precursors generated *Albertine.*) There is, in fact, a play of proper names in *La Prisonnière* that highlights the different roles played by the gaze in Gide and in Proust. In Gide, the use of the gaze in the attempt to establish purity, i.e., an absolute difference from the other, does not work; when one uses the gaze to make a world in which all is purely masculine, all purely similar to the conception one has of one's own self, this gaze eliminates the other as well as the self. Michel eliminates the feminine; to make up my own word play, Marceline becomes Marcel. However, in Proust, even though the narrator, Marcel, would like to see and control the feminine, Albertine, even though he would like to see and eliminate any difference between her and his idea of her, he learns that his gaze at her can never be complete, can never grasp the totality of her being. There is always a displacement; he can never see the entirety of what she is; there is always a space, symbolized perhaps by the fact that it is not Marcel who spies on Albertine directly. Marcel can gain only indirect and thus imperfect knowledge of her through the gaze of the other, who is (significantly, in relation to André Gide) Marcel's spy, *Andrée.* Thus in Proust we will see a

turning away from the elimination of difference toward a new relationship to it.

## Perceiving Difference: Seeing Albertine Seeing in Barbey and Proust

*"However, I will often think of that window slightly opened, of that shutter which
was as poetic for me as Le Rideau cramoisi and in front of which M. de
Beaumont passed and played so well into the anecdotal beginnings of Barbey
d'Aurevilly, beginnings that lead apparently to nothing."*
          —Letter from Proust, Correspondance générale

The most obvious scenes of voyeurism in Proust are so well known
that they need only be mentioned briefly here: Marcel, hidden in
some bushes, sees Mlle Vinteuil and her friend through the window
as they make love; he sees Charlus being whipped through a little
oval window. These two scenes reconfigure the primal scene of the
parents' lovemaking in a single sex scenario. Two genders do exist,
but in two different scenes rather than in one primal scene (of
course, Proust radically questions the nature of the two genders
throughout his text). In this gender configuration, the difference
between the sexes is both affirmed and denied.

In these primal scenes of the viewing of lovemaking, the origin in
question is that of the nature of sexuality: what does one desire? It is
also a question of the role of gender in sexuality: how does the
difference between, and similarity of, genders function in love? As a
rewriting of the primal scene of parental lovemaking, it is also a
question of the origin of the self: how does the individual come to
exist? what is the individual? Finally, both scenes involve questions
of domination, sadism, and mastery (with Mlle Vinteuil, it is her
cruelty to the image and memory of her father). These are the three
areas of investigation that will be important as we turn our attention to the representation of the voyeurist gaze at the woman in *La
Prisonnière:* the origin of the self (and through a metaphoric construction, the origin of the work of art), gender identity and its
relation to desire, and the need to master.

The topic of the repetition of the semes of names with which the last essay on Gide concluded is not a mere game but an important link to the "primal scenes" in Proust of the origin and nature of the self and the origin and nature of the work of art. First, the narrator asks himself whether the "individual" human being really exists or not, whether a person can be unique or is, rather, merely composed of a conglomeration of traits (semes) from others. One of the observations made by the narrator is that certain family traits reappear in different generations; thus the individual is perhaps only a repetition. The individual is perhaps not different, but the same as his ancestors. Second, the notion of "heredity" is linked through rhetorical structures to the notion of literary and artistic influence, and thus to the question of the origin of the work of art. In certain reflections made by the narrator, he notes the repetition of artistic traits from author to author. To what extent is an artist original, to what extent repetitious? Can one not recognize a particular and peculiar personality in the voices of great artists? (In this discussion, Proust significantly cites the scene in *La Chartreuse de Parme* in which Fabrice secretly gazes out his window at the "band" of young women with their flowers—Fabrice is "à l'ombre des jeunes filles en fleurs").

It is here that the function of intertextuality in Proust's own work, intertextuality as constitutive structure (Proust rewrites Balzac and Barbey) as well as theme (Proust discusses Barbey and Balzac and the role of artistic influence), can give us insight into the unique way in which Proust rewrites the primal scenes of voyeurism in his text. In the multilayered intertextuality of his work, we will see that Barbey and Balzac, in their representation of the voyeurist desire to unveil the woman to learn her truth, should be placed alongside of Gide. For these three writers, the voyeurist gaze at the desired other is not really an attempt to understand the other; it is only an attempt to reinforce the definition of the (male) self through its difference from the other. It is an attempt to eliminate the female so that the male can see his own mirror image.

In Proust, however, the male gaze at the woman attempts to see, understand, and control the female object. The scene that best represents the Proustian voyeurism I will investigate here is the scene in *La Prisonnière* in which the narrator takes pleasure in spying upon Albertine while she sleeps, a spying that epitomizes all the other scenes of surveillance in that novel. The pleasure in this scene involves the knowledge that Albertine is present, under his gaze, and that she is unable to manifest her otherness. Thus even though Proust's text does focus the gaze on the other, the aim of the gaze at the other remains at first the elimination of her difference, specifically her difference in the sense that she does not conform to the idea that the gazer has of her. Nevertheless, the way in which Proust "resolves" this problem is surprising and invaluable for any investigation of self and other, voyeurism, and individuality. We must first investigate the elements of voyeurism in Barbey and Balzac that Proust rewrites, and then study that rewriting in the terms of origin, originality, and difference posed by Proust's text both thematically and structurally.

In *Le Temps retrouvé,* Gilberte informs Marcel that she is reading the Balzac tale *La Fille aux yeux d'or,* and that she finds the plot of the story implausible: it could never really happen, or, at the very least, if a *woman* might imprison the woman she loved, a *man* would never imprison the woman he loved. This is a nice bit of irony, because, as Marcel argues, it *is* true that a man might imprison a woman; in fact, he knew a woman who had been imprisoned. Of course, the reader understands that the woman's jailkeeper was Marcel himself; the prisoner, Albertine; and the tale of this imprisonment the subject of one of the preceding volumes, *La Prisonnière.* We have here, in the discussion between Marcel and Gilberte and in the intersection between the two texts (Balzac's and Proust's), both a terse summary of *La Prisonnière* ("I knew a woman who was loved by a man who succeeded in confining her; she could never see anyone, and she went out only with devoted servants" [*Le Temps retrouvé* 706]) and that novel's themes: desire, surveillance, imprisonment, the chiasmus of genders—all themes related to the structure of voyeurism, as we have seen.

Another text interposes itself between the Balzac and the Proust texts: Barbey d'Aurevilly's *Le Rideau cramoisi.* Also mentioned in *A La Recherche du temps perdu,* specifically in *La Prisonnière, Le Rideau cramoisi* carries on those same Balzacian themes that later reemerge in Proust: the themes of secret love in an enclosed space (with the significant change in Barbey and Proust that it is the woman who comes to the man's room to make love, and the man who limits himself to the domestic space), the themes of gender ambiguity (which abound in Balzac's corpus),[7] and the covert or overt theme of homosexuality. In all three texts the women who desire die, while the men live on.[8]

But it is the title of Balzac's text that provides the one theme that structures all three texts and that regulates the vagaries of the plot: the image of the eyes of the woman who desires. In *La Fille aux yeux d'or*, Paquita's eyes draw the gaze of her suitors, and it is ultimately because of her eyes that she dies at the end of the novel. Her death comes about not because those golden eyes reflect the admiring gaze of those who desire her nor because they represent the ultimate signified of the Balzacian world, gold. It is rather because those eyes do not remain passive, reflecting surfaces but gain the depth of otherness when Paquita desires to see, to flee her domestic prison in order to gaze at men; when she desires to *know*, to break out of the prison of her concubinage, and to discover what her own desires are. Her activities arouse in those who desire her a parallel desire to know her, to reveal her secrets, as we see when Henri resorts to melodramatic espionage methods to learn who she is and thus to solve the enigma of her identity. Her gaze at the outside world and her investigation of her own desire set up a network of significations between woman, seeing, knowledge, and desire, raising important questions that are ultimately silenced when she dies at the end of the story.

The nineteenth-century texts of Balzac and Barbey differ in a significant way from the twentieth-century opus of Proust, however (a difference that is not simply one of length). Barbey's and Balzac's texts continue to propagate the "myth" of the enigma of woman and of her desire, but Proust's text ends up by treating that theme in a very different way. Let us work through the Barbey text, whose female protagonist goes significantly by the name of Alberte *and* Albertine (the "semes" rewritten in Proust), and then turn to *La Prisonnière* to see how Proust's Albertine is similar yet different.[9]

Gender ambiguity, much discussed in analyses of Barbey's work, functions mainly at a symbolic level. A chiasmatic exchange of gender characteristics takes place between the male protagonist, Brassard, and the woman Albert(in)e. Brassard is young and innocent, is "like a beautiful woman at a ball" (50), has a forehead "white like a woman's arm" (52; *bras*, "arm," forms a significant part of the name that identifies him, *Brassard*—perhaps this white forehead/ woman's arm is a kind of a feminine phallus?), and himself describes his dandyish nature as follows: "I was like those women who still make themselves up when they are alone and expect no one" (61). Albert(in)e, on the other hand, has a hand "large and strong like that of a young boy" (69), and, as the narrator claims, she has "as many muscles as I" (75). Since she is the one with the strong hands and muscles (the strong "bras"/phallus perhaps), it is a bit amusing that her lips should be described as "red and erectile" (82).

In the story's frame, when the narrator and Brassard travel together in a coach and pass by the house in which Brassard and Albert(in)e were together many years earlier, gender ambiguity is related to the darkness that surrounds them and thus to the impossibility of *seeing*: "Not a sound troubled the profound silence . . . but one, the sound of a monotonous and tired broom, of someone (of man or woman . . . it was not known)" (55). Indeed, the impossibility of seeing and of seeing gender engenders the now familiar voyeuristic need to see and to know the solution to that mystery, more specifically the mystery of the woman's identity.[10] This is thematized in the text in the immortal image of the curtain or veil that hides a secret behind it. One would like to see the curtain drawn back so as to be able to peer through the window and reach the truth within: "Not knowing what makes someone stay up at night behind a window with drawn curtains, where the light indicates life and thought, adds the poetry of dreams to the poetry of reality. At least, for me, I have never been able to look at a window, alight at night, in a sleeping town through which I passed, without attaching to that frame of light a world of thoughts" (54). And when the two men in the coach spy the crimson curtain in the frame of the story, the narrator guesses why Brassard is so affected by it: "I would wager heavily that you have kept this window that shines over there so present in your memory only because a woman was there for you behind its curtain!" (58). Here we have two men, sitting before that veiled window, who discuss the nature of the woman who was, and perhaps is, behind that veil, a woman described later as mysterious, Sphinx-like (84).[11]

The desire to see behind the curtain is linked to the narrator's (and our) desire to hear Brassard's story, which the narrator subtly seduces from Brassard. Françoise Gaillard links this shared desire for the truth of the plot to a position of voyeurism that the reader shares with the narrator in "Le Bonheur dans le crime": "It is always necessary for the narrator to 'make one see as if one were there.' To tell a story is to draw the other into the situation of voyeurism that was the situation of the narrator" (267).[12] The narrator's desire, born from Brassard's hint at knowledge about what goes on behind that curtain, reflects Brassard's desire to "know" Albert(in)e. But in both frame and story, that desire to pierce the veil threatens the person who is behind it. Albert(in)e is the secret Brassard wants to learn, and in trying to learn that secret he unwittingly kills her (she dies while making love to him). In the story's frame, the narrator desires to learn Brassard's story and, in a reversal of positions (the narrator is the "man" who tries to learn Brassard's secret), he does not see the answer but instead an image of death, when Brassard, in recounting the desired story to the narrator, is described as "pale, not like a corpse . . . but like death itself" (56).

There is a threat, then, in revealing the secret behind the curtain, the threat of death. In speaking of some different windows, windows which Brassard had to pass when he was a soldier (and the use of the metaphor of war for love is repeated over and over again), he speaks of the death that is ready to pour forth from them: "These windows, masked by their blinds, were on the verge, in a few moments, of spitting out death" (49). Brassard is the kind of person who goes too far—"*trop loin*," in italics, in the text (52)—in his loves; he goes too far in his attempt to learn the solution to the woman's mystery. Here we begin to see the story we have heard told so often, the story of the man who seeks vision, knowledge, and domination of the mysterious female object of his desire (death being the ultimate domination).

And Albert(in)e *is* a mystery in this text. She is incomprehensible to Brassard, who cannot fathom how a young woman, obviously well brought up, could throw herself at him with no guilt or remorse, with no blushing or trembling: "I felt a hand that boldly took mine beneath the table . . . My eyes sought the other of those two hands I had never before noticed, a hand which, in this perilous moment, coldly turned up the lamp that had just been placed on the table" (69–70). She is a mystery, impassible, proud, whose origins are "impossible to explain" (67).

Part of her mystery stems from her double nature, as seen in that image of the two hands, one of a young woman who lights the lamp in the presence of her parents in a gesture of domestic peace, the other of a strong, desiring woman who lights the desire of Brassard, who takes the lead in the relationship, and who has no qualms about doing so literally in the presence of her own parents. The mystery lies perhaps in the fact that she combines the mutually exclusive images of the innocent, young, desireless woman with the seductive, desiring, "fallen" woman. She represents woman's desire; not just the desire of prostitutes or mistresses, but of all women.

Her mystery is thus generated in part by the ambiguity of her identity and by the reversal of roles that takes place between man and woman in her love affair with Brassard. As Brassard says: "So it was not a woman who was taken here: it was I!" (59). But her mystery resides most of all in her eyes and in her gaze, which represent her desire. Normally, as this text makes explicit, the woman is meant to be seen: "Mothers would parade and exhibit their daughters until two o'clock . . . Almost always we would place ourselves behind the prettiest women who came to Mass, where they were sure to be looked at" (61–62). Albert(in)e, however, looks, gazes, stares: "She finally paid me the honor of looking at me with two black eyes, very cold, to which her hair, pulled together in curls on her forehead, provided the kind of depth that this hairstyle gives to the gaze" (66). She even looks at him as they make love: "Her first move had been to bury her face in my chest, but she raised it and looked at me, her eyes opened wide—immense eyes! . . . Her mouth opened . . . but her black eyes, of deepest blackness, and whose long lids almost touched mine, did not close at all" (82). Like Paquita, she manifests qualities that belong to the male sphere.

It is not surprising that on the next page the image of Medusa should appear (83), for her gaze is not one that admires the man and reassures him of his masculinity, but is rather one that is independent, one that shows otherness not similarity, one that as a result is seen by Brassard as a threat that will turn him to stone, will nail him to his place: "But this air . . . that separated her not only from her parents but from all others, with whom she seemed to share neither the passions, nor the feelings, nailed you . . . in surprise, to your place" (67). Indeed, her gaze is one that looks, acts, has otherness and subjectivity, and that refuses to be a mirror for the other: "The painting of the Infanta with the spaniel, by Velasquez, can, if you know it, give you an idea of that air, which was not proud, nor despising, nor disdainful, no! It was quite simply impassible, because a proud, despising, or disdainful air says to people that they exist, since one takes the trouble to disdain or to despise, whereas her air says tranquilly: 'For me, you do not even exist' " (67).

This mention of Velasquez is particularly interesting, because his portraits of children are often strangely similar in that they have that odd, impassible stare. There is another Velasquez painting, however, in which it is a woman who stares at the viewer, the painting called the *Rokeby Venus*, in which Venus reclines, with her naked back to the viewer (a "back-turning" similar to Albert(in)e's refusal to acknowledge the existence of Brassard) and in which Cupid holds up a mirror to Venus, whose gaze is not directed at herself (as it would be in *Manette Salomon*), but is directed out at the viewer. Like Albert(in)e, her body presents itself, but is accompanied by an active glance which, according to Pam Cook, is a threatening one ("Reflections"). The viewer of the painting is surprised in his/her perpetration of an act of voyeurism (looking at the back of the naked woman) when his/her voyeurism is seen by the woman in the mirror. Similarly, the woman behind the crimson curtain, the mysterious Albert(in)e, returns the gaze of the men who would like to see her truths.

This aggressivity of her stare is countered in the rhetoric of the text by a similar aggressivity on the part of Brassard, although this aggressivity is only rhetorical. In that hackneyed metaphoric equation constantly repeated, love is likened to war, and Brassard is a soldier. In speaking of his relation with Albert(in)e, he says: "I did not however lay *siege* . . . As for taking a woman with or without an *escalade*, I told you, at that time, I was perfectly incapable of it" (58–59, emphasis mine). And the metaphor is reversed also: "I told you, except for the feeling of my uniform . . . and the hope of hearing the cannon roar in the first battle in which I was to lose (allow me this soldier's expression) *my military virginity*, all was the same to me!" (63, emphasis added).

In this equation of love and war, one image is particularly revealing, because it shows how the field of love is as dangerous as the battlefield: "When the July Revolution made them the masters of a country they did not know how to keep, it found the captain in his bed, sick with a wound on the foot that he had gotten while dancing—as he would have while charging in battle—at the last ball of the Duchesse de Berry" (49). Brassard is significantly wounded on the foot, another of the rather overt symbols of the phallus and of castration much discussed by readers of this text. It is not surprising that the aggressive, masculine Albert(in)e should make her pass at Brassard with her foot (which replaces her hand), for she is, in his terms, more masculine than he. In recognizing this, he wounds himself on his lips (we recall that Albert[in]e's lips were "érectiles"; here Brassard's are wounded): "Ashamed, however, at being less of a man than this bold young woman who was taking such a risk, and whose wild conduct was covered by an incredible sang-froid, in a superhuman effort I bit my lip until it bled" (70).

Thus in the rhetoric of the text a battle wages between Brassard and Albert(in)e for the rights to activity, to the gaze, to sexuality. Although it would seem that Albert(in)e dies of the fear of being discovered, the rhetoric of the text in fact shows that she dies because she looks, because she desires; she dies in the act of making love—she dies because she makes love. Brassard is victorious, he is the man who triumphs in this battle of love and he survives, just as he is the man who triumphs (although rather ambiguously) in the memory of the marquise de V . . . , explicitly likened to that other aggressive, castrating woman, Delilah: "The Marquise de V . . . , who knew young men well and who would have clipped a dozen the way Delilah clipped Samson, wore with much pomp, on a blue background, on a very wide bracelet, made of gold and black checks, a small piece of the mustache of the Vicomte" (46).

Thus, following the standard fate of desiring females, Albert(in)e dies, a death described significantly by the absence of her gaze and by the cold of her feet and lips: "I looked at her as she was, linked to me, on the blue sofa, and I watched for the moment when her eyes, which had disappeared under large lids, would show me again their beautiful orbs of black velvet and of fire. . . . But her eyes did not return, and her mouth did not open. . . . The cold of Alberte's feet had risen all the way to her lips that lay under mine" (89). Desire in the nineteenth century can belong only to the male, and Albert(in)e's deprivation of her desiring attributes, which in this text must be phallic, return desire to the man. This story tells the same old tale of the fate of female desire.

And indeed, if we look closely at just what the two men finally "see" in the text in their voyeurist search for the truth of the Sphinx, they in fact see nothing at all but that same old curtain that continues to hide the woman behind: "You would think that it is still the same curtain!" (56). The story ends as it began (as Proust says, it leads nowhere), with the curtain hiding a woman's form, and the carriage leaves before the men can attempt to see behind it. Similarly, the story does not leave us in any kind of suspense about its revelation at the end, for we know from the beginning what will happen. Before he even begins his tale, Brassard tells of his role in the story—he flees (59).

In fact, it seems that the purpose of the story is to leave the curtain in place, to leave the myth of the truth behind the curtain intact. The story seems to promise to reveal the mystery, but it fails to do so because we never find out who is behind the curtain. The tale propagates the belief in the existence of that truth, and it implies that we are prevented from knowing it merely by circumstances, chance (the carriage leaves before the two men could make any attempt to draw back the curtain). The mystery of the identity of the silhouette of the woman remains intact, and it is the continuation of the mystery of woman that is important. Her truth exists and is there to see; the two men simply fail to reach it.

And what, then, is revealed by the story? If Alberte's death figures her castration, which in turns ratifies Brassard's masculinity, then it is his masculinity that he displays to the narrator in his recounting of his story. Brassard, who admits the extent to which he loves himself and the way he looks in his uniform, also shows that he not only does not attempt to get behind the veil that covers the window but also enjoys the veiling. His uniform, representing his narcissism, is significantly the thing that veils: "That uniform, for which I was mad, veiled and embellished all things for me" (61). He really aims at veiling the woman so he can display, exhibit, himself.

Indeed, the two men display a kind of rivalry in this exhibitionist storytelling, a kind of one-upmanship that is evident when the narrator twice implies that Brassard's tale is not so unusual as all that, and when he himself tells a mini-tale. They do not look behind the curtain, they significantly remain in the dark in the carriage together, because they are busy displaying their masculinity to each other, mirroring each other both in their places in the carriage and in their roles as narrators. In a telling phrase, the narrator says that Brassard was so attractive that he seduced not only women but also—circumstances: "This beauty, which, moreover, seduces not only women but also circumstances themselves" (47). It is as if they are attempting to seduce each other, as the narrator attempts to seduce the story from Brassard. If the metaphor of hunting is used for the search for good stories, then the narrator and Brassard are the hunters whose prey is the veiled, dead body of the woman, which makes a good story and which verifies that they are, in fact, men.

If Barbey's text then leaves intact the belief in the truth behind the curtain, Proust's text, although it begins with this belief, moves on to a different understanding of the quest for the truth of Albertine. To return to Balzac's *La Fille aux yeux d'or* for a moment, the main problem for Mariquita is to imprison Paquita and to keep her ignorant of men; for Marcel in *La Prisonnière* it is to imprison Albertine and keep her from women, and more importantly, to learn the truth about her desires, a truth that she seems to keep hidden from him (if the genders are mixed up between the two texts, something that is commonplace in Proust, the characters who die are still in both cases women: Paquita and Albertine). Marcel's need is to know the truth about Albertine's point of view, her perspective on desire, her desire for other women. How does this woman desire? How does she look at others? What is the nature of the desire of the other?

It is significant that Marcel never learns the final answer to the question of the woman's gaze, of her desire. He may learn bits and pieces about what that gaze might mean, but he is never sure of understanding it completely. He is like Charlus, in a way, who has available to him poems that look at love from the wrong point of view, with the wrong gaze, the gaze of a man who loves women. Charlus is described as an "invert who was able to nourish his passion only with literature written for men to women, who thought of men while reading the *Nuits* of Musset" (242–243). Marcel can look at Albertine's desires only through the wrong perspective, and as one who loves the opposite sex, he cannot understand her love for women, as Charlus cannot understand Morel's "lesbian" love for women. (This is also an interesting comment on the gender of readers and writers: how do women writers read those poems written about the love of men for women? How do these women write of their own love? Do women read the *Nuits* of Musset while thinking as desiring subjects about men, or do they see themselves as objects of the man's desire? Do women read while identifying with the male author who desires women, or do they imagine themselves as the object of a female author's desire for women? Similarly, if Saint Loup tries to comprehend Rachel's desire by attempting to see the attractive men as she does (Bersani, "Proust" 66), is this not how women view women, by putting on the man's desire? We will leave these questions to the next chapter.)

The need to know the truth goes by the name of jealousy in this text: "How many people, cities, roads jealousy makes us avid to know! It is a thirst for knowledge" (86). If it is first the need to learn the truth of Albertine's desire and the identity of the object of her desire (he must constantly ask himself the question, whom *did* she desire, "Who could that young woman have been?" [86]), it is also the need to know the truth about the everyday events of her life, past and present, the truth about another's "time": "I had remained preoccupied with the way she spent her time" (21). In Lacanian terms, it could be seen as the search for the Real ("the real life of another person" [62]), and the attempt to locate the desire of the other (as in *La Peau de chagrin*, Raphaël tries to see gender in the Real).

More than any other author, perhaps, Proust investigates the link between desire and knowledge, and his character pursues investigation to the borders of epistemophilia: he has "an inquisitorial sense that wants to know, that suffers however in knowing, and that seeks to learn more" (57).[13] Indeed, the definition of desire in this novel seems to be the as yet unattained truth, for when one does attain a truth, when there ceases to be an unknown and unexperienced novelty, desire dies: "I am not saying that a day will not come when we will assign very distinct characters even to these luminous young women, but then they will have ceased to interest us, and their entrance will no longer be the apparition that our heart was expecting to be other, one that leaves it astounded, each time, by new incarnations" (66). And this epistemophilia manifests itself in a kind of voyeurism.

Scenarios of voyeurism, of course, occur in important scenes throughout the different volumes of the *Recherche*, most notably in the two scenes mentioned at the beginning of this essay. And they appear in smaller, less well-known scenes, such as that in which Françoise attempts to kill a chicken in the kitchen, and Marcel observes her cruelty and insensitivity (*Swann* 121–122; again sadism and domination). It seems that the scenes of voyeurism reveal those socially unacceptable traits which must normally be hidden from the world. And it is a voyeurism that feeds upon itself, for Marcel "loves" Albertine, in other words, develops a possessive jealousy for her and a need to spy on her, when she reveals that she, Mlle Vinteuil, and Mlle Vinteuil's friend were as close as sisters. Marcel transposes his voyeurist gaze from the Mlle Vinteuil (when he spied on her and her friend through the window) to Albertine (*Sodome et Gomorrhe* 1113–1114).[14]

This is *the* quintessential scene of voyeurism as we have analyzed it throughout these readings, because it is a male gaze that aims to see the woman—a structure which seems all the more crucial since, as so many critics have pointed out, this is a text written by a man more interested in men than in women. It is particularly curious in the light of Barbey's text that, in one little scene, it is a fetishistic unveiling of a foot that Marcel wants: "If she would permit me to take off her shoes before she went to bed, that would give me great pleasure" (78). He also gazes at her eyes, which he describes in one passage as veiled, "curtained": "When she closed them, it was as when curtains keep one from seeing the sea" (18).

However, although it appears that Proust would continue the voyeurist trend of the novel in a fetishist vein, and although spying and prying are certainly key elements in the relation between Marcel and Albertine, there also seems to be a continuous undermining of the voyeurist gaze and a desire for another type of relation. For instance, there is a small scene in which Marcel at first seems to succeed in unveiling Albertine's body. Here her body is compared to that of a man's, and although the smooth surface of her shape is valorized, lack is emphasized both in the mode of comparison (she lacks something that belongs to a man, and her "sun" has disappeared), and in the description of breasts which seem not to be integrated into her body:

> Her two small, uplifted breasts were so round that they appeared less to be an integral part of her body than to have ripened there like two fruits; and her stomach, covering the place that is ugly on the man's body (like a metal clamp left sticking out of a statue pulled away from its place), closed, at the junction of her thighs, into two valves with a curve as sleepy, as restful, as claustral as that of the horizon when the sun has disappeared. (79)

Ultimately, however, this scene veils the woman's body, because from Marcel's point of view (he is looking down at her) he cannot actually see her sex because her stomach swells slightly to block his vision. The woman in this scene is not completely exposed; a man's gaze cannot unveil just what a woman is.

Of course, as we have seen before, this physical veiling is a metaphor for the inner truth she hides from Marcel. The relation between physical exposure and inner unveiling is neatly represented in a scene in which Marcel questions Andrée about Albertine's activities, while Albertine is *undressing* in her room: "I continued to question Andrée while Albertine, being discreet and allowing me (did she guess all this?) to question Andrée at my leisure, prolonged her undressing in her room" (62). Indeed, as Marcel says, it is not her body he is aiming to possess but her thoughts and desires: "I would have liked not to tear off her dress to see her body, but, through her body, to see the whole notepad of her memories and of her upcoming ardent rendez-vous" (94). Before he develops his jealous possessiveness, he does not worry about "seeing" into the obscure parts of her life which she leads when away from him: "Then, one fine day, suddenly arose Albertine, whose rosy apparitions and silent visits told me very little about what she could have done in the interval; it remained plunged in the obscurity of her life, which *my eyes* were scarcely concerned with piercing" (*Guermantes* 353; emphasis mine). But, in one of the final scenes of *La Prisonnière*, when Marcel has just about perfected his imprisoning tactics and when Albertine seems at last to be fed up with his spying and maintains a distance from him, Marcel feels that if only he could undress her, he could reduce that distance: "It seemed to me that if I had been able to undress her and to have her in her white nightshirt, in which she seemed rosier, warmer, in which she stimulated my senses more, the reconciliation would have been more complete" (399).

Marcel's problems are complicated further because if his gaze is his desire, he can also see that others gaze at Albertine, others desire her: "I remembered the suffering I felt in seeing her face looked over by active gazes, like those of a painter who wants to make a sketch, her face entirely covered by them, while she endured this contact, because of my presence no doubt, without seeming to notice it, with a passivity perhaps clandestinely voluptuous" (149). What Marcel finds most unacceptable is that she, in fact, like Paquita and Albert(in)e, gazes also. As Marcel's gaze at her is driven by his desire to know, hers is driven by her own desire and seems to be a kind of physical caress: "Her narrowed, velvety look glued itself to the passing woman, adhering so well, so corrosively, that it seemed that to pull it back would be to take her skin with it" (150).[15] He cannot bear the fact that she takes a voyeurist pleasure in looking, specifically in looking at women (her desire is like his own). Marcel cannot tolerate, as he is practicing his own voyeurism, that she too practices it, and he cannot bear her *regard*, both active (she looks) and passive (the expression on her face as she looks): "That look which . . . gave her a serious expression, and even made her seem to be suffering" (150).

Even more intolerable than this, however, is that she enjoys a kind of exhibitionism in displaying her body to the gaze of women, and again he cannot stand the look on her face as she exhibits herself to two of them, and, in a secondary way, to him: "I would have preferred the somber expression of the desire that she felt at times, to the laughing expression caused by the desire she inspired" (150). Thus, although Marcel practices and continues the network of voyeurism (he looks at the look on her face as she looks at the pleasure others feel when they look at her), he would like to escape from it, and this is why he imprisons Albertine: he wants to withdraw her from any gaze that is not his own or a substitute for his own.

This is how his desire differs from Charlus's, because Charlus is pleased with his voyeurist relation to Morel and Jupien's niece: "Nothing was more pleasing to the baron than the idea of this marriage; the baron thought that this way Morel would not be taken from him" (49). Charlus goes so far as to boast about the way Morel inspires desire in the eyes of the prostitutes: "Everywhere the whores most in view have eyes only for him" (218). As long as Morel has relations with a sex different from the baron's (biological and psychological women), the baron is happy. It is only when he displays a "lesbian" desire for another lesbian (215–216) that Charlus becomes jealous. For Marcel, however, as long as Albertine shows desires for a sex different from Marcel's, he is miserable.

It is difference itself that he cannot tolerate in desire. He cannot bear the distance put between him and Albertine when she engages in exchanges with others, and the distance of her type of desire from his: "During those hours, I sometimes saw floating over her, in her gazes, in her pout, in her smile, the reflection of those interior spectacles, her contemplation of which, on those evenings, made her unlike me, separated from me, to whom they were refused" (384). And since their desires are different, a space of ignorance will always remain. He can never know her desire, and her eyes will always show to him how many things he does not know: "The eyes that we see, are they not penetrated through and through by a look that carries images, memories, expectations, and disdains that we do not know, a look that we cannot separate from them?" (169).[16]

He does try to "know" it, however, as he tries to eliminate that distance between them by understanding her desire: "What else can a woman mean to Albertine?" (308). This he attempts to accomplish by controlling her and possessing her completely so that she can have no desire but for him. He needs, in effect, to eliminate her desires, because they do not correspond to his own. In eliminating her desires, he would remove her from subjectivity (the state of seeing and desiring) and reduce her to an object to be possessed and viewed.[17] This is most evident in our representative scene of voyeurism, the one in which Marcel watches Albertine sleep. Eyes closed, she can no longer gaze ("I was no longer watched by her" [70]), and it seems as if the outside world of dangerous desires has been eliminated: "Her sleep was but a kind of erasure of the rest of life" (115).[18] Significantly, it is when she is sleeping most deeply that Marcel can touch her, almost as if any desire or resistance on her part keeps him from her physically (70). She becomes pure object: "Her self did not constantly escape, as it did when we chatted together, through the openings made by hidden thoughts and by gazes. She had called back to herself all of her that had been outside; she had taken refuge, was closed in, reduced, in her body. Holding her under my gaze, in my hands, I had an impression of possessing her entirely that I did not have when she was awake. Her life was submitted to me" (70). The images of her are of a plant, of the sea, of a "domestic animal" (15). She becomes for him, as the women Bergotte brought to his room, "an object of contemplation" (184), and he feels he possesses her, as one would an object (156), a possession which is even better than "love" (51).

In fact, the narrator understands that what he was trying to do with Albertine was to make her into a special image of absolute knowledge that had nothing to do with the real Albertine: "The image that I was seeking . . . was no longer of Albertine with an unknown life, it was of an Albertine as known to me as was possible . . . , it was an Albertine who did not reflect a distant world, but who desired nothing else—there were moments when, in fact, it seemed to be this way—than to be with me, just like me, an Albertine who was the image precisely of what was mine and not of the unknown" (75). If, when she sleeps, she has "a rigidity of stone" (359), then it is clear that Marcel is the reverse of Pygmalion: instead of turning a statue into flesh and blood, he tries to turn Albertine into his own stone creation: "We are sculptors. We want to obtain from a woman a statue completely different from the one she presented us" (142). [19] If Eileen Sivert, in her excellent article on *Le Rideau cramoisi*, says that Brassard, by drawing Alberte and by describing her when she first appears as if describing a group of drawings, creates the effect of "suspending life for a moment, of holding Alberte still within the frame of the room and of the story so that she may be examined" (151), then Proust may indeed have been heavily influenced by this attempt to "create" a fictional, still, controllable woman out of a real one. [20]

His imprisonment of Albertine is an attempt, if not to eliminate the outside, where dangerous desires lurk, at least to bring that outside in. As he says, he would not mind it if Albertine would bring those she desired into his house so that he could know, understand, and see all that happened (30). At the end it seems that he has succeeded in bringing that dangerous outside in when he says that "her beautiful legs, which I had rightly imagined that first day to have pushed bicycle pedals throughout her adolescence, went up and down in turn on those of the pianola" (382).

In an extension of the desire to bring the outside in and to make her his, even in a sense to make her *him* ("just like me" [75]), her physical imprisonment seems almost an attempt on his part to incorporate her into himself in a bizarre sort of union. First he aims to "imprison her in a part of my brain" (29). And nearer to the end of her imprisonment, she has become like a part of his own body: "If I came to think of her, it was as one thinks, with the irritation of being tied to it in complete slavery, of one's own body" (328). Indeed, when she kisses him good night and slips her tongue into his mouth, he "incorporates" a part of her as if taking a Communion host: "Albertine slipped into my mouth, giving me the gift of her tongue, like a gift from the Holy Spirit, she gave me a viaticum, left me with a provision of calm almost as gentle as when my mother, placed, in the evenings at Combray, her lips on my forehead" (10). [21] This, along with the famous madeleine scene, could be seen as a metaphor for artistic creation: one takes a bit of the real world, imbibes it, and from its digestion comes the work of art. It also links the desire for Albertine's tongue, writing, eating, and knowledge, if, as Roger Shattuck says, "the surest way of knowing a thing is to eat it" (*Binoculars* 5). [22]

In an image similar to this Communion-tongue, the uncovering of a body, possession, and desire are linked as Gilberte pronounces the narrator's name:

> Later recalling what I felt at that time, I discerned the impression of having been held for a moment in her mouth, myself, naked, no longer with any of the social coverings that belonged either to her other friends, or, when she said my family name, to my parents; her lips . . . seemed to strip me of them, undress me, like the skin of a fruit whose pulp alone can be swallowed, while her gaze, situated at the same degree of intimacy as her words, also reached me more directly.
>
> (*Swann* 403–404)

Incorporating him into her mouth is like gazing at his stripped body and soul. Thus later, when he holds Albertine's tongue in his mouth, it is as if he controls her desire and individuality. He controls her tongue, imprisons her speech and desire, so that she cannot do as Gilberte does; she cannot pronounce his name, cannot gaze at him naked, cannot imbibe him into her world and strip him of his own little universe. He controls her, her speech, her gaze, and her desire. In terms of seeing, incorporation means eliminating her gaze (her desire for others) in order to make her see with his eyes, see what he sees and what he wants her to see.

In a significant passage, he links the absence of her gaze while she sleeps with a kind of plenitude and beauty possible only when her eyes are closed: "Those lowered eyelids gave to her face that perfect continuity that her eyes did not interrupt. There are beings whose faces take on unaccustomed beauty and majesty when they have no more gaze" (71). Linked with the previous image, by holding her tongue in his mouth, he prevents her from stripping him and gazing at him (as Gilberte does), explaining why he enjoys so much the contemplation of her closed eyes. When Albertine sleeps, she displays a continuity without interruption from the manifestations of self or desire that is perhaps assimilable to the description of the smooth surface of her naked body, deprived of the attributes of the male sex. To bring Albertine into his house and make her a part of himself is to "domesticate" her, to give her that nineteenth-century female identity which is relegated to the home, to domesticity, to a desireless and passive state.

If what Marcel is seeking is to incorporate Albertine, perhaps to make her eyes his own in terms of the gaze, then his perplexing refusal to read her letters when he perpetrates every other manner of spying and surveillance (the word *surveillance* actually appears in the text) can perhaps be explained by the fact that her letters and the record of her correspondence with others come too close to being evidence of her selfhood and desire, and would show that Marcel has not succeeded in capturing her gaze and locking it within himself, would show that the woman is not castrated from self or desire. Just as Albertine's body remains essentially veiled when it is naked, so too Marcel never makes the final attempt to "see" her desire by reading her letters.

If Marcel attempts on the one hand to make Albertine's eyes his own, to bring the outside in, he attempts on the other hand to take his dominating gaze and transplant it to the outside, to put his eyes in another in an "exterior prolongation of the sequestration" (126). When the chauffeur whom Marcel has asked to spy on Albertine says, "Don't worry . . . Nothing can happen to her because, when I am not driving her around, my eye is following her everywhere" (133), Marcel transplants his eye into his "private eye" who follows her.[23]

It must be made clear, however, that in the recounting of this tale of imprisonment, perhaps even in the actual "living" of it, the narrator is aware of the futility of his own project, and of the fact that the attempt to so control the life of another simply makes of oneself the same kind of prisoner and even a slave (177). There is a certain poignancy to this tale of imprisonment which Marcel, both jailer and prisoner, is unable to escape, even knowing its disastrous effects as well as its futility.[24] *La Prisonnière* is the history of a mistake, one which one cannot escape making, the mistake of believing in plenitude and wholeness. As Deleuze says, it is the revelation that "we are wrong to believe in truth" (90).[25]

Of course, there are many reasons given to explain how the plenitude of knowledge and desire Marcel seeks is impossible. In order to know Albertine, she would have to be an object, fixed, immovable. But of course, she is a subject: she desires, she changes, she is "insatiable for movement and life, which troubled her sleep in her movements" (131); she will always escape captivity (23). She is the woman who will always be veiled, "a goddess in the clouds" (140), not because there is no truth, not because she wants to hide the truth, but because the truth is not closed, is not finite, is not complete, but is rather an unending process of interpretation: "the task is to be taken up again ceaselessly" (151). Jealousy, like analysis, is "interminable" (87).[26]

Furthermore, because interpretation takes time, there is always a space between fact and understanding, between reality and knowledge. On the one hand, one cannot see into the future to know which details of the present to store (153); on the other hand, one can only know the past "after the future" (87). One needs all the details in all the places at every moment to have the desired plenitude of knowledge, but that is impossible (357). Thus the real is true, but the real for each person is different; each position in time and space, each point of view, changes it. "The universe is true for us all and different for each one of us . . . It is not just one universe, it is millions of them, almost as many as there are human intelligences and eyes that awake every morning" (191).

If one is able to map out a series of facts about a person, as Marcel does with Albertine, when these facts are put together they do not make a nice coherent, logical story, but contain contradictions, as does Albertine: "Even if she told me the truth every time about, for instance, what she thought about people, she would have said different things each time" (98). How can one know the truth when it seems to contain its own negative, its illogical counterpart, when memory turns it around or drops it altogether? The real life of another person is simply unknowable: "I had succeeded, while exploring a parcel of that great zone that spread out around me, only in pushing back that unknown that is for us, when we indeed seek to represent it for ourselves, the real life of another person" (62).

Even when one does learn some isolated facts here and there, that knowledge makes no difference in the way we act and desire: "The disappointment I had felt because of women I had known or cities I had visited did not keep me from allowing myself to be taken up by the attraction of new ones or from believing in their reality" (171). We understand what we want to (189–190). Sometimes we simply do not remember correctly, or at least we cannot be sure that we do (61).

Thus this novel is about the mistaken belief that one can see the truth, the whole truth; that truth is revealed to the eyes, that it can be unveiled. The search for truth itself blinds one: "Jealousy . . . wears a blindfold" (151). It is not a coincidence that Brichot, the learned Sorbonne professor, is half-blind. One's perspective, which changes with time like Albertine's, causes one to have "fragmented eyes" like hers (92): eyes are multiple, multivisionary. Conversely, as Marcel believes that there is a "knowledge by means of lips" (*Guermantes* 364), and as he approaches Albertine to kiss her, he does not confront a single individual whom he can dominate and control; rather "it was ten Albertines that I saw" (*Guermantes* 365). He sees many individuals and learns that that knowledge by the lips, that knowledge he seeks, is impossible, for one approaches "the barrier of the impenetrable and desired cheek" (*Guermantes* 364). And, as the narrator claims at the beginning of *La Prisonnière*, the most profound of our selves is not one that looks out the window and *sees* the weather, but rather that little barometer-man, who is a feeler and who works without the active participation of our intelligence, who mechanically acts according to certain laws (like the unconscious) without being in the exterior world, who does not see but who is contained "deeper" than sight, within sight, within the *optician's* store at Combray: "But last of all, I sometimes asked myself if it [the most essential interior self] were not the little man . . . that the optician of Combray had put in his window to show what the weather was to be, and that, taking off his hood as soon as there was sun, would put it back on if it was going to rain" (11). The inner workings regulate our knowledge, and run counter, sometimes, to the logical, seeing, deductive world of outer reality: "Moral uncertainty is a bigger cause of difficulties in exact visual perception than a physical defect in the eye would be" (140). In terms of the voyeurist scenario, the truth that one seeks is not available in the "visible" real world; Marcel learns a "truth" that Raphaël never does. Gender identity, the truth of the primal scene, woman's identity is not "visible."[27]

It is especially in the image of Pygmalion reversed that we see, not only the mistake of Marcel's search for the truth of Albertine, but also the mistake in his choice of object. He attempts to do the opposite of what he should do, because he is attempting to make the real Albertine into his creation, a work of art. Indeed, numerous allusions to Albertine as a work of art point to his realization of this inversion of goals: "But did my room not contain a work of art more precious than all of those? It was Albertine herself" (382). She is, more specifically, a novel which he has spent much time writing (350). The "incorporation" and incarceration that he would like to perform literally is one which really takes place in his own inventive, creative imagination: "Because Albertine's possible actions happened in me" (252).

Thus in one sense he is mistaking reality for fiction; he is doing with reality what he should attempt with fiction instead (Madame Bovary's mistake, perhaps). Rather than trying to learn Albertine's reality, he should be interested in the multiplicity of fictions she generates in him. He tries to eliminate what he calls his "hallucinations" (22) about Albertine's life (hallucination being, significantly, the mistaking of fiction for reality) when he should be attending to the various hallucinations (fictions) themselves, while recognizing their fictional and hallucinatory character.

Furthermore, he attempts to reduce the plurality of selves and desires in Albertine to one controllable image, the one he creates for her. The "love" he has for her is one that demands unity, plenitude, oneness: "Love, in painful anxiety as in happy desire, is the need for a whole" (106). However, the reduction to sameness, to the one, to the snapshot is a "captured flight" that is no longer interesting or desirable. It is almost as though Marcel cannot see that it is the very irreducibility of Albertine that is important, that generates his fictions. It is the multiplicity of noses (in that incongruous but psychoanalytically significant Proustian image) that one wants, not the reduction to the single nose:

> Alas! Once she was near me, the blond dairymaid with streaks in her hair, stripped of so many imaginings, and so many desires aroused in me, was reduced to herself. The quivering cloud of my suppositions no longer enveloped her dizzyingly. She took on a contrite air because she had (rather than the ten, the twenty, that I remembered one after the other without being able to fix my memories) but one nose, rounder than I had thought, which gave the impression of stupidity and which had, in any case, lost the power of multiplying itself. This captured flight, inert, annihilated, incapable of adding anything to its pitiful self-evidence, no longer had my imagination with which to collaborate. Fallen into immobile reality, I tried to rebound. (143)

Instead of reducing the multiple fictional possibilities of the real Albertine to one prisoner under his eyes, he should attempt to multiply those fictional possibilities in art. Instead of combining

Albertine's eyes with his own, substituting his for hers, reducing vision to one perspective, he should attempt to multiply those visions, those eyes, and thus to embark on the only true "voyage," a voyage possible only, perhaps, in art: "The only true voyage, the only fountain of youth, is not to go to find new scenery, but to have other eyes, to see the universe with the eyes of another, of a hundred others, to see the hundred universes that each of them sees, that each of them is; and this we find with an Elstir, with a Vinteuil, with their counterparts, we really fly from star to star" (258). He should become Scheherazade and tell stories rather than acting out that role in his life with Albertine (131).

Indeed, at the end of *La Prisonnière* there occurs an episode in which Marcel does not try to unveil Albertine in order to reduce her fictional possibilities to one banal reality, but rather realizes that her very veiling, the impossibility of reduction, gives rise to his dreams:

> The Fortuny gown that Albertine wore that night seemed to me to be the tempting phantom of invisible Venice. It was invaded with Arab ornamentation like Venice, like the Venetian palaces hidden like sultans' women behind a veil of stone laced with openings, like the bindings of the Ambrosian Library, like columns whose oriental birds, signifying alternately life and death, were repeated in the sparkling fabric. (394)

Later in *La Recherche* it is not surprising that Marcel says he will construct his book like a dress (*Temps retrouvé* 1033).

It is distance itself that gives rise to desire: "If we seek to contain our amorous curiosities in a formulation of law, it would be necessary to seek the maximum distance between a woman seen and a woman approached, caressed" (142). It is also that space of incomprehension that makes a work of art enjoyable, and when one feels one has penetrated all the obscurities, one is no longer interested (371); the loss of interest that results is called the learning of a new "truth" [372]).[28] And significantly, at the beginning and end of the text, we find two passages in which Marcel is extremely happy, not because he sees Albertine, but because she is separated from him by a barrier that makes her invisible. In the first, she bathes while he is separated from her by the "cloison," which enables them to speak but not to see each other, and this moment generates memories and another "earlier young man" in him. In the second episode, he is in his room, behind the curtains; it is still dark, and he does not see the dawn but hears it in the voice of an unknown and unseen songbird (388; the image of the bird has, of course, frequently been used in this volume to designate Albertine). Finally, after Albertine's death, as he continues to try to discover the truth of her desire, he eavesdrops on two laundresses making love, and admits that there will always be that "barrier," here a curtain both literal and figural, that separates the truth-seeker from knowledge: "[The pleasure] must have been strong to upset to such an extent the being who felt it, and to draw out that unknown language which seems to point out and comment upon all the phrases in the delicious drama lived by the little woman, a drama hidden from my eyes by the curtain drawn forever closed to others, closed to what goes on in the intimate mystery of each creature" (*La Fugitive* 550–551).

The goal of the work of art thus presented in *La Prisonnière* is not one that will sing, after the fact, the praises of plenitude, as Marcel sees the works of Balzac and Wagner doing, but rather one that sees the impossibility of plenitude and the beauty of plurality; that does not make of the "unknown," or as we would say the "unknowable," a "névralgie" (jealousy, epistemophilia) but rather "art" (the story of Marcel's failed search for Albertine's truth, this novel itself): "A phrase . . . so vague, so internal, almost so organic and visceral that one did not know, at each of its reprises, whether it was of a theme or of a neuralgia" (260). The work of art is neither nihilistic nor naive, but rather generates positivity from impossibility and art from the inevitable space that separates one from knowledge and from the fulfillment of desire. It is the comic offspring, for instance, in that image of Françoise, who can never be right about the time, can never *know* the exact time of her own existence, but whose mistake makes us laugh: " . . . Françoise, having thus looked at her watch, would say, if it were two o'clock, it is one o'clock or it is three o'clock" (155–156). It is the humor in the error made by Marcel's maître d'hôtel who, whenever one says the word *pissotière* (urinal) hears the word *pistière* (which contains the word *piste*, meaning path or track). He, of course, is on the wrong track (*piste*) because not only does he misunderstand the word, he thinks that Charlus is a "coureur de femmes" (someone who runs after women), and that he must spend so much time in the "pistière" because he contracted a disease in his excursions (he is probably staying in the "pistière" for other reasons). But all these mistakes generate laughter, as well as meaning, because one could see, in a comical representation, Charlus as a "coureur de femmes," running into/on that "pistière." A new meaning is generated from all these mistakes— old mistakes at that, since Charlus has long had the reputation of a womanizer. The new meaning is generated as an offspring from the old situation.

Let us take what we have learned from the structure of voyeurism in Proust's text one step further to discuss our original problematic of artistic originality and similarity, both in thematic terms of the new individual in the family and the new work of art in the artistic world and in linguistic terms of the family name and the artistic word. How does the recognition of the radical difference of the other relate to originality, to individuality? It has often been said of Proust's work that through repetition of events, traits of character, memories, what was lost in the past is regained, and as Deleuze shows, a certain "essence" is transmitted from person to person, generation to generation, past to present, through memory; one might call this the effect of transference. Albertine "repeats" the role of Albertine's mother for Marcel, complete with the bedtime drama, the desperate note sent to call her back to him. Albertine becomes the mother in *La Prisonnière;* she can give him that "appeasement such as I had not felt since the faraway evenings at Combray when my mother, bent over my bed, came to bring me rest in a kiss" (77). It is sometimes wonderful, sometimes painful to see the patterns of one's experience in the experience of others, who are sometimes not even family relations: Marcel repeats Swann's pattern of love; Charlus's possessiveness parallels Marcel's.

But in *La Prisonnière,* repetition does not seem to be the most important structure. In this novel about the discovery of a mistake, it is difference that seems most elemental: Albertine's irreducible difference; difference in the way Deleuze describes it, as the "essence," or what I would call the unique, and in this novel, the "inconnu" (unknown). Thus, what is most surprising is not that things repeat themselves, but that the product of that repetition of the same is the creation of something different and unique: from repetition comes difference.

This movement from repetition and similarity to difference can be seen first in the "genetic" images of family resemblances. This is seen in the importance of heredity (not just biological but literary—

one thinks of Zola, perhaps): "The oldest women end up by showing, in a bumpy red nose, in a deformed chin, the specific signs in
which each one can admire the 'race.' But among these persistent
and ceaselessly aggravated traits, there are those that are not visible:
these are tendencies and tastes" (47). Marcel is his grandmother
(290), his mother and his father (79, 107), his aunt Octave
(353).[29] Even those who are not related by blood pick up on those
essential tics that make up one's personality: one can always tell
when Andrée has spent time with Marcel because she takes on
those tics (20); Albertine learns how to compose a literary discourse
on ice cream from Marcel. The laws of heredity and the code of
individuality are "unknown laws" whose codified form we must
obey. The essence of others, whether conveyed through biology or
social communication, transmigrates to our soul: "What had trans-
migrated in me, despotic to the point of sometimes silencing my
jealous suspicions, or at least of keeping me from going to verify
whether or not they were well founded, was my aunt Léonie" (78–
79). One wonders what Proust would have made of the scientific
findings on the genetic code, because it so aptly incorporates the
notions of the "laws" and codes of transmission that are elemental
to his notion of repetition.

But these essences repeated in life do not come back in exactly
the same form, because they combine with other essences, situations, moments, and they return as different, "the same and yet
different, as things in life return" (259). If Marcel mistakenly tries
to make of Albertine a statue in *La Prisonnière* by eliminating in her
all trace of her difference, it is significant that at the end of *Le
Temps retrouvé*, the offspring of Robert and Gilberte, Mlle de Saint
Loup, is also a "masterpiece," with features that would enable one
to "recognize one statue among thousands" (*Le Temps retrouvé*
1031–1032). She, however, is a statue that does not reduce the
living difference to a lifeless sameness, the sameness of memory that
"suppresses precisely that great dimension of Time" (*Le Temps
retrouvé* 1031). She is rather the embodiment of the difference
made by time, the difference achieved by those same elements as
they combine in a new individual. The narrator recognizes in her
Saint Loup's and Gilberte's nose; Saint Loup's eyes; and, in the
sense that Saint Loup is present in her even when he is dead, that
wonderful ability Marcel noticed in Saint Loup: the ability to occupy so many different positions in space in such a short time. She

embodies the difference of time that memory erases: "Colorless and ungraspable time, in order for me to see it and touch it, so to speak, had materialized in her, it had shaped her like a masterpiece" (*Le Temps retrouvé* 1031). It seems then, that what is quite amazing and wonderful is not that heredity should pass on the same traits, but that those same traits combine to make something unique, individual, different, a new "world." The repetition and combination of the same elements create unique difference.

The metaphor of heredity was not chosen by chance, for the child represents the same kind of offspring as the work of art: Vinteuil's septuor, his artistic offspring, even perhaps reflects the peace of his daughter's sleep (253). Proust is mother: "It [the work] was for me like a son, whose dying mother again took upon herself the fatigue of ceaselessly caring for him" (*Le Temps retrouvé* 1041–1042).[30] Indeed, the notions of heredity, of the repeated code, and of uniqueness fit precisely the situation of art as presented in *La Prisonnière*, and although the elements of the metaphor are certainly not "new"—the notion of immortality through children and through art—the emphases Proust gives to certain of the elements in the comparison are new.

The transition from physical heredity to artistic heredity is made in the notion of a repeated language, code, pattern. There are certain expressions used in a family that are passed on from generation to generation: "This kind of expression is generally the current remainder of a previous state of the family" (325). In the same way, each artist uses a certain "genetic code" from previous artists. While listening to Vinteuil's work, Marcel says: "I could not keep myself from murmuring '*Tristan*,' with the same smile that a family friend has when finding something of the ancestor in an intonation" (158–159).

Yet in this very same passage, the narrator emphasizes that Vinteuil's work, even though it repeats those previous patterns, is completely individual, unique: "Each great artist seems, in fact, so different from the others, and gives us such a feeling of individuality" (158). What is amazing is not the repetition of these coded patterns, the "genealogy," but rather that "despite the conclusions coming from science, the individual existed" (256). So too, we might see in the same "Charlus" that Balzacian character "Carlos Herrera," one of the incarnations of the sexually ambiguous Jacques Collin. And we might see in "Morel" that Frédéric Moreau of

Flaubert, who played the feminine part in his friendship with *Charles* Deslauriers (as *Charlus* plays the feminine part in his friendship with *Charles* Morel—both characters, of course, being more or less bisexual). The narrator discusses repetition and individuality in the world of Barbey d'Aurevilly's *Le Rideau cramoisi*, where certain key phrases of an author form a theme that identifies the author time and again, examples being the blush in some of Barbey's stories or the hand in the *Rideau cramoisi*. Proust, of course, then uses some of Barbey's themes in this very work, *La Prisonnière*, as we saw above.

Again, in art as in family heredity, what is extraordinary is that, as in our present knowledge of genetic coding, a limited number of these "same" elements can come together in different combinations to make the unique, the different, the new work of art. The breathtaking originality of several musical phrases of Vinteuil is built merely of "the same four notes, four notes that [the public] can play with one finger on the piano without finding any of the three pieces" (400). A limited number of notes, colors, letters, words form the proliferation of unique worlds and works of art.

This family link of creation is perhaps clearest in the case of Vinteuil and his daughter's friend. This young woman is responsible for the "immortality" of Vinteuil because she is the only one who can understand Vinteuil's scribble, and because she scrupulously transcribes and makes available his posthumous works. His work can come to fruition only through her, and thus her work becomes an intimate part of the work of art, her talent an "offspring" of his. As a child permits the body and spirit of a parent to live on, she allows the body and spirit of Vinteuil's genius to live on. If she is perhaps one of the reasons for Vinteuil's inability to put his work into proper form (his suffering on account of his daughter's behavior perhaps causes his death), she is also perhaps a part of its creation (the suffering Vinteuil endured on account of his daughter's behavior inspires his work). Indeed the "immortal and compensating glory" is made possible by her labor and her closeness to Vinteuil, which is called a "parental line" even closer than the ties formed by marriage (262). She is a true "daughter-in-law" of Vinteuil—the only offspring possible in this homosexual union being the work of art she allows to be born. She later becomes the "parent" of Marcel's artistic vocation: "It was thanks to her, as in compensation, that the strange call was able to make its way to me, a call that I will never cease to hear as the promise that something else exists, realizable in art, no doubt" (263). In this light, the image of Niobe, whose children were murdered, that appears in *Le Rideau cramoisi* and the horrible image of the dead child's heart in *A Un Dîner d'athées*[31] link Barbey's texts to a kind of sterile narcissistic circularity (the two male rivals face to face with each other at the end of the tale) that aims at killing off any acknowledgment of difference and strives merely to perpetuate the image of the truth behind the veil. Proust's texts go beyond that narcissism to acknowledge the impossibility of truth. Yet through that acknowledgment is born difference, the work of art.

The lesson of *La Prisonnière* is that plenitude is impossible, that one cannot imprison and assimilate the other's difference. One cannot see and know the truth of the other, cannot reveal it by casting furtive glances, nor by seeking the one true answer in the myriad hypotheses formulated about that truth. One cannot possess plenitude, cannot enjoy the constant repetition of the same in a cozy domestic contentment. The Real is the true in Proust, but that truth is utterly other, inaccessible; it might as well, in fact, not even exist. But from the recognition of the impossibility of any knowledge of the real, any possession of the truth, should come the remarkable understanding of the eternal return of difference in our glance at the real, and of the fact that the repetition of the "same" produces the unique and new fictions of our imagination, the offspring of impossible plenitude. It is this important role of difference in the creation of art that will be studied in the next chapter on women's writing and voyeurism.

**8**

# Voyeurism and the Recognition of Difference: Women's Writing and the Space of Identity

*Therefore Stendhal has perfectly instructed us on the two major difficulties that women writers encounter: she must steal culture without being seen for fear of passing as knowledgeable, and if she wants to write, she must again hide.*
                                                    —Claudine Herrmann,
                                                    *Les Voleuses de langue*

IN THIS FINAL CHAPTER, the gendered structure of the gaze is re-versed, and women look in secret at the objects of their desire. In the two texts to be studied here, women write as well as look; they are not the passive objects of the male gaze and pen; they look, desire, and write. In both *La Princesse de Clèves* and *Le Ravissement de Lol V. Stein*, traditional scenes of voyeurism are also present; in other words, men spy on desired women in order to learn their truths. However, both texts rewrite these traditional scenes in their own "female" reconfigurations of the voyeurist scenario. In these two novels, separated by such an enormous distance of time, women write of woman's desire, a desire that is linked to her gaze and to her *different* way of looking and writing.

## Seeing, Imitating, and Differing in *La Princesse de Clèves*

*"She was in love with Léon, and she sought solitude so that she could delect in his image at her ease. The sight of his person troubled the voluptuousness of that meditation."*
—Flaubert,
*Madame Bovary*

In turning back in time to what is often considered one of the first French novels, we see in Madame de Lafayette's seventeenth-century *La Princesse de Clèves* a story written by a woman about a woman who flees the constant male gaze.[1] The princess is trapped in a world of investigations in which she fails to guard her inner being from exposure. She is trapped in a structure in which gazes constantly determine her activities and limit her freedom, even in her own home. The two infamous scenes of Nemours's voyeurism show that this early novel firmly situates voyeurism as a novelistic problem. Nemours spies on the princess, whom he desires, as she speaks to her husband at her home about the secrets of her desire; later he spies on the princess in her home as she symbolically expresses the object of her desire.

If the princess chooses to live in this world of prying gazes, she can never pursue her own desires and objectives; she can only react against the invasiveness of others. In *La Princesse de Clèves,* this necessarily reactive posture is also related to woman's artistic creativity, and to her attempt to express the difference of her creations as well as her gazes. As we study the princess and the structures of the gaze in this novel, we will see how woman's gaze and her writing are limited by the voyeurist scenario, and also how they go beyond it.

Certainly, this is a novel in which several specific scenes of voyeurism appear. These scenes can be separated into three sets of parallel scenarios. The first sequence of scenes involves a strange kind of voyeurism in which a character looks at a portrait rather than at a real person. In the first of these scenes, Nemours steals a portrait of the princess, which belongs to her husband, in order to be able to look at it at will. In this novel of gazes, the princess sees him steal it, and he sees her seeing him. At first sight (as has been noted so often), it appears that what the princess is constantly "exposed to" is the gaze of others: *exposer* and its cognates are used frequently, as in "ne se pas exposer à être vue," "not to expose oneself to being seen" (156). Here it is her portrait that is subjected to Nemours's gaze, and her recognition of his desire that is viewed by him. Indeed, the princess first appears in the novel as an object of view and in a rather passive grammatical construction: "There then appeared a beauty" ("Il parut . . ." [40]).

This theft of the portrait is closely preceded by another scene involving a portrait: the princess is wondering about Queen Elizabeth, who is purportedly interested in Nemours, and, unable to ask direct questions about their possible marriage, the princess, innocent in her deviousness, instead asks about Queen Elizabeth herself. To please the princess, a portrait of Queen Elizabeth is brought before her. Now, if Nemours steals the portrait of the object of his desire (the portrait of the princess) in order to look at it, in this previous, less well-known scene, something similar but significantly different takes place. The princess does not look at the portrait of the object of *her* desire (Nemours) but rather at the purported object of *his* desire (Elizabeth). Thus although the two portrait scenes appear at first to repeat each other exactly, as two lovers make devious attempts to view a portrait that relates to the object of their desire, the scenes are really different because the subjects of those portraits stand in different relations to the viewers.

Furthermore, in the first scene, when it is the woman who looks, there is an element significantly absent from the more famous second scene. The princess's viewing of the portrait is followed in the text by a woman's creative act of representation and embellishment: the dauphine recounts the story of Anne de Boleyn. The gaze of the princess, not visible to Nemours, is linked in a contextual way to a woman's creative act of storytelling. In this metonymic relation, the absence of the image of the princess as the object of desire in the scene involving Elizabeth's portrait, and the "invisibility" of the princess's gaze to Nemours, signify then a type of invisibility which is contextually related to a woman's creative act (the dauphine's story), similar perhaps to the anonymity Joan DeJean relates to Lafayette's creative act, this novel itself.

Curiously, just as the first scene involving Elizabeth's portrait is doubled by the second scene involving the princess's portrait, the second scene is itself involved with two portraits of the princess, one belonging to the dauphine and one belonging to the prince (the portrait Nemours steals). The characters in the novel compare the two portraits of the princess much as we compare the two portrait scenes, and the single portrait of Elizabeth in the first scene becomes, in the second scene, two portraits which mirror each other, in the sense that they portray the same person (the princess). This doubling, mirroring, and multiplying is again mirrored in the exchange of glances: when Nemours steals her picture, she first sees him do this; then he sees that she sees. As they look at each other seeing, the gaze seems to double itself "en abîme," as do the portraits.[2]

But just as the princess is mistaken when she thinks Elizabeth is the object of Nemours's desire, so would we be reading things too simply in thinking that the princess is the ultimate object of Nemours's desire. When the princess, hoping to learn something about the object of Nemours's desire, looks at the portrait of Elizabeth, Nemours never sees her look. But when he looks at her portrait, the most important part of the scene is that she sees him look; he becomes a spectacle for her, he "exhibits" himself to her in a certain way. Ironically, the scene which seems to make possible Nemours's portrait-voyeurism actually generates the reverse of voyeurism, in the psychoanalytic sense, because it is most importantly a scene of exhibitionism. Just before this scene, it is stated that Nemours takes pleasure in seeing the princess but that he fears making that pleasure visible: "He dared not, however, let his eyes remain on her when her hair was being combed, for he feared he would let be seen the pleasure that he took in watching her" (91). What is really suggested in this scene, however, and what becomes clear in the third scene we shall discuss, is that his "fear" of being seen is really a desire to be seen. The princess's mother, who is her daughter's teacher, points out this structure of desire when she tells her daughter that what is important is that the princess recognize and appreciate M. de Clèves's desire. Here her daughter's desire does not enter into the discussion: "She took great care in attaching her to her husband and in making her understand what she owed to the desire he had for her before even knowing her and to the passion he had shown in preferring her to all the others, at a time when no one dared to think about her" (51). It is thus not a question of the object of the princess's desire, for she desires no one at the moment of this conversation with her mother; it is rather a question of the recognition, the viewing, of the man's desire.

The third portrait scene, in which the princess looks at a painting which includes an image of Nemours, a painting which she had had copied from one which belonged to Mme de Valentinois (152), is again filled with doubling. It is first a viewing of that secondary, copied painting of a copy of Nemours's image. It is, second, a structural doubling and displacing of the physical positions of the characters in these scenes. When the duke stole the portrait of the princess, the dauphine was sitting on the bed, Nemours took the object-portrait from a table, and the dauphine performed the creative act of historical storytelling (in the Elizabeth portrait scene).[3] In this third scene, when the princess looks at Nemours's portrait, she is the one resting on a "lit de repos" (daybed), she takes an object from a table (the cane), and she performs the creative act (knotting the ribbons around the cane). She takes the others' places (those of Nemours and the dauphine), thus repeating, doubling, and slightly displacing the structures of those scenes.[4]

Furthermore, there are, one could say, two representations of the objects of her desire here, the cane and the portrait of Nemours (just as there were two portraits in the theft scene). And there is a triple scene of voyeurism, for Clèves's representative spies on Nemours spying on the princess looking at Nemours's cane and portrait.

What makes it clear that Nemours's ultimate object is not just to see her is that he wants to be seen seeing her. Surely, as he looks at her, he thinks not only that his act of voyeurism ("to come to see Mme de Clèves without being seen by her") is a bit crazy but also, and even more so, that it is crazy that he should "think about being seen by her" (155). Yet, at this point, when he wants to make himself seen but is still troubled by the bizarre nature of that desire, he mistakenly makes a noise that *assures* that he will be seen: "He was convinced that she had recognized him" (156; this noise could be thought of as that "click" of the camera that belongs to the primal scene; here, in its exhibitionistic structure, it is the child-onlooker that makes the noise and involves himself in the scene). Apparently being convinced was not enough, however, for later he overtly tells her he saw her, when he says two days hence that he had already been in her garden: " 'I was there not long ago, also,' Nemours continued while watching her, 'And I do not know if I should be pleased that you have forgotten seeing me there' " (159). Clearly his object here is to make his seeing seen; he must be the object of her gaze, and he must be able to see her recognition of this.

M. de Clèves's voyeurist act has the same outcome. He must eventually reveal to the princess that he saw Nemours in her garden (albeit through an intermediary). This occurs when, just before his death, M. de Clèves asks his wife: "Was not M. de Nemours at Coulommiers with his sister? And did he not stay the two preceding nights with you in the forest garden?" (163). Although he never reveals just how he came to know this, he nevertheless confronts her with this knowledge and makes her know he knows, makes her see that he saw.

In comparing these three portrait scenes we find that, beyond their similarities in the many mirrorings and doublings, there are important differences. To reiterate, Nemours and M. de Clèves, especially Nemours, seem to be striving not so much to see the princess, as has been said before of this novel, as to make their act of seeing seen, to make themselves the spectacle of the gaze. As Nemours says to himself in an imaginary conversation with the princess: "Look at me at least in the same way [avec les mêmes yeux] as I saw you look at my portrait that night" (157). This then relates to the more literal fact that what Clèves and Nemours want is not simply to love (see) the princess but to be loved by her (to be seen by her). If in Freud the exhibitionist act is essentially a narcissistic act ("the narcissistic subject is, through identification, replaced by another extraneous ego" ["Instincts" 32]), what we might say is that, inasmuch as what Nemours wants is for himself to be seen, he is the ultimate object of his own desire. Thus it is significant that when the princess looks at the supposed object of Nemours's desire, she does not see herself but sees instead another subject (Elizabeth): she is not the direct object of desire here. In another way, she is symbolically subtracted as the object of Clèves's desire when her portrait is stolen from him. In a symbolic way in these portrait scenes, she is not the object of their desire; they themselves are.[5]

Finally, the princess's reaction to this third portrait scene is fundamentally different from that of Nemours and Clèves. If these two men constantly seek to satisfy their curiosity by verifying her desire, by seeking constantly to learn the truth of her desire for them by spying on her, she, on the other hand, prefers doubt and uncertainty over knowledge: "She found that it was better to remain in doubt than to take the chance of becoming enlightened" (156). She does not seek to make herself seen, does not seek to pry their secrets from them, but prefers invisibility and doubt.

If the first set of parallel scenes is involved with the viewing of portraits, the second set is involved with speaking: these are what we will call the "aveu" (avowal) scenes. The first and oft-discussed one takes place at Coulommiers, where Nemours spies on the prince and princess and she reveals to both men that she loves someone. This scene of the revelation of desire opens as Nemours wanders, in a kind of dreamlike, automatic state, through the forest: "At the mention of Coulommiers, without thinking at all and without knowing what his plan was, he went as fast as possible in the direction showed to him. He arrived in the forest and let himself wander at random on carefully made roads which he judged must lead to the castle. He found at the end of these roads a pavillion" (120). Again, it is the princess who later doubles this dreamlike state, first when she utters her "aveu" and can barely believe she has done so—"She wondered why she had done something so risky, and she found that she had begun it almost without planning to do so" (125)—and then again later, as Butor notes, when she looks at Nemours's portrait and enters a dreamlike state (74–78).

Furthermore, in this first "aveu" scene, Nemours hides in the isolated room of the pavillion during the princess's avowal to her husband; later we see that, in the portrait scene at Coulommiers, the princess takes Nemours's place in that room when she looks at his portrait. Thus the role of the princess is again to double another's position. What is interesting in the "aveu" scene, though, is that both Nemours and Clèves seem to take the same stance, in the sense that they both want her to reveal the object of her desire. If, as we saw in the portrait scene, Nemours, and also M. de Clèves (although to a lesser degree), feel the need to make themselves seen, the princess does the opposite. She reveals that she desires but does not reveal the object of her desire. Of course, Nemours can interpret the situation to learn that he is the object, but she never says his name directly. She tries to keep her secret and her distance.

This distance which she keeps (or has created) between herself and her husband by her "aveu" she terms an abîme ("abyss," 125).

This is, in fact, in miniature, what the princess constantly does in this novel: as so many have noted, she creates a distance of difference between herself and others. She and her mother make her into someone "où l'on ne pouvait atteindre" (52), someone "unattainable," at a distance. Indeed, it is this distance that makes her desirable to her husband: "It was also the case that, while being her husband, he did not tire of being her lover, because there was always something to desire beyond her possession . . . He continued to have a violent and uneasy passion for her that troubled his joy" (52). And part of what Nemours loves about the princess is her difference: "He found glory in making himself be loved by a woman so different from all the others of her sex" (126).

Indeed, the princess knows this. As she says, the distance she keeps from M. de Clèves explains, perhaps, why he continues to love her: "My destiny did not want me to profit from this happiness [M. de Clèves's love]; perhaps also his passion subsisted only because he did not find any in me" (173). And she feels that this is why Nemours retains his passion for her, too: "But I would not have the same means of preserving yours: I even believe that obstacles were the cause of your constancy" (173). It seems that she understands that the nature of desire is not in its object but in its unbreachable distance from that object—desire is the unfilled gap. Just as the story of Mme de Valentinois shows that it is "neither merit, nor fidelity" (55) that made the king continue to love her, but their opposite (her desire for others and her intrigues), what the princess understands and what this novel shows is that it is not fidelity and plenitude that sustain desire but distance. If distance sustains desire, then the words pronounced by the king concerning Nemours's marriage to Elizabeth ironically present what might be the ideal marriage in this text: "to marry the Queen of England by ambassador" (82).

Thus far we have seen the object of the men's desire and the nature of desire in this novel, but as yet we have not seen the object of the *princess's* desire. What is it? We can discern it in the seldom-mentioned scene at the end of the book in which it is the princess who spies on Nemours, a scene that is followed by the ultimate mutual "aveu" by both the princess and Nemours.

In this scene, the princess learns that Nemours still loves her and, she believes, has been watching her from a room which he rents across from her dwelling. In order to think over these discoveries, she takes a walk in the woods, and whom should she encounter but Nemours? The first thing to notice about this scene is, again, its doubling of the previous "aveu" scene, with the princess and Nemours as before, switching places. In the first "aveu" scene, the princess is in a dreamlike state in her woodland "cabinet," when Nemours traverses the forest; here it is Nemours in a different "cabinet" and a dreamlike state, and it is the princess who traverses the forest: "After having gone through a small wood, she saw, at the end of an alley, in the farthest spot in the garden, a kind of small building [*cabinet*], opened on all sides, toward which she headed. As she approached, she saw a man resting on the benches, who seemed engrossed in a profound reverie, and she realized it was M. de Nemours" (166). Furthermore it is now Nemours who does what the princess usually does: he puts distance between them, that is, he avoids her (although he does not know whom he avoids). But in this scene she never serves as the reflector of his desire, for he never sees her.

It is precisely this that the princess likes:

The prince appeared to her in her imagination, more lovable than all else in the world, loving her for so long with a passion full of respect and fidelity, disdaining all else for her, respecting even her grief, dreaming of seeing her without dreaming of being seen by her, leaving the court, when he was so liked there, in order to come to look at the walls that enclosed her, in order to come to dream in places where he could not expect to meet her. (167)

In this scene at the end of the novel, when it is the princess who is the "voyeuse," when she sees Nemours without being seen and sees him without becoming a tool in his own self-viewing, she comes the closest to deciding to love him: "No more duty, no more virtue opposed her feelings; all the obstacles were gone, nothing remained of their past state but Nemours's passion for her and hers for him" (167).

Indeed, early in the novel it seems that all those who love her, even Nemours, understand that to please her they must keep their desire far from view: "She saw M. de Nemours at Mme la Dauphine's; she saw him at M. de Clèves's, where he often came with other people of quality of his age, in order not to be noticed" (88). And what she finds unforgivable in Nemours's behavior, when he tells the Vidame de Chartres about her "aveu" to her husband, is that he needed to *expose her desire for him*, and the extraordinary circumstances surrounding it, to public view: "How could she excuse such great imprudence, and what had become of the extreme discretion of that prince, which had so touched her? . . . I was wrong to believe that there was a man capable of hiding what flatters his glory" (138). What she desires, in a sense, is no longer to be a tool for Nemours's own self-contemplation but herself to see, as she does in her "voyeuse" scene, and to be seen herself, in a mutual "spectacle" which would not involve the simple mirroring of the two partners for their own individual glory and narcissism but would be a real gaze at the other (a gaze that is also idealized, as we saw, in Stendhal's *La Chartreuse de Parme*). For instance, near the end of the novel, Mme de Clèves, instead of looking for Nemours's desire for her, simply shows her own desire while enjoying her contemplation of his person: "Mme de Clèves gave in for the first time to the attraction she felt for M. de Nemours . . . looking at him with eyes filled with gentleness and charm" (169).

In contrast to Nemours, the princess never allows her viewing to itself become a spectacle; when she plays the "voyeuse" in the forest, Nemours doesn't know that she is spying on him. The two lovers, we could say, seem to have two different systems of desire. On the one hand, Nemours desires that she do as he does; he wants to make her and her desire a spectacle for his contemplation. " 'Let me see that you love me, beautiful princess,' he cried, 'Let me see your feelings; if only to let me learn them from you once in my life . . . I know my happiness; let me enjoy it' " (157). And most importantly, he wants to make visible, and make her recognize, his own gaze. Even in her "voyeuse" scene, when it seems that at last he adheres to her mode of desire and tries to remain invisible, we learn that he has always wanted to be seen: "She went there, she saw M. de Nemours. This sight surprised her, and she drew back with such haste that the prince realized that he had been recognized. He had often desired to be" (168).

On the other hand, the object of her desire is, first, to be able to see in an active way, to contemplate the person she loves. It is, second, to be able to do this without becoming a tool in the process of self-visualization of the other. In a sense, she wants to become invisible, so as not simply to be a mirror for the other: "There was nothing left for her to use as a defense, and there was no security for her except in departing. But, since it was not up to her to decide to leave, she found herself in terrible straits and ready to fall into what seemed to her to be the greatest of troubles, which was to let M. de Nemours *see the attraction* she felt for him" (93, emphasis mine). This becoming invisible is symbolized in a rather paradoxical scene in which the princess is happy to be able to express her feelings for Nemours when she decides not to be seen at the ball given by Saint André. She does this to please Nemours, who had said that men suffer when their lovers are at a ball, because their lovers "want to please all who look at them" (62). Thus in this unique scene, where the princess decides not to make herself into a spectacle, she is ironically fulfilling both of their desires.

But through most of the novel they always seem to be "a phase apart" in their love for each other, because, just as Nemours tries to force the princess into his "exhibitionist" mode of desire, so the princess would like Nemours to adhere to her "invisible" mode. The princess holds her love hostage and makes Nemours adhere to her system. Again, in the disjunction of their two systems of desire, it is the impossibility of desire itself that is the point. As Claudine Herrmann says: "She knows that love *as she envisions it* is not attainable. What is attainable is a counterfeit that she does not want. Her education permits her to realize this: men and women exchange feelings that are not equivalent" (78).

What are the implications of this difference of the feminine mode of desire from the masculine? The third and final series of scenes helps us to understand the nature of the princess's desire and its relation to her identity, the nature of the creative process in this text, and the relation of both to the gaze. The first of these scenes is one of the first scenes of "seeing" in the text. Here the princess (at that time still Mlle de Chartres) goes to the shop of a Florentine merchant to match some gems, and the prince of Clèves sees her there and immediately loves her, both because of her beauty and because of her difference. Here the introduction of the princess to the world of desire is also an introduction to the search for the truth of her identity: "M. de Clèves looked at her with admiration, and he could not figure out who this beautiful woman was whom he did not know" (42). This scene itself gives some clues to that identity:

she is the one who is different, indeed opposite, "contre l'ordinaire" (42). This is later, in fact, a matter of pride and glory for her: " 'Ah, Monsieur,' she said, 'There is no other adventure like mine in the world; there is no other woman capable of the same thing' " (136).

Finally, in this "matching" scene, her difference is a refusal to take pleasure in exhibiting herself, for she is not one of those "young women who always view with pleasure the effect of their beauty" (42), and her response to the gaze of others, here of M. de Clèves, is to flee: "He [M. de Clèves] noticed that his gaze embarrassed her . . . it even seemed to him that he was the reason for her impatience to leave, and in fact, she left quite promptly" (42). This is the response she repeats again at the end of the novel, when she flees to her convent. One could view this retreat as both a means of avoiding the "loss of authority that accompanies every public appropriation of fictionalized female desire" (DeJean 887), as well as her refusal to engage in the narcissistic, exhibitionist mirrorings in the novel. What she would like is that Nemours share her difference and distinction by refusing to exhibit his conquest of her, but she learns that instead of becoming distinctive, as she is, he has made her similar not only to him but to all others: "It is, however, for this man, whom I thought to be so different from the rest of men, that I find myself to be like other women" (138).

The second scene in a "shop" both doubles this scene and alters it slightly. Let us quote the entire scene:

The next day, this princess, who was looking for activities appropriate for her state, went to see a man near her home who did a certain kind of silk work; she went there so that she would be able to do similar work. After they were shown to her, she saw the door to a room where she thought there would be more silk work; she asked that it be opened. The craftsman answered that he did not have the key and that the room was occupied by a man who came there sometimes during the day in order to make drawings of the pretty homes and gardens that could be seen through his windows.

"He is one of the most handsome men," he added. "He does not have the look of someone reduced to earning a living. Each time he comes in there, I see him looking at the houses and gardens; but I never see him working."

Mme de Clèves paid great attention to his words. What Mme de Martigues had told her, that M. de Nemours was sometimes in Paris, joined, in her imagination, with this handsome man who would come near to her home, and gave her the idea of M. de Nemours, and M. de Nemours occupied in trying to see her. (166)

The first things one notices is that this scene doubles the early merchant scene. But beyond that, we see that the princess herself is here engaged in doubling structures (two of them, in fact: a double act of doubling). She is trying to match precious stones, searching for "doubles," and at the same time, she is setting out to learn how to imitate the work done by the second "merchant."

This scene also doubles and reverses the cane and portrait scenes at Coulommiers. There Nemours spies on the princess while she secretly looks at a representation of him, and he thus confirms that she desires him; here she discovers the place where he has been looking at her cladestinely, and she thereby rediscovers his desire. In the Coulommiers scene, Nemours makes the noise that causes the princess to see him; here the princess makes a noise when she is walking through the woods and happens upon Nemours, but Nemours does not look up.

Furthermore, in this later scene the princess again ends up assuming all the possible positions of viewer and viewed, as she did in the cane and portrait scene. First she goes over and puts herself in Nemours's place, the shop from which he views her: "She went toward the windows to see what they overlooked; she found that from there one could see her whole garden and the front of her quarters" (166). Then she goes back to her position as the one viewed, who looks over to the vantage-point of the viewer: "And, when she was in her room, she saw quite easily that same window where she was told the man came" (166). Then she puts herself into the place she usually occupies when dealing with Nemours: she makes his viewing a spectacle for herself and him. "In the morning, the first thing she did was to go and see if there was no one at the window across from her rooms; she went there, she saw M. de Nemours there. This sight surprised her, and she drew back with such haste that the prince realized that he had been recognized" (168). (At the end of this passage, which we cited before, we recall that Nemours makes his desire visible; he makes his voyeurism seen; he exhibits it.) In psychoanalytic terms, what the princess does in her reconstructions of the primal scene of viewing is to point out the interchangeability of positions in the scene, interchangeability that can entail taking the position of the other gender.

Even though this scene doubles and mirrors previous scenes, it does so, again, with several important differences. There are, of course, the substitutions of one subject for another and the reversals of roles, but what is perhaps the most significant feature is that, when the princess goes to the room where Nemours spies on her, the door to that room is closed. This door, closed on the place of Nemours's desire, symbolizes her refusal of his love, which follows just after this scene, and repeats her constant gesture of distancing and differentiating. Thus, when the princess's role is to repeat, to double, previous scenes, she imitates them, but with a difference.

Indeed, one of the central structures of the novel appears to be this "differential" doubling, and if we have already mentioned several doubling scenes in the text, we must add there are an incredible number of other similar structures. Consider, for instance, the fact that the princess's mother lost her husband, retreated from society, and then returned; subsequently, the princess loses her mother, retreats from society for a short time, then returns; yet later, the princess loses her husband, retreats from society, then returns and speaks with Nemours. But the real difference the princess introduces into this series of repetitions is, of course, her ultimate retreat at the end and her refusal to return to continue the mirroring.

Perhaps the most remarkable scene of mirroring between two different intrigues is the episode of the dropped letter, which is a mirroring involved with the princess's *writing* and a mirroring which thus leads into a concept of women's writing. In this scene, a letter which speaks of desire falls out of a pocket, and it is seen by persons for whom it was not destined. In this same episode, the princess exhibits her desire in spite of herself (just like the letter of desire that escapes from the pocket) when Nemours is hurt; her desire is also seen by the wrong person, the chevalier de Guise. In the letter, a woman who was successful in hiding her true desire, as well as her knowledge that her lover was unfaithful, finally reveals both. As for the princess, she likewise shows her affection for Nemours (which she had previously hidden) when he is injured, and now she learns, (from the existence of the letter itself, which she supposes is destined for Nemours) that he loves another, or so it appears. The following words from the letter can be applied both to the princess's situation and (obviously) to the situation of the woman who wrote the letter: "I thought that you had a violent passion for me; I no longer hid the one I had for you, and, at the time that I let you see it in its entirety, I learned that you betrayed me, that you loved another" (98). The results of the letter are the same at both levels, for at the level of the intrigue involving the real author of the letter, the dauphine is eventually forced away from France, and at the level of Nemours and the princess, both the chevalier de Guise and the princess (at the end of the novel) leave the court. But again, although the princess seems to mirror the situation of the letter writer perfectly, she changes it, displaces it; because when she re-writes that very letter in the presence of Nemours, she deforms it, makes the copy unlike the original, makes it different, so different in fact that no one believes it is the same.

The princess's creative act thus seems to be involved with copy-ing, with mirroring, with representing, but in this mirroring pro-cess, she does not merely imitate the original exactly, but rather changes something, adds difference, distance. Her re-presentation emphasizes the distance and difference in the similarity.

Is this not also the task she seeks to perform in the shops of the two merchants? In the first scene she comes to match stones, to add to, to copy the original stones with ones that are similar but belong to a different batch. In the second scene she wishes to learn to imitate "in her own hand" the creations of the worker in silk. Such copying in difference is the gesture of this text itself, as we have seen, which continually doubles in a slightly askew, off-centered way, its own scenes. And it is also the gesture of historical fiction: to imitate history but with a difference. This rewriting of history becomes particularly important from the feminist point of view, in light of Faith Beasley's new work on Madame de Lafayette. Beasley shows how Lafayette rewrites history, repeating it but changing it, with the result that she highlights a tradition of women's writing (a genre specifically linked to *portraiture*) (190–243).

Thus we could say that the text constantly makes visible its own "mise en scène," which is the nature of the creative act, and the difference (in Derrida's sense) of the creative act, specifically that of woman.

The scenes of voyeurism in this text have shown us how looking and creating are linked: the princess puts a space of difference into the mirroring of Nemours's narcissistic desire for exhibitionism, and she puts a space of difference both into her identity as the one who is different and into her imitations, which are both the same and different.[6] This text thus tells of the difference of woman's creation in the princess's imitations and doublings, and of the difference of woman's identity (the princess's identity is to be the one who is different). It is the tale of the difference of woman's desire, which is not to be involved in narcissistic mirroring but actively to see (Susanne Kappeler says that in pornography "The look between man and woman—both looking as active subjects—has been extinguished" [81]); and of the relation between a woman's creation and her desire (think of the two creative acts of storytelling in which women, the princess's mother and the dauphine, tell stories about the desire of women, Valentinois and Anne de Boleyn). For the princess, vision, desire, identity, and creation are distance; they uphold distance. Just as the gaze itself cannot be seized, her gesture is to show how it is impossible to seize a perfect mirror image of oneself through the other, through desire, or through creative representation. If, as Joan DeJean says, the princess's language is one of gaps (889), what the final action and creative process in the text show is that very gap, the gap inherent in desire itself (never realized, always elsewhere), the gap of the princess herself (her identity), and the gap of writing, specifically of woman's writing (imitation and displacement in this text).

The notion of a copy that copies, but not exactly, of an imitation that, in a sense, does not imitate, brings us to the paradox of this text. Indeed, the princess's desire is paradoxical: one the one hand, in her desire for Nemours, she desires to see and to be seen, but on the other hand, she desires to remain invisible in the game of mirroring for the other. In order to fulfill the desire for invisibility she removes herself from Nemours, but this ironically renders impossible the fulfillment of her other, conflicting desire to see. This parallels the paradox of her behavior when she confesses her desire to her husband: she wants to make her passion invisible, to withdraw from Nemours's demanding eyes, and to do this, she makes her desire visible by telling, showing it to her husband and ultimately to Nemours. The princess's dilemma shows the impossibility of her desire in the voyeurist structure of her society, and thus she must escape to the convent in the end.

In my view, it is this impossibility of a woman's desire in the structure of voyeurism that gives rise to the paradoxes in the text. The princess feels contradictory things: "Mme de Clèves had at first been angry that M. de Nemours had reason to believe that it was he who had kept her from going to the Maréchal de Saint-André's; but then she felt a kind of discontent" (64); "She thought she should speak and thought she should say nothing. M. de Nemours's discourse pleased her and offended her almost equally" (85). Nemours recognizes the paradox of his desire: what makes him happy in the "aveu" scene is exactly what makes their love impossible: "He abandoned himself at first to this joy; but it did not last long when he realized that the same thing that had just informed him that he had touched Mme de Clèves's heart must also convince him that he would never receive any mark of it, and that it was impossible to enter into a relationship with someone who had recourse to such an extraordinary remedy" (125). It is a paradox that the princess's coldness gives Nemours pleasure (114). It is a paradox that the liberty M. de Clèves gives to the princess is the strongest of "limits" (128). It is a paradox that the princess finds it impossible that her husband could have spoken of her "aveu," and impossible that he could not have spoken about it (137). It is, paradoxically, as with Madame Bovary in her initial love for Léon, when he stays away that she loves him best: "He dared not speak to her, even though the confusion of this ceremony gave him several opportunities; but he made her see such sadness and such a respectful fear of approaching her that she did not find him quite so guilty, even though he had said nothing to her to justify himself" (141). It is the fact that when all obstacles are gone the love between the princess and Nemours becomes impossible (167).

It is, finally, this paradox, this copresence of opposites that is expressed in the use of negative linguistic expressions to express a positive thing: "It was not impossible that she had seen what he had just done" (92); "It was not impossible that he could see Mme de Clèves there without being seen by her" (153). And there is a certain irony of point of view, which makes one smile, in the sentence: "They ran to him [Nemours], and they thought him to be seriously wounded. Mme de Clèves thought that he was wounded more seriously than the others did" (95). It is the irony of finding the truth in words said in jest: "These words, even though said in jest, made a deep impression on Mme de Clèves" (93).

Finally, there is the paradox of the last word of the text, "inimitables," for the princess copies, imitates, but with a difference which shows a certain inimitability in the nature of copying itself.

A copy is always different; writing is always involved in difference. Nemour's desire to find an object that can mirror his desire back to him fails, because the mirroring always involves distance and difference, the difference of the princess's desire.

*La Princesse de Clèves* represents the impossibility, the double bind of woman's desire in a world in which her desire is always only a mirror of the man's identity. Its paradoxes make evident to us the contradictions involved in a voyeurist structure that purports to be an erotic gaze at the woman but that is, in reality, a narcissistic, autoerotic male gaze at himself.

## Triangulations of the Gaze: *Le Ravissement de Lol V. Stein*

*"Triangulation: any trigonometric operation for finding a position or location by means of bearings from two fixed points a known distance apart."*
—Webster's Seventh Collegiate Dictionary

*"Nothing will have taken place but the place. Except perhaps a constellation."*
—Mallarmé,
"Un Coup de dès"

In many ways, Marguerite Duras's twentieth-century novel, *Le Ravissement de Lol V. Stein,* is a very traditional narrative. After all, the basic plot is the voyeurist quest made by a male narrator to learn the truth about a mysterious and inexplicable female character, to learn the solution to the mystery of woman. Tatiana Karl, another female character, draws attention to this quest when she asks, aloud and silently, the following questions: "How do you know these things about Lol? She means to say: how do you know them in a woman's place? In the place of a woman who could be Lol?" (151). How could he know things that a woman knows about herself? Not surprisingly, he has followed Lol, spied on her, become a voyeur in order to learn the truth about her. He literally places himself outside of her window in several scenes, to watch Lol and Tatiana when they cannot see him: "I take a few steps around the house and I arrive behind some of the lateral bay windows of the living room. Lol is seated facing this bay window. She does not yet see me" (90). He follows Lol in the street (128); he spies on Lol and her daughters again through the bay window (129). This spying on the woman is linked to the desire to possess and "know" the woman completely, and to a vague implication of death and finality accompanying that possession, when just after the narrator spies on Lol, he says "In a little while, in a little while, in scarcely two days, I will possess all of Tatiana Karl, wholly, until her end" (91). Indeed, during his possession of Tatiana, he symbolically "decapitates" her, taking away her identity and her thought: "He hides Tatiana Karl's face under the sheets and thus he has her decapitated body under his hand, entirely at ease" (134).

This theme of decapitation ties in to another "traditional" nineteenth-century narrative structure: the resolution of the Oedipus complex as the plot of fiction. The "primal" scene near the beginning of the novel, in which Lol's fiancé abandons her for the older woman, Anne-Marie Stretter, resembles perhaps the oedipal primal scene in which the little girl must give up her love for her father when she sees that he "belongs" to the older-woman/mother, when she understands them as a formed couple.[7] This resemblance is further reinforced by the inexplicable appearance of Lol's real mother on the scene and by the aggressivity manifested by Lol toward her mother: "The screen of her mother between them and her was the sign that preceded it. With her hand, very hard, she knocked it down to the ground" (22).

This text is also conventional, in the postmodern tradition, in its ambiguity and word play. For instance, the word *ravissement*, which appears in the title, is derived from a verb that means "to steal," "to ravish," and "to delight." The repeated word *vol* (both "flight" and "theft") suggests with the title *viol*, meaning "rape," and resonates with the sense that Lol's love has been stolen, that she has been stolen, both her identity and her body (in the rather violent scene in the train near the end of the novel). And her love was stolen, not so much in the sense that another woman stole the object of her love, but rather in the sense that Lol lost her love, the love she experienced for Michael Richardson, a surprising fact that she reveals to the narrator: "I no longer loved my fiancé when the woman came in" (137). Lol's voyage into insanity, then, results from the death of her love, and the emptiness that ensues is the absence of that love.

Furthermore, the "male," whose goals are so firmly affixed to the nineteenth-century quest for knowledge, questions his own authority as he attempts to reveal the truth, and again traditional elements are undermined by the postmodern ambiguity of narrative authority and narrative truth. In his quest for the truth about Lol, Jacques admits that his story, this truth about Lol, is a combination of Tatiana's copy and his invention (the mixing of fact and interpretation in the experience of the primal scene): "There is here, throughout, mixed in, all together, both that false semblance that Tatiana Karl is telling and that which I am inventing about the night of the Casino on T. Beach" (14).[8]

This narrative, like the narratives of the decadent period at the end of the nineteenth century, actually takes the clichéd conventions that form narratives and repeats them to such an extent that it reveals its strategies aimed at simulating truth and thus undermines the truth it purports to seek. This happens in particular in the quest for the truth of woman as represented by Lol: she exemplifies and crystallizes the definition of woman as "not-all," yet she does this in such an exaggerated fashion that the clichéd nature of this definition is revealed. Lol exemplifies Irigaray's analysis of the nature of woman in the Western tradition.[9] Something is "missing" in Lol's "castrated" nature: "Already something was missing in order for Lol to be—she says—there" (12); "Lol was missing something, already she was strangely incomplete" (80). When Michael Richardson looks for "someone" at the ball, he does not find her—"He had not discovered Lol" (20)—for in fact she is almost no one. She is the nothing, the not-all, that makes plenitude possible, and when one knows "nothing" about Lol, one already knows her: "To know nothing of Lol was to know her already" (81). Even the form of Lol's name, when written in small letters, figures the emptiness of her nature (O or 0) surrounded by two *l*s, or two 1s, perhaps the two males Michael Richardson and Jacques Hold. She is almost a child, too young and without a voice: "She had remained fraily young. . . . She pleased him. She piqued the desire that he liked, the desire for little girls not quite completely grown, sad, immodest, and with no voice" (29–30). She is passive, effaced, a perfect domestic housekeeper (33). Her identity is a masquerade, a "seeming": "She gave the impression of enduring in tranquil boredom a person she obliged herself to be" (12). Man, on the other hand, is the all, as when Jean Bedford sees Lol smiling at him for the first time. As he sees her watch him arrive, he is called the "tout-venant," both the indiscriminate arrival of things, and in a literalization, the "all" coming to encounter her "not-all": "What made him stop was certainly the fearful smile, but a smile that burst with a very vivid joy at seeing the arrival of things, him, that evening" (26).

Anne-Marie Stretter, on the other hand, represents the other figure of woman, the one who is "more than one," too much, too many identities and organs, not the simple "one" of man. Anne Marie Stretter is represented as complete before she meets Michael Richardson: "Nothing more could happen to this woman, thought Tatiana, nothing more, nothing. But her end, she thought" (16). But this book (her meeting with Michael Richardson and Lol's story) is the surplus that is added to her completeness. Tatiana Karl, too, goes over the limit of plenitude, surpasses the "one," in the quantity of her hair: "People said then that she would be obliged, one day or another, to cut it, that hair, it tired her, it threatened to round her shoulders with its weight, to disfigure her by its mass too overwhelming for her large eyes, for her small skin-and-bone face. Tatiana Karl did not cut her hair, she accepted the risk of having too much" (59). Thus woman, as Irigaray theorizes, can be less than one or more than one, but only man can be "one."

But is a hyperbole of tradition all that this narrative presents? Does it do no more than display the clichéd nature of woman without suggesting a shift out of that cliché to a different concept of woman? It is actually from within this cliché that a decidedly different narrative structure emerges, along with a different structuration of the male and female self, the male and female gaze. Let us first examine the way the self is structured, and then turn to the various scenes of voyeurism which reconfigure the typical narrative scene of the search for the truth of the other-than-the-self.

In Lacan's theory of the structuration of the subject, the mirror stage, when the self can recognize itself as a human in the mirror, represents the inauguration of the subject. In this Imaginary stage, the gaze is the means by which the child can control the other in a one-to-one correspondence in the mirror, a relationship that is (even though the child moves jubilantly) static, because the self is riveted in one space before the mirror and, for the self to be recognized, it must remain fixed there. It is as if there is no room, in Lacan's early writing, for the space of a third term in this binary stage, whether that be the mother or father, or simply the space of

symbolism itself. (I am using here the early description of the structure of the mirror stage in Lacan, and not his later revisions of it.)

If Lacan uses this rather symbolic "scene" as a structural representation of the early formation of the subject, I would like to take an
early scene of Duras's novel, early both in the sense that it happens
on the first page of the novel and in the sense that it happens early
in the narrated life of Lol, as a "primal" scene of the construction of
the Durasian subject. It is not a mirror scene, but it is a scene in
which two selves, Lol and Tatiana, similar in their gender and in
their age, face each other in a kind of mirror relation:

> Both of them danced, on Thursdays, in the empty schoolyard.
> They did not want to go out in lines with the others, they
> preferred to remain at school. People let them have their way,
> they were charming, they knew better than the others how to ask
> for this favor, it was given to them. Shall we dance, Tatiana? A
> radio in a nearby building played outmoded dance songs—an
> oldies program—with which they contented themselves. With
> the guards gone, they were alone in the large schoolyard where,
> that day, between the dances, they heard the sound of the street.
> Go on, Tatiana, come here; let's dance, Tatiana, come here.
> That is what I know.

What is striking here in this early scene is that the mirror relationship
of the two young girls, so similar one to the other, is a relationship
that contains an other. This "otherness" does not remain static and
fixed in its place in space before the mirror. Rather the couple dances;
the mirror relation between self and mirror-self-other moves in space
and time, is displaced and changes. The agent that puts the dance
into motion, the music, is significantly an "émission-souvenir," an
"oldies broadcast," but also the word *souvenir* evokes the idea of time
always already at work, putting the present at a distance from itself,
just as each "snapshot" of the dancers in motion is displaced from
what precedes and follows. The dance is the situation of the subject
and its relation to others in space and time, and shows that a static
notion like the mirror stage could be overlooking the already "dis-
tanced" and symbolic status of the identification of the self. Although Lacan, in his essay on the mirror stage, does emphasize the
alienating nature of the identification with the mirror-self, he
does not, in that essay, allow that relation to be Symbolic, for the

Symbolic comes only with the Oedipus complex (this changes later in Lacan's work, as we shall discuss in the conclusion). The spatial and temporal nature of the identification of the self on this first page of Duras's novel is further emphasized in the switching of personal pronouns at the end of the paragraph. As the dancers move in time and space, circling and changing position but facing each other, the pronouns dance and change, from the third person "elles" (the two girls alone), to "on" (one), to the colloquial imperative *vous* form with the *tu* form following ("allez viens," "go on, come here"), to "on," and finally, to the narrator, "je." The self here is enmeshed in a spatial and temporal dance with other subjects and selves, and is not fixed in place.

The most prominent dance scene in the novel is the second one, in which Lol goes to the dance with Michael Richardson and he encounters, and leaves with, Anne-Marie Stretter. The introduction of this scene by the narrator is important, for it shows the "thickness" of the present moment, exemplified by the present of the narrator's life. As he says, he wants to begin with the dance scene and not with the part of Lol's life that precedes it because so much past biography might obscure the importance of Lol in his present: "The nineteen years that preceded this night, I do not want to know more about them than what I say . . . I do not want it because the presence of her adolescence in this story risks attenuating a bit in the eyes of the reader the crushing actuality of this woman in my life" (14). In order to emphasize Lol's present role he recounts the scene of the past dance, a dance already formed in Lol's life and in this narrative by the "primal" dance on the first page of the text, because the "present" is the dance between past and future, here and there. Lol begins to come to the narrator, as he says, far back in the past when Anne-Marie Stretter came to that ball at T. Beach: "So I am going to look for her, I take her, there where I think I should, at the moment when she seems to me to begin to move to come to meet me, at the precise moment when the last ones to arrive, two women, pass through the door of the ball room of the Municipal Casino of T. Beach" (14).

The dance begins with the empty space of the floor: "The dance floor had slowly emptied. It was empty" (15). This empty space sets the stage for the dance between subjects, in the sense that a restructuring will take place: Lol's place in relation to the others will change, her position in the couple will be altered. Then Lol and

Michael Richardson dance, and Lol already knows that he has changed, that the positioning has changed. It is as though change were already inscribed in Richardson and the dance itself and is not a surprise: "Without a doubt, Lol perceived this change. She found herself transported before it, it seemed, without fearing it, without surprise; the nature of this change seemed to be familiar to her: it had to do with the very person of Michael Richardson, it had to do with the one Lol had known until then" (17). The nature of the dance and of the subject is its shifting form and the substitution of selves: Tatiana and Lol in the first dance scene, Lol and Michael Richardson in the second dance scene, Michael Richardson and Anne-Marie Stretter in the third. Each subject is like the dance floor, the place where this intersection and crossing of partners takes place. The fact that the narrative makes clear that this is not a painful experience for Lol (she does not suffer from this; she is merely changed [17]) emphasizes its symbolic nature, its "formative" function in Lol's and the narrator's lives. Lol is fascinated with the dance of Michael Richardson and Anne-Marie Stretter; she does not want it to end. It is almost as if she were the child fascinated by its own image in the mirror or an image of its parents, an image of the formation of the self as a constantly shifting position in a relation of couples; a child who does not want to face the end of the spectacle that is its own formation. Indeed, one could view the initial scene of the dance between two female subjects as a dance between the mother-daughter couple; here, the child, after forming the father-daughter couple, must forego that "dance" to allow for the mother-father couple (as we saw, Anne-Marie Stretter is an older woman, a mother of a daughter very similar to herself). What Lol shows is how important the dance of substitutions is, for as she returns to it every day in her memory, she finds there her very place as subject, and it is by displacing herself in space during her walks that she "relives" the ball: "Thoughts . . . come to Lol V. Stein while she walks. . . . 'So it was for that reason that she would take walks, in order better to think about the ball.' . . . She goes in there every day. . . . And in this enclosed space wide open to her gaze alone, she begins the past again, she orders it, *her real abode,* she arranges it" (45–46, emphasis mine).

The next dance scene is more complicated: Lol and Jacques Hold, the narrator, dance together, along with Tatiana Karl and her husband, Pierre Beugner. This already represents a change in position, since, because Tatiana and Jacques are lovers, he has taken his new position with Lol. As Jacques and Lol dance, they speak of the earlier dance scene at T. Beach and of their plans to go there together, thus superimposing onto the current dance floor a conversation about the location of a previous dance. Finally, Jacques and Tatiana dance, another shift in partners.

The concept of the self as a space or location in which partners, identities, places come together, meet, and leave becomes most concrete when Lol watches Tatiana and Jacques dance, and when her understanding of a certain "time," perhaps the time of the self, is represented as an alternative filling and emptying: "She thought a time was possible that would refill and empty alternately, that would fill and unfill, then be ready again, always, to serve, she still believes it, she will always believe it, she will never be cured" (159). And this "time" of the self, as it is filled and emptied or as the dancers change partners, passes, and in the first dance scene the partners are described as having aged: "Tatiana had seen how they had grown older" (19).

If the identity of the subject can be compared to the dance floor, the empty space to be filled and emptied, then it is a kind of hole, an absence across which identity is written and erased. Identity itself is not a word or a definition, but is that "mot-absence" ("word-absence") the "mot-trou" ("word-hole") so often associated with Lol's quest. Identity is this absent word that one would like to hold and pin down, affix so as to understand it and contemplate it, just as Lol never wants the ball at T. Beach to end: "Immense, without end, an empty gong, it would have kept those who wanted to leave, them, the future and the very instant" (48). It is a word that would bury all other words because it would make them unnecessary: "It would have been a word-absence, a word-hole, dug out in its center with a hole, that hole where all the other words would have been buried" (48). But this "word" does not exist; it is the space of the intersection of all the words, positions, partners. Its absence, the space of identity, is what joins, or here "contaminates," all other words: "Lacking, this word, it spoils the others, contaminates them, it is also the dead dog on the beach at high noon, that hole of flesh" (48). This word, this absence of a fixed identity for Lol, is a dead dog by the sea. Duras makes this link in another place when she speaks of her writing and of Lol: "Evidently, I can show Lol. V. Stein in the movies, but I can show her only when she is hidden, when she is like a dead dog on the beach, covered with sand, you see" (Duras and Porte 100). Just as Duras, and Martha Noel Evans in her excellent analysis of the novel, "Marguerite Duras: *The Whore*" (*Masks*: 123–156), speak of the prostitution of Lol in the sense that she is substitutable, can take many partners, and is what all the words written about her make of her, so identity itself is substitution, is all the words that cross in the space of the subject, all the relationships that form in time and space just what the subject is. For Duras, this formation of the self by others and by the outside is fearful: "It has no meaning, Lol V. Stein, see, it has no significance. Lol V. Stein, that is what you make of it, it does not exist otherwise. I think I have just said something there about her. . . . When I was writing it, I experienced a moment—I told you this, I think—a moment of fear. I cried out. I think that some threshold was crossed" (Duras and Porte 101).

If the self is composed of a crisscrossing of various words, positions, and identities, then the self has no real fixed place, no secure location where it can always be found. It is constructed as a relationship in space between other subjects/relationships. Lol sees herself as the space formed by the triangulation of people and time (dawn): "She sees herself, and that is her true thought, in the same place, in that end, always, in the center of a triangulation with dawn and them as the eternal terms" (47). Her subject is composed of others: "She who does not see herself, she is seen in that way, in others" (54).

There is no "fixed" self, but the constructed selves can choose to manifest one or the other of those various "discourses" that compose the subject. The subject can display a certain identity, and can create identities by selecting a particular spatial relationship, just as Lol is described as "creating" the couple by her gaze: "Lol V. Stein watches, incubates, fabricates these lovers" (60). This is where the gaze becomes important in the structure. It is related to the way the self selects and creates its various structures. Lol is described as having an unfixed nature and as being able to hide or reveal that unfixed identity: "She thought she had flowed into an identity of an indecisive nature that could be named by names indefinitely different, and whose visibility depended on her" (41). In the dynamics of the gaze in this novel, the fluidity of identity is precisely what Lol makes visible, both to the reader and to the male narrator of the text.

As we have seen so often, the voyeurist gaze is one that aims to dominate and to steal the truth of the other. It is a gaze that one subject directs to another subject in a relationship of power and control. It is the gaze that the narrator casts upon Lol when he wishes to understand her, when he spies on her to see if he can learn her true nature. In this novel, as in *La Princesse de Clèves*, the woman who has been the object of the gaze takes it over, becomes the gazer or the "voyeuse." And, as in Lafayette's novel, the woman who looks does so in a different way. When Lol becomes the voyeuse, she does not simply reverse the dynamics of traditional voyeurism in order to dominate and control Jacques Hold; she changes the dynamics of the gaze.

When she first sees Jacques, she follows him and he does not see her. But this scene is not one of domination and control of another, of Jacques by Lol. It is rather a repetition, a replay of the ball scene, because what Lol watches is the way Jacques looks at women, just as, in the beginning of the ball, she watched the way Michael Richardson watched Anne-Marie Stretter: "She feels the suffocation of the summer only when he makes an added gesture to this walk, when he passes his hand through his hair, when he lights a cigarette, and above all when he watches a woman go by" (56). Just as when Michael Richardson looked for someone but did not see Lol, Lol once again occupies the position of being for Jacques "a woman whom he still never sees" (56).

Later, Lol posts herself outside of the hotel window where Tatiana Karl and Jacques Hold meet to make love. Her position is the same as the one she occupies at the ball, for she can watch a couple form, a couple that forms and affects her. And as she places herself in an open field, again a kind of empty space, the field is associated with the maternal image of milky darkness, which repeats the maternal structure of the ball at T. Beach: "This field, several meters from her, plunges, plunges more and more into a green and milky darkness" (62). What Lol seeks to see is the construction of the self, the layering of scene upon scene, discourse upon discourse, triangle upon triangle. Her somnambulistic state, the "sleep of Lol V. Stein" (63), the description of the scene that she watches as an "invisible, nonexistent spectacle" (63) reveal that she is not seeing a concrete spectacle of present identity, and that she is not dominating others by means of her gaze (Jacques, in fact, seems to know that she is there, and in the second, third, and fourth scenes in the hotel room [120, 162, 191] he actually looks for her in the field). Rather, what she is letting stand forth is the space, the void, where identities cross: "With eyes riveted to the lighted window, a woman hears the void" (63). What this act of "voyeurism" entails is not a penetration of the secret truth of others, but rather the risk of an even greater "separation," a multiplication of the numerous positions and spaces in Lol's identity and relation with others (63). Lol is different from others because she seeks out that space as "identity," and is not driven off by the fear such lack of place brings with it:

> And perhaps Lol is afraid, but just a bit, of the possibility of an even larger separation from others. She knows even so that some would fight—she herself did yesterday—that they would return home running as soon as any remains of reason would surprise them in this field. But that is the last fear learned by Lol, the one that others would have in her place, this evening. They would imprison it in their heart, with courage. But she, on the contrary, cherishes it, tames it, caresses it with her hands in the rye. (63).

Lol seeks out her identity as the end of identity, the space that separates her from the couple at the ball, the space that is the self and that is revealed by triangulation: "In the multiple aspect of the ball at T. Beach, it is the end that Lol retains. It is the precise instant of the end, when dawn arrives with an unheard of brutality and separates her from the couple that Michael Richardson and Anne-Marie Stretter formed" (46). She wants to *see* that space, the spatial relation that defines subjects in their relations to others. When Tatiana and Jacques ask her just what she wanted that night of the ball at T. Beach, Lol answers, "To see them" (103).

Indeed, what Lol reveals about the gaze is that it, like identity, is not present but is the relation between self and other in space. The look cannot be seized, is not an object in reality; it is not "there." Thus, when Jacques looks at Lol's eyes to see her gaze, he does not see it: "I push her back a bit in order to see her eyes. I see them: a transparency looks at me. Again I do not see" (155). And in a paragraph that rather ambiguously describes Anne-Marie Stretter's or Lol's gaze (one can not really tell which is the subject, which is the self whose gaze is being described), the difficulty of "holding" the gaze is emphasized: "The gaze, her gaze—up close one understood that

this defect came from an almost painful discoloration of the pupil—
was lodged in the whole surface of her eyes, it was difficult to capture
it" (16). What this might add to Lacan's theory of the gaze and the
mirror stage is that the "space" of the Symbolic is always already
present in the gaze of the mirror stage; the space of symbolism is of
course operative as soon as the self identifies with the nonself. If the
mirror stage, the Imaginary, and the relation to the mother are Symbolic, then the psychoanalytic definition of gender must be revised.
The relation to the mother and the identity of woman are no longer
excluded from the Symbolic, no longer exiled to the prehistoric,
preSymbolic realm, and must be explored in their Symbolic nature.
This is perhaps what Duras's text does.

Lol's relationship with Jacques Hold is one that aims to divert
him from the dominating gaze of one-to-one control to the spatial
gaze she exemplifies. Early on in their relationship, Jacques describes his gaze as voyeurist. He tries to penetrate Lol's mystery, and
he describes her story as if he saw her even though he could not
have seen her: "I see how she arrives there" (62). And he begins to
understand that she wants him to see her in a different way, in a
different "space": "She wants, I understand it clearly, to be met by
me and seen by me in a certain space that she prepares at this
moment" (105). Lol wants also to see how the space of the others
has changed now that she has come into it: "Perhaps it was not
thoughtlessly that Lol got us together that night, perhaps it was to
see us together, Tatiana and me, to see where we were since her
irruption in my life" (146). When Lol places herself outside of their
window again, in the field, repeating a previous scene, the window
is described as a mirror that reflects nothing, the nothing of the
space that is the subject: "We must have been there for an hour, the
three of us, for her to have seen us in turn appearing in the frame of
the window, that mirror that reflected nothing and in front of
which she must have felt deliciously the hoped-for eviction of her
person" (124).

Lol makes Jacques Hold succumb to the divestiture of the subject.
Once he places himself in the triangulations of selves, he understands
that he will lose his supposed stability: "At the moment when my
hands touched Lol, the memory of an unknown dead person came
back to me: he will serve the eternal Richardson, the man of
T. Beach, he will be mixed with others, pell-mell, all will make one,
no one will be distinguished from any one else, not before, not after,

not during, all will be lost from view, from memory of names" (113). According to Lol, Jacques too has "disappeared." If Hold's original goal was to "hold" Lol—"My hands become the trap with which to immobilize her, to keep her from always coming and going from one end to the other of time" (107)—to isolate her identity and contemplate it, through his relationship with her he has become like her, absent, "holed." The crisscrossing of subjects, positions, voices becomes Hold, too, just as when he hears Tatiana's and Lol's voices and they become his own internal and feminine voice: "Suddenly here their voices interlace, tender, in the nocturnal dilution, made of a femininity likewise joined in me" (93).

Lol, too, seems to undergo a transformation in the novel, from an unconscious routine of existence to a kind of consciousness of her spatial identity. When she lived the life of a "frozen order," she made the mistake of creating paths in the garden that did not intersect each other, and thus one could not take walks, could not move about in space, nor "connect" the various lines related to each other in the garden (35). But then she had cross paths constructed that permitted one to walk, and immediately thereafter (on the next page) Lol goes out and takes walks in the city, and discovers the cross paths of her own identity (35–36).

This loss of the subject's place and "home," although fearful, is not tragic. On the contrary, there is a recurring image of the smile, almost like that of the Cheshire cat, whose smile remains behind when its "self," its body, has disappeared. Lol's wandering is described as an "errance bienheureuse" (42). She laughs when she does not find what she is looking for (179); she smiles at the ball at T. Beach; she smiles during her walks (42). We will consider this smile in the conclusion.

# CONCLUSION

## The Comic Gaze:
## A View Beyond Voyeurism

THE FUNCTION of voyeurism in literary texts is obviously not confined to the world of French literature. In our conclusion, let us explore two stories from the English-speaking world. The first is an early English legend that exemplifies many of the issues at stake in the gaze at the woman. This legend, partly history, partly folklore, and originating some time between 1038 and 1057, is the famous ride of Lady Godiva through the town of Coventry.[1] Although several versions of the story exist, there is a central core that varies only slightly: Lady Godiva wished to unburden the people of Coventry from a tax, and when she asked her husband to lift that tax, he said he would do so only if she would ride through the town naked. In a significant symbolism, the well-being of society, the town of Coventry, is established by means of the naked female body. Godiva gives over her body to view in exchange for the economic security of the town, and the authority of her husband, who is also the lord of the town, commands her to do so. Her body is exchanged for money, but this is not prostitution; it is a transaction sponsored by the family and the "state."

What is also of interest in this legend is that no one sees her as she rides. It is almost as if it shows that a certain good for society is built upon the body of a woman, but that this structure must remain "invisible." This is similar to the "blind spot" that we discussed at the end of part I, the blind spot that prevents one from seeing what is really there. Furthermore, art, sculpture, and poetry have never tired of showing us Godiva's naked female body in representations of her ride, imitating the position of Peeping Tom, who appears in several of the versions. Art takes a contradictory stance, reiterating the necessity of the invisibility of the structure and at the same time taking pleasure in revealing the naked body of the woman, assuming the dangerous position of Peeping Tom, who is blinded by his own gaze, who looks on at the forbidden body/text that should remain invisible. The texts we have studied for the most part also take up a contradictory stance, both repeating the pleasure of the gaze at the naked woman and making visible the repressive ideological forces at work in that gaze.

But where does the woman fit into this structure? Must she acquiesce and take up the position of the body to be viewed? Does she also take pleasure in being in the other position, that of the viewer? What kind of pleasure would this be? Is there any way of changing the structure of this gaze? Before turning to some concluding remarks about the texts we have studied and how they might help us formulate answers to these questions, I would like to discuss the second English text, a short story by Anaïs Nin, "The Veiled Woman," to help us situate ourselves in this problematic, as well as to provide a counterpoint to the Godiva legend.[2]

In this brief tale, told in third person narration, the main character, George, a handsome, athletic man, catches sight of an attractive couple in a bar, and the three of them seem to share the same outlook. George is very taken with the woman, who is quite beautiful under her veil, and is disappointed when she gets up to leave. His disappointment fades, however, when her male partner invites George for a drink; as they talk, they discover that George may be the perfect person to perform a certain task for money. This task is the following: he must make love to the veiled woman, who must even then remain veiled in a metaphoric sense, because George must never try to find out who she is or to repeat the experience. When George and his male friend arrive by taxi at the place where the woman awaits him, he is paid fifty dollars, and then he enters a lavishly decorated house filled with mirrors. After he encounters the woman, she is physically unveiled, and after he fulfills his task, he leaves. Several months later, he runs across a friend who tells him that he (the friend), a confirmed voyeur, paid one hundred dollars to watch an attractive couple make love in a lavishly furnished, mirrored room. The center of this story, as in so many of the stories we have seen, is the veiling and unveiling of woman. But this story is also a kind of "mise en scène" of its own coming into being. In the collection of tales published by Nin, the preface explains the very material, monetary conditions of its generation. According to Nin, Henry Miller was asked to write erotica for one hundred dollars a month, but feeling he did not want to perform this task, he gave it to Nin. Thus the one hundred dollars puts Nin, the writer, and George in the same position—each is paid one hundred dollars for a "performance"— showing how Nin perhaps equates writing women's private erotica (this was put forth by her as a woman's diary) with performing a sexual act while being spied on by an invisible voyeur. When woman writes, she cannot escape the structure in which she is viewed as a woman, where her gendered identity is the place where the truth will be found, and by writing, she and her desire are automatically implicated in the voyeurist structure. When the reader reads her texts, it is with the expectation that they will reveal "woman," the real secrets, just what a woman is and just how a woman writes and desires.

But Nin does not simply succumb to this structure, she shifts it in an interesting direction. The shift is first of all a narrative one, since George is not a first-person narrator, and the "fictional" narrator is the woman writing the diary. And it is a shift generated by exaggeration. As Nin says in discussing the difficulties involved in such a writing project: "I began to write tongue-in-cheek, to become outlandish, inventive, and so exaggerated that I thought he [the anonymous man commissioning the works] would realize I was caricaturing sexuality" (ix). What this story by a woman writer does is to make highly visible the underlying motives behind the unveiling of woman's desire, and it does so by exaggerating male and female identities and roles, by "masquerading" and parading. First, the veiled woman has no identity, just as woman does not attain the status of a subject. She does not need an identity, because her sole function is to reflect back to man his full identity as opposed to her empty one: thus the house of mirrors. The man goes to her house not to see her but to satisfy himself, to see himself: "He was glad that he could bear these repetitions of himself, infinite reproductions of a handsome man, to whom the mystery of the situation had given a glow of expectation and alertness he had never known" (90).

This structure revealed by Nin, in which the woman serves as a mirror to man, is a familiar one. To reiterate, the woman's image here, as we saw in numerous analyses of voyeurism, is but man's desired plenitude reflected back to him. Woman is placed in a hall of mirrors, as when, in *La Fille aux yeux d'or*, she is merely the golden mirror in which the man can construct his own plenitude. In keeping the woman nameless and almost speechless, Nin reveals that in this story it is the men who talk to, and look at, each other, who enter into financial transactions surrounding the woman, who end up spying on each other—let us not forget the final scene of voyeurism. The woman is a kind of screen for male financial dealings and relations; it is through her that the capital grows from the fifty dollars paid to George to the one hundred dollars paid to view George's performance. In our textual analyses, we saw how these structures of identity involve the quest to construct a closed visual version of sexual difference, to establish a perceptual identity, specifically a visual one. It is a gaze that believes that one can go and look and see things as they are; it believes that the real is not articulated, that the truth is visible in the world. As Françoise Gaillard points out, this is the essential confusion that the realist illusion upholds: "The carefully retained confusion between seeing and knowing serves as an (ideological!) substratum to the realist enunciation" ("La représentation" 267).

As well as exaggerating, and thus rendering visible in a new way, the issues involved in the unveiling of the veiled woman, Nin also looks at the male position, which is that of the invisible spectator. In so doing, she points out that his invisibility is not assured, and that he can in turn become the object of the voyeurist gaze, just like George. As Sartre showed, there always can be another subject to view the first subject as an object. This other viewer is also the reader, and as dramatized in Nin's recounting of the way in which she came to write these tales, it is the anonymous "reader"/ commissioner of the works.

After his episode with the veiled woman, George has been changed: "Poor George. For months he was wary of women. He could not believe such perfidy, and such play-acting. He became obsessed with the idea that the women who invited him to their apartments were all hiding some spectator behind a curtain" (96).

The male, put in the position that the female must always occupy, the position of the object of the gaze, finds this position intolerable. The intolerability of being viewed parallels the intolerability expressed by Henry Miller (according to Nin) of the position of the male writing erotica for money: Miller felt that "writing to order was a castrating occupation, because to be writing with a voyeur at the keyhole took all the spontaneity and pleasure out of his fanciful adventures" (vii). Both George and Miller cannot accept the feminine position, the "castrated" position, of being the object of the gaze. Nin shows, however, that this position is that of any subject, male or female—there is always an Other who looks.

In addition to showing that the male is in the vulnerable position as well, Nin shows that he is in his own way a victim of this construction of gender identity in the visual field. The common enemy of both male and female is that anonymous old man, consumer and commissioner of the unveiling, who orders the difference between genders in his request for "facts" not poetry, the anatomical description of sex not the emotions involved. He separates body from emotion, and both the male and female contributors to these stories hate him: "We sat around, imagined this old man, talked of how much we hated him because he would not allow us to make a fusion of sexuality and feeling, sensuality and emotion" (xiii). For him, sex and gender are visible, marked, "out there" as facts in the world.

Finally, Nin does not just tell a story; her story tells the story of its own writing, which originates in money paid for the revelation of the female. This mise en scène of its own generation is echoed in the preface (from her diaries) that tells of her desperate economic needs, and how survival depended on this exposure (Lady Godiva again). This text, rather than presenting itself as a simple reflection of reality, shows how it was produced, and how it produces meanings.

What is especially interesting in this tale by Nin is its strategy. To return to our earlier questions, when we ask if the woman takes up the position of the object to be viewed, we must say yes, but we must also add that the male does too. When we ask if she takes pleasure in looking at the woman being unveiled, the answer must also be yes, because in this story it is, after all, the woman who is unveiled by a woman writer. But it is also the man who is unveiled, as well as the economic apparatus behind that unveiling. To ask another question: when woman writes does she take up the male position? Nin gives us a complicated answer to this question. It is "yes" insofar as Nin takes over the male structure of voyeurism, but "no" insofar as she displaces, exaggerates it. Nin expresses the necessity of assuming a certain gendered point of view when writing (certainly a point of view that is constructed as male in our culture), while displacing it so that it is not purely male. In the preface she talks about this in terms of women's and men's writing, maintaining that her text is not just derived from the male, but also manifests her femaleness: "I believed that my style was derived from a reading of men's works. For this reason I long felt that I had compromised my feminine self. I put the erotica aside. Rereading it these many years later, I see that my own voice was not completely suppressed. In numerous passages I was intuitively using a woman's language, seeing sexual experience from a woman's point of view. I finally decided to release the erotica for publication because it shows the beginning efforts of a woman in a world that had been the domain of men" (xvi). What this story shows is that the woman's point of view in writing must begin as a kind of strategy of distanciation, on the one hand, of the male from the male role (showing the man as object to be viewed); on the other hand, of the female from the female role (woman as subject of writing, viewing). If the woman's problem in representation is being too close to the image (she *is* the image; she *is* the object of the gaze), Nin provides her with a strategy for taking up distance. And it is a distance that involves pleasure, the pleasure of laughter. In discussing Miller's inventions and exaggerations, Nin says that when he attempted to write these erotica: "Henry started out gaily, jokingly. He invented wild stories which we laughed over" (vii).

Nin's story brings out several structures that permit us to look at the ideology informing certain psychoanalytic texts and the way they relate gender identity to the gaze, so that we can find a possible way out of the bind of femininity as absence, castration, otherness. The first of these involves the mirroring in Nin's text, which in psychoanalytic terms immediately conjures up the notion of the mirror stage. In the past, there seemed to be a division between the Imaginary and the Symbolic in Lacan's work, a division as impossible to mediate as the division between male and female. By division, I do not mean that they are mutually exclusive, for Imaginary and Symbolic do interact. Rather, there is a "temporality" to their stages: "At this [earlier] stage in Lacan's work the relation between

the Imaginary and the Symbolic was often posed as a sequence—
from the image (fixed, stable) to language or the word (the means
of intersubjective communication)" (Rose, *Vision*, 176n.21). The
Imaginary precedes the Symbolic, is necessary for the development
of the Symbolic, and the Symbolic, once functioning, is, in a
certain way, inescapable. The Symbolic is the place of the law of
the father, of the assumption of gender identities, of the construction of femininity as the null set. Woman was seen to have no way
to gain access to her own language, because in language, in the
Symbolic, she has no being. This led some feminist writers, such as
Cixous and Irigaray, to seek a "body language" that would get back
in touch with the Imaginary, back in touch with a feminine essence
that preceded the phallocentric Symbolic order, but this was a
contradictory stance, since their language, as language, is always
already Symbolic.

Recent psychoanalytic theorists, however, have picked up on
certain trends in Lacan's later work that show his revision of the
strict temporal distinction between Imaginary and Symbolic. The
concept behind this revision parallels the structure of mirroring in
Nin's text: when the man sees himself in the mirror, it is not just a
ludic affirmation of his own identity, because there is an other who
is already looking at him. Thus, his reflection is not merely a one-
on-one, clean-and-clear identification; rather there is already the
space involved in the third term, the gaze of the other (the
mother).

In psychoanalytic theory, it is specifically Jacqueline Rose who
has emphasized Lacan's shift away from the unity, however illusory,
of the identification involved in the mirror stage: "The movement
away from a stress on illusory totality and identity, to identity as a
function of repeated difference can thus be seen as representing a
shift in Lacan's emphasis from the Imaginary, to the structure of
linguistic insistence as already underpinning moments prior to its
intervening symbolisation" (*Vision* 185). Rose also describes this as
a shift "from the concept of *Gestalt* to one of identity as a function
of repeated difference" (*Vision* 194). For Lacan, it is the notion of
appeal and desire that always already inhabits the mirror stage,
appeal to and desire for the other, the third gaze (the voyeur in
Nin): "For the Other, the place of discourse, always latent to the
triangulation that consecrates that distance, is not yet so long as it
has not spread right into the specular relation in its purest mo-

ment: in the gesture with which the child in front of the mirror, turning to the one who is holding it, appeals with its look to the witness who decants, verifying it, the recognition of the image, of the jubilant assumption, where indeed *it already was*" (Lacan 678). As Rose says, "This Other is now even referred back to the primary moment of the mirror-stage" (*Vision* 186), and the presence of that Other reveals "the irreducible place of desire within the original model" (149).

This revision then undoes much of the differentiation between the Symbolic and the Imaginary, and since the Symbolic has been thought of as the place in which the castration complex assigns nonidentity to the girl, her female identity as castrated needs to be rethought if the "splitting" and distance, the "linguistic insistence," is already present before the castration complex develops (here, in the mirror stage, which developmentally precedes the Oedipus complex). For this means that the symbolic, linguistic structures are in place in the child's pre-Oedipal relations to the mother. Nancy Chodorow, similarly, shows how even before gender identity has been established, "gender personality differentiation begins" (50).

It is the work of Kaja Silverman that picks up on the revisionary potential present but not articulated in Rose's work. Since there is a kind of linguistic structure already present in the earlier mirror stage, there is little to distinguish earlier distances and desires from later ones, little, as Silverman argues, but the protection of the male from castration. She, using Rose's analysis, finds a similarity between the work of Metz and Comolli on the cinema and Freud's discussion of the difference between the sexes because they all refuse even to consider that earlier sacrifices might also be castration: "I would like to suggest that his refusal to identify castration with any of the divisions which occur prior to the registration of sexual difference reveals Freud's desire to place a maximum distance between the male subject and the notion of lack. To admit that the loss of the object is also a castration would be to acknowledge that the male subject is already structured by absence prior to the moment at which he registers woman's anatomical difference—to concede that he, like the female subject, has already been deprived of being, and already been marked by the language and desires of the Other" (*Mirror* 15). This acknowledgment of losses and differences that precede the Oedipus complex fits in in an interesting way with current claims of psychoanalysts "that genital awareness develops in the second year, in what would have formerly been called the pre-genital period" (Chodorow 181).

What does distinguish the earlier castrations from the Oedipal is that "the various pre-Oedipal castrations catalogued by Lacan . . . are realized only retroactively, with the entry into language" (16). Then the anatomical difference between the boy and girl can take on its weighty significance, can be dichotomized in the clichés of socialized and infantile gender difference. The important point to emphasize, as Silverman does, is the *cultural* nature of this assumption of gender identity. The girl has not undergone the loss of the penis (nor has the boy); thus "it can only be through a cultural intervention analogous to that to which the male subject is exposed that the female subject comes to perceive herself as lacking a privileged organ" (15). If gender identity is assumed through culture, then it is not some unavoidable, immutable thing in reality, but is subject to the transformations and mutations of culture—and to revision. Studies such as Nancy Chodorow's become very important because they look at the ways in which culture comes to determine gender, and they can hypothesize about ways to change a determination that so brutally crushes woman. This is the first real step beyond the essentialist—one could say biological—distinction between the genders based on anatomy, based on *seeing the anatomical difference of the woman in the Real*, to one that recognizes the all-pervasive influence of culture, language, and ideology that makes difference meaningful.

These new developments in psychoanalytic theory force the rethinking of male and female gender identities. First, the male is seen to be just as much defined by castration and loss as is the female: as we saw earlier, "the male subject is already structured by absence prior to the moment at which he registers woman's anatomical difference" (*Mirror* 15). This involves emphasizing male lack of plenitude, rather than simply denying woman's lack. As Steve Neale states: "Both men *and* women are subject to Symbolic castration . . . men and women are *both* susceptible to the wish to occupy a position of control and to find an object for the drive" (130). Just as in Nin's text, male gender identity does not enjoy a comfortable, closed totality but is fractured by otherness.

Second, it involves a substantial reevaluation of the mother's role in both male and female Oedipal complexes, as well as a reformulation of the female castration complex. On the one hand, the importance and power of the male child's relation to the mother has been downplayed in many respects. After all, at first, as Nancy Chodorow emphasizes, "the child does not differentiate herself or himself from her or his mother but experiences a sense of oneness with her" (47). She goes on to show how masculine identity is founded on the necessity of differentiation, the necessity of distinguishing the male and distancing him from this identification with the female, which is primary: "A boy's masculine gender identification must come to replace his early primary identification with his mother. . . . A boy, in his attempt to gain an elusive masculine identification, often comes to define this masculinity largely in negative terms, as that which is not feminine or involved with women. . . . He does this by repressing whatever he takes to be feminine inside himself, and, importantly, by denigrating and devaluing whatever he considers to be feminine in the outside world" (50–51). We could formulate this in "gendered" terms to say that the first "relationship" that the male child must renounce is not a masculine desire for his mother (the Oedipus complex) but rather an identification with her that is precisely parallel to that of the little girl in her negative Oedipus complex. Thus masculinity, too, can be called a masquerade, which, as Mulvey claims, can crack (130).

What must be reemphasized and not denigrated or downplayed is the basic "feminine identity" of all males. What needs to be made "visible" is that "the threat of femininity is internal as well as external: as a result of being socialized by women, men retain within themselves feminine qualities, a partial identification with women, and often a desire to be a woman like one's mother" (36). Furthermore, Chodorow shows how male dominance that grows out of this exclusion of the feminine is "a masculine defense and a major psychic cost to men, built on fears and insecurity; it is not straightforward power" (177). To return briefly to Nin and to literature, in her preface, Nin spoke of the shared hatred of both male and female "victimized" writers for the necessity imposed by the anonymous commissioner of the works, the structural voyeur, who demands the visual difference between the sexes.

On the other hand, the nature of the female child's negative Oedipus complex, her love of her mother, has been analyzed for the most part through the derogatory lens of this denigration of the feminine. Kaja Silverman points to one way in which this identification of the girl child with her mother must be rethought:

"Identification with the mother during the negative Oedipus complex is at least in part an identification with activity. The equation of femininity and passivity is a consequence only of the positive Oedipus complex, and the cultural discourses and institutions which support it" (*Mirror* 153). Female gender identity must be rethought, too, while attempting to pinpoint ideological blind spots in previous formulations of theory.

The relevance of this revision of the "anatomical" and visual foundation of gender for a discussion of voyeurism is clear. Voyeurism aims to see gender identity in the visual field; it aims to see how the subject comes to be gendered as male or female by looking at the real. But current psychoanalysis shows the inadequacy of this visual foundation of gender difference, and many of the literary texts we have studied show not only the insistent desire to determine gender in this way but also the impossibility of this enterprise. The texts show also that the project of fixing gender identity goes hand in hand quite often with the desire to represent, in a one-to-one correspondence, reality with language in order to fix meanings, to exclude the other. In Robbe-Grillet the true identity of the murderer *is* there in the text to be found, and the body of the woman is there to be viewed. In *La Peau de chagrin*, Raphaël tries to unveil the woman's identity, but the fantastic nature of the text and of language seem to get in the way. In *Manette Salomon*, the belief in the ability to fix the identity of the other is related to a belief in the painterly representation of reality in language, in other words, in realism, and to the unveiling and "painting" of woman. In *L'Oeuvre* the painter of woman finds out that his quest to represent the truth and the true image of woman, unencumbered by ideology, is impossible. The belief in the ability to unveil the truth of woman in physical reality, to make visible as a "thing" her gender identity and her desire, seems to go hand in hand with a need to give a clear, unambiguous representation of that truth in language.

As Jacqueline Rose has emphasized, our gender identities are not fixed, yet we seem to need to nail them down: "The lines of that division [between genders] are fragile in exact proportion to the rigid insistence with which our culture lays them down; they constantly converge and threaten to coalesce" (*Vision* 227). Rose, citing Freud and Lacan, links our need for fixed meanings precisely to representation and gender:

Freud often related the question of sexuality to that of visual representation. . . . as if Freud found the aptest analogy for the problem of our identity as human subjects in failures of vision or in the violence which can be done to an image as it offers itself to view. For Freud, with an emphasis that has been picked up and placed at the centre of the work of Jacques Lacan, our sexual identities as male or female, our confidence in language as true or false, and our security in the image we judge as perfect or flawed, are fantasies. (*Vision* 227).

What she says of art is true of several of the texts we have studied. They "expose the fixed nature of sexual identity as a fantasy and, in the same gesture . . . trouble, break up, or rupture the visual field before our eyes" (*Vision* 228). *L'Immoraliste* shows the disaster of the elimination of gender ambiguity, and *La Religieuse, La Fille aux yeux d'or,* and *Le Rideau cramoisi* show the violence and error involved in the desire to unveil the "truth" of woman, a truth that is not an essence in the physical world, but rather a construction of human culture. In the literary texts we have studied, it is indeed true that "the fixing of language and the fixing of sexual identity go hand in hand" (*Vision* 228). As Irigaray also notes, the desire to define the woman as a man missing a penis fixes this "truth" upon which is based "metaphysical coherence and 'closure' " (28).

In literature, the illusion that realism is a representation of reality—it is not "literary," poetic, ambiguous, ideological—is a blind spot which, when ignored, runs the risk of continuing to propagate the unjust repression of the "other." Linda Williams has shown how in film too the desire to make "true-to-life" movies is equated in some films with the perverse structure of voyeurist seeing: realism and the belief in visual identity go hand in hand (92). To believe that language does not carry with it a whole array of cultural ideologies, that it simply and purely represents in a one-to-one correspondence a recuperable reality, is a dangerous mistake.

What Nin's text does, as do many of the others we have studied, is to show the process of production that goes into the construction of the story: as we recall, it is a kind of "mise en scène" of its own generation. It does not try to erase its status as text and as construction but rather makes that process visible. It shows itself as constituting meaning and knowledge, it shows many of the processes of that construction, and does not pass itself off as a reflection of some preexisting truth and reality. Proust's text *is* the description of its generation; Zola's description of the artist's life and the financial necessities that vie with the desire to paint what one wants, his description of himself as Sandoz, and his description of the generation of the *Rougon-Macquart* draw attention to the production of literature and art.

It is this notion of the construction of meanings and of genders that can enable us to think of the woman's position in a different way. Rather than looking for the essence of what a man is, what a woman is, we should look at how they are constructed, and in those constructions, what contradictions exist. We should not abandon the notion of gender differences but rather explore their configurations, study their effects, attempt to eliminate their injustices. There are differences between men and women, between men's and women's uses of language, and we should attempt to explore those differences as the constructions of culture, not as the expression of some gendered essence. Even if there are biological differences between male and female, those differences can never be divorced from their cultural meanings and effects.

Thus I would like to conclude with a suggestion that there is at least one identifiable difference that can be said to exist in "feminine" writing, one that is not exclusively the property of women, but is found in male writers also. It is one that relates to woman's position as subordinate in a phallocentric culture; it is necessitated by her use of a language that is coded as belonging to the male. This difference is one of textual strategy, a strategy that we find in the texts of Lafayette, Duras, and Nin, as well as in those of Stendhal and Proust. The notion of "differential doubling" in *La Princesse de Clèves* and that of "triangulation" and space in *Le Ravissement de Lol V. Stein* partake of the strategy of distancing. The differential doubling involves the taking up of a preexistent "place," and then the revelation of one's difference from that place. The distancing in Duras involves the revelation of the spatial nature of identity itself, the fact that identity is not a thing that exists in reality but rather a relationship between positions, as between places in Lafayette. In Nin, exaggeration and masquerading distance the text from realism.

It is logical, as Nin makes clear, that a woman who takes up a man's pen is putting herself in a certain position that is and is not hers. It is logical that she would need to express a certain uncomfortableness with that position, and this expression, I argue, takes the form of a strategy of doubling and displacement. The structures and content of the world are represented in the text, in much the same way that Nin uses voyeurism, but a strategy is used to put a distance between onself and those structures so as to point out their functioning. Nin exaggerates; the princess doubles with a difference; Duras reveals the space already inherent in any identity structures. That this is a strategy that is used, perhaps, because of one's position in culture is borne out by some recent discussions of black writing, such as that of Henry Louis Gates, Jr., concerning "signifying" as a repetition of formal structures, and their difference. He also states that Zora Neale Hurston "is the first author of the tradition to represent signifying itself as a vehicle of liberation for an oppressed woman, and as a rhetorical strategy in the narration of fiction" ("Blackness").

This strategy of distancing is closely related to irony, and indeed, one would certainly call Stendhal's and Proust's texts ironic in certain ways.[3] The questioning of identity is perhaps the essence of both the ironic consciousness manifested in these texts and the questioning of the realist understanding of truth in which they engage. We need only to contrast the "ironic" doubling of Lafayette's and Duras's texts with the paranoid exclusion of otherness of the Goncourts' text to see the essential difference between the representation of identity's purity and the undermining of that belief. We need only contrast Proust's and Stendhal's revelation of the impossibility of seeing the truth with Robbe-Grillet's violent imposition of the voyeurist nature of that truth to understand their difference. The texts of distancing do not do away with seeing and its attendant pleasures, but rather point out the separating distance inherent in the gaze, as well as the fact that the gaze itself is not a thing to be seized and dominated.

Indeed, this is a strategy that has been emphasized by certain film theorists as a way to engage in feminist expression. Claire Johnston speaks thus of the role of irony in Dorothy Arzner's films: "In all these cases, the discourse of the woman fails to triumph *over* the male discourse and the patriarchal ideology, but its very survival in the form of irony is in itself a kind of triumph, a victory against being expelled or erased: the continued insistence of the woman's discourse is a triumph over nonexistence" (44). Pam Cook, writing also on Dorothy Arzner, speaks also of the woman's entrapment in a system of representation in which her options are limited to playing with the system:

> The films of Dorothy Arzner are important in that they foreground precisely this problem of the desire of women caught in a system of representation which allows them at most the opportunity of playing on the specific demands that the system makes on them. This concept of play permeates every level of the texts: irony operates through the dialogue, sound(s), music, through a play on image, stereotype and gesture, and through complex patterns of parallels and reversals in the overall organization of the scenes.
>
> ("Arzner" 47).

And in an analysis that comes closest to identifying a strategy of distancing, Judith Mayne shows how Dorothy Arzner and other women filmmakers often "turn around" structures of classic Hollywood films. For instance, Arzner turns around the voyeurist look to show the perspective of the woman who is the object of the gaze. This distances the convention of male voyeurism from itself (55–60).

Similarly, Jacquelyn Suter believes that "feminine expression" should aim to point out contradictions, what one could call the space of a text from itself in its double meaning. This would entail "an intervention into patriarchal order by generating a text which foregrounds contradiction and by positioning the spectator in such a way that throws into question his/her voyeuristic relation to the image" (101).

In art history, too, Griselda Pollock sees one of the differences that mark Berthe Morisot's work, as opposed to much of the work of the other (male) Impressionists, as "the juxtaposition on a single canvas of two spatial systems—or at least of two compartments of space often obviously bounderied by some device such as a balustrade, balcony, veranda or embankment" (62). This would seem to parallel Duras's emphasis on the spatial construction of identity. Pollock goes on to remark that both Cassatt and Morisot, although painting scenes that are traditionally those of the domestic space assigned to women, take up that space to question it: "One of the major means by which femininity is thus reworked is by the rearticulation of traditional space so that it ceases to function primarily as the space of sight for a mastering gaze, but becomes the locus of relationships" (87). In my reading of the novels, I have attempted to juxtapose two texts, to read them together in an attempt to do textually what Pollock sees Morisot and Cassatt doing on the canvas. I have attempted to have the structural and thematic relationships between the texts influence my relation to them.

I would finally link this differential and spatial doubling to laughter and to the kind of irony that Candace Lang calls "humor," as opposed to straight irony that "is intended to transmit a message, communicate an idea, or express a thought or sentiment" (5). The ironists she labels as "humorists" differ from the above because their emphasis is not on the transmission of an idea but on something else:

> It is those authors who do not subscribe to the essentially Platonic notion of language as a mere representation of ideas, or of writing as a necessary but potentially dangerous supplement to conceptualization, and who work out the consequences of their anti-metaphysical presuppositions in their texts, whom I call "humorists." The humorist writes with the conviction that language is *always* an essential determinant of thought (not only accidentally or when used perversely), and that its semantic ambiguities and connotative resonances are to be explored and actualized rather than limited or suppressed. (6)

In particular, it is Lang's notion of laughter that I believe is an important strategy in a feminist critical position. Lang discusses Barthes's strategy by saying he wants "to dispense with the ego, not with a sign, but with laughter, not with irony, but with humor" (13). Humor retains pleasure and is affirmative even in the face of the negativity that one must encounter.

Obviously, as Lisa Merrill has said, "satire, irony and comedy pointedly directed can wield enormous social and political power" (272). This is not a humor that uses women or other "others" as victims, that takes individuals as the target, but rather one that points out incongruities and contradictions in the ideologies involved, one that creates a spark of laughter—as when Linda Nochlin describes the juxtaposition of a nude female holding an apple with a nude male holding a banana. Finally, it is a humor that takes the invisible ideologies of culture as the objects to be unveiled.

# Notes

### 2. The Primal Scene of Seduction, Voyeurism, and La Religieuse

1.    This shift in Freud's thought has been the subject of several recent studies. For three different interpretations see Jeffrey Moussaieff Masson, *Freud's Suppression of the Seduction Theory*; William J. McGrath, *Freud's Discovery of Psychoanalysis*; and Martha Noel Evans, "Hysteria and the Seduction of Theory."

2.    The desire to know what woman does in secret, when she is on her own, is especially prevalent in soft-core pornography, whose aim is to "find out what a woman gets up to when she is on her own, (to) find out what women are really like, what their pleasure really is" (Kuhn 30).

3.    Herbert Josephs discusses her transgressive nature in the realm of sexuality and in the convent in his "Diderot's *La Religieuse*: Libertinism and the Dark Cave of the Soul" (742).

4.    Jeffrey Mehlman also makes this link between Foucault and *La Religieuse* in *Cataract: A Study in Diderot*.

5.    Jay Caplan analyzes this "in-between" state as a kind of shuttling motion back and forth in *Framed Narratives: Diderot's Genealogy of the Beholder*.

6.    Beatrice Fink analyzes the fertile metaphor of eating in this text in "Des mets et des mots de Suzanne."

7.    In a similar vein, Elisabeth de Fontenay suggests, in *Diderot: Reason and Resonance*, that Suzanne is not as innocent as she appears.

8.   As Jeffrey Mehlman says, "Diderot's contemporaries were transfixed by the spectacle of a blind sensibility emerging into light, he, on the contrary, was above all concerned with the new understanding that might accrue by sharing philosophically the experience of the blind" (7).

## 3.   The Primal Scene of Castration, Voyeurism, and La Fille aux yeux d'or

1.   See my discussion of this reversal in *Fictional Genders: Role and Representation in Nineteenth-Century French Narrative.*
2.   For a description of one case see Charles S. Grob, "Single Case Study: Female Exhibitionism."
3.   See Fenichel. The copresence of oral/anal and genital modes is discussed by Fenichel in his analysis of the symbolism of the eye itself: it is both genital (as discussed by Freud, it can symbolize the phallus) and oral (to look at is to devour) (373–374). For Rose, this kind of ambiguity is between Imaginary and Symbolic (*Vision* 182–187).
     The ambiguity between self and other is described by Fenichel, when he says that to look at an object can mean for the unconscious to grow like it (to be forced to imitate it) or to force it to grow like oneself (since to look is to devour).
4.   Three studies that discuss these ideas are Mary Ann Doane, *The Desire to Desire: The Woman's Film of the 1940's* (39); E. Ann Kaplan, *Woman and Film: Both Sides of the Camera* (14); and Laura Mulvey, *Visual and Other Pleasures* (129).
5.   Shoshana Felman, 24.
6.   In the women's films studied by Mary Ann Doane, this male gaze becomes the ultimate "scientific" gaze of the doctor who aims to learn the objective truth about women (*Desire*, 43).
7.   When saved or forgiven, she is reintegrated into the correct social order. As Catherine Clément describes the possibility in opera, "The prima donna will be saved, married, and silenced, deprived of her song" (27).
8.   See Pléiade edition, 1562.

## 4.   The Primal Scene of Parental Intercourse, Voyeurism, and Le Voyeur

1.   This is not to suggest that literature must be the one or the other, but texts usually "represent" what they do as either one or the other (when, in fact, what they do is usually a combination of both).

2.     *Gonade* is a word that is bisexual, in a sense, because there is the *gonade mâle* (testicle), and the *gonade femelle* (ovary). Thus the word would include a kind of bisexuality that becomes female (missing).

3.     See Ned Lukacher for a discussion of this intricate interweaving of fiction and reality in the concept of the primal scene, in his *Primal Scenes: Literature, Philosophy, Psychoanalysis*.

4.     The person often thought to be the voyeur in the text, Julien, has a strange film over his eyes, almost as if he were "aveugle."

5.     Bruce Morrisette calls this the "stop motion" of Robbe-Grillet's work (99).

6.     Peter Wollen tells how Yvonne Rainer describes Robbe-Grillet's films "as starting with a whole and then 'cutting it up like a puzzle and re-assembling it.' Her own films, in contrast, are like puzzles that cannot be put together properly, riddles that have no simple answer, or mazes whose center can never be discovered" (37).

7.     John Fletcher notes that Robbe-Grillet himself claimed that the void generated this book (31).

8.     Here we agree with Stephen Heath when he says that the "problem of reading poses itself thematically" in Robbe-Grillet's works (133).

9.     McDougall gives a remarkable example of disavowal in a different type of case, when a child who taps on his mother's pregnant stomach claims that she is not really pregnant ("Pleine comme une bouteille" [58]).

10.    Jacqueline Rose discusses this admirably in *Sexuality in the Field of Vision* (170–184).


**5.**     *Romanticism, Voyeurism, and the Unveiling of Woman*


1.     *Mal du siècle* is the term used in French to describe the general unease of the Romantic sensibility. *Mal* and *mâle* (male) are pronounced quite similarly.

2.     All citations of *La Peau de chagrin* will be from the Garnier-Flammarion edition of 1971, unless otherwise noted.

3.     See Pierre Danger, "La Castration dans *La Peau de chagrin*," 246, for a thorough discussion of the images and function of castration in this novel.

4.     Curiously, Pauline's father is also associated with a key when her mother holds one above the Bible (the law of another Father) to see if Pauline's father is still alive.

5.     It is curious that the woman whom he ultimately loves in this text, Pauline, does not become an object of desire for him until her *father*

returns: in her fatherless world of life with her mother, there is again no possibility of sexual discrimination, and desire is not possible until the return of the father, who brings power and money with him.

6.     There are other small scenes of voyeurism. There are times when Raphaël would look into a window and see a young woman: "In the frame of a rotten window [I could make out] some young girl getting ready, thinking she was alone; I could see only her attractive face and her long hair raised up in the air by a pretty white arm" (143). In another, he watches Pauline sleep (270–271), (as Proust's Marcel watches Albertine; see chapter 7).

7.     This is, of course, a commonplace in Balzac: women are novels, and body language can be read.

8.     Another scene of symbolic blindness accompanies Raphaël's gambling loss: "The stranger closed his eyes softly, his lips blanched" (65). Raphaël also remarks that after losing everything, his body has nothing of worth: "Dead, he was worth fifty francs, but alive he was but a talented man without protectors, without friends, without a place to lay his head, a veritable social zero, useless to the State, which did not care about him at all" (68).

9.     Translations of these technical terms were gleaned from the Penguin edition (225).

10.     The quotation from Sterne is taken from the Penguin translation of this novel.

11.     Bersani labels this side "the alliance of women and youth . . . Stendhal's paradisiacal world of mothers and children" (*Balzac* 100).

12.     Even though this text by Stendhal proposes a new symbolic order, it continues to blame the woman for failure; it is Clélia that brings about the tragedy.

**6.**     *Realism, Voyeurism, and Representation*

1.     Robert J. Niess names the following, among others: Nodier's *Le Peintre de Saltzbourg*, several Balzac texts, Musset's *Le Fils du Titien*, Gautier's *Le Berger*, Flaubert's *Education sentimentale* (6).

2.     Film theorists who pursue a similar line of argument concerning the female gaze in cinematic structures are Linda Williams, "When the Woman Looks" (92); Constance Penley, *The Future of an Illusion: Film, Feminism, and Psychoanalysis* (47); Mary Ann Doane, "*Caught* and *Rebecca*: The Inscription of Femininity as Absence" (198) and "Film and the Masquerade: Theorising the Female Spectator" (79); Janet Bergstrom, "Enunciation and Sexual Difference" (180).

3.    I place this word in parentheses in order to question from the beginning its status as a thing in reality and to emphasize its linguistic, rhetorical nature. As Henry Louis Gates, Jr., writes: "In 1973 I was amazed to hear a member of the House of Lords describe the differences between Irish Protestants and Catholics in terms of their 'distinct and clearly definable differences of race.' 'You mean to say that you can tell them apart?' I asked incredulously. 'Of course,' responded the lord. 'Any Englishman can' " (*"Race"* 5). On the insignificance of the biological differences between populations in different parts of the world, see Anthony Appiah, "The Uncompleted Argument: Du Bois and the Illusion of Race" (21–22).

4.    Coriolis is not "pure" French, however, and is referred to as having a creole origin. Could this "contamination" be the reason why it is he who is destroyed?

5.    The erotism of monkeys appears in another place, in which a white woman is the target of a monkey's desires: the pet monkey, Vermillon, develops a passion for the concierge of the building.

6.    In the latter part of the nineteenth century, there was an increasing fear of "degeneracy" in a France whose birthrate had fallen behind. See Robert A. Nye, *Crime, Madness, and Politics in Modern France.*

7.    See my discussion of Balzac's "Le Chef d'oeuvre inconnu" in *Fictional Genders* for an analysis of this "nothing," painting, and woman.

### 7.    Voyeurism and the Elimination of Difference

1.    All references to *A la recherche du temps perdu* are from *La Prisonnière*, unless otherwise indicated.

2.    *Règles* in a general sense means "rules" and in a specific sense "menstruation."

3.    Another scene that could be investigated from this angle is the one in which, after Bachir's mother shows up, Bachir is no longer attractive to Michel.

4.    Annette Kuhn, in *The Power of the Image*, shows that this desire to know what the other does when alone is a common theme in pornography.

5.    A similar analysis could be made for the scene at La Morinière in which the harvesting of the trees on Michel's land is discussed.

6.    These "phallic" scissors actually belong to Marceline; significantly, they are stolen from the woman and later destroyed, just as Marceline's health is stolen from her, and she is later destroyed.

7.    For a discussion of the problem of gender in nineteenth-century French fiction see my *Fictional Genders.*

8.    Another minor resemblance between the Balzac and Barbey texts

is the English background of the protagonists. Although Barbey credits Balzac's *Le Réquisitionnaire* as having the greatest influence on him, Jacques Petit recounts, in his *Essais de lectures des 'Diaboliques' de Barbey d'Aurevilly*, that Barbey made a "lecture d'ensemble" of Balzac in 1849 and that there are certainly other Balzac texts which influenced Barbey's writing. For a discussion of other connections between Barbey and Proust see Philippe Berthier's "Barbey D'Aurevilly et Proust."

9.    If, as has so often been suggested, "Albertine" should be read as "Albert," then "Alberte" provides an interesting midpoint between the feminine and masculine forms of the name.

10.    Eileen Boyd Sivert studies voyeurism from a narratological point of view in "Narration and Exhibitionism in *Le Rideau cramoisi*"; Jacques Petit discusses voyeurism briefly in *Essais de lectures des 'Diaboliques' de Barbey d'Aurevilly* (136–147); and Marcelle Marini studies a typical primal scene in which a male character peers through a window at a love scene inside and learns a certain truth by doing so, in "Ricochets de lecture: La Fantasmatique des *Diaboliques.*"

11.    Significantly, Brassard says that at the time when he lived behind that curtain, respectable women were for him "dreams hidden, more or less, *under veils*, seen from a distance!" (62, emphasis mine).

12.    This mirroring of positions fits nicely with the mirrors in Proust's and Gide's texts.

13.    Malcolm Bowie has an excellent section on knowledge and *La Prisonnière* in *Freud, Proust and Lacan: Theory as Fiction.*

14.    Roger Shattuck's study, *Proust's Binoculars*, maps out the importance of vision in the texts in his study of optical images and metaphors.

15.    It is of course not only her gazes that reveal her desire but her memory lapses and slips of the tongue, and, as in the Balzac story, Albertine mistakenly pronounces the name of a lover of another gender (134). Curiously, in the Barbey text, Albert(in)e pronounces a word that is never understood.

16.    Bersani puts it this way: "It is true that Marcel devotes most of his energy to trying to find out how Albertine spends her time, but he does this in order to know what kind of desire is separating her from him, to possess the images that possess Albertine" (*Proust* 61).

17.    As Bersani notes, he wants the other women in his life to have the fixity of gaze which his mother had for him (*Proust* 56).

18.    As Gilles Deleuze says: "There is an astonishing relation between the sequestration born of jealousy, the passion to see, and the action of profaning: sequestration, voyeurism, and profanation—the Proustian trinity. For to imprison is, precisely, to put oneself in a position to see without being seen, that is, without the risk of being carried away by the beloved's viewpoint, which excluded us from the world as much as it included us

within it. Thus, seeing Albertine asleep. . . . Seeing therefore transcends the temptation of letting others see, even symbolically" (125).

19.     Bowie shows how the narrator's "commemoration of his mother's tenderness takes a provocative form: in a world where everything else is exuberantly in process, he turns her to stone" (85)—he makes her into a statue.

20.     Philippe Berthier studies the theme of the woman-statue throughout Barbey's texts in *Barbey d'Aurevilly et l'imagination* (Genève: Droz, 1978), 157–164.

21.     See Serge Doubrovsky for an analysis of vampirism or cannibalism in *Writing and Fantasy in Proust* (40–41).

22.     This also fits nicely with Doubrovsky's notion that the madeleine concerns "a question of 'filling' the vacuity of a faltering self with the memories that restore its substance" (11).

23.     Marcel is simultaneously the object of the "jealous" gaze of Françoise (441). And Charlus "contents himself with having the deeds and gestures of Morel unscrupulously spied upon by a detective agency, just like a husband or a lover. . . . The surveillance by the agency that he had charged an old servant with enlisting was so indiscreet that the valets thought they were being followed, and a maid no longer dared to go out in the street, because she thought she always had a policeman on her heels" (216–217).

24.     If Marcel confines himself to his room in a kind of takeover of the woman's role, then this is also a theme from Barbey that perhaps attracted Proust's attention, since Brassard says of himself: "I spent most of my time at home, lying on a great devil of a dark blue sofa" (63).

25.     Bowie also says that Albertine shows that "our other notions of what it is to know are the products of a lingering infantile wish for comfort or mastery" (59).

26.     As Kristin Ross states, the major drama of this volume is "the continuing work of interpretation." See "Albertine; or, The Limits of Representation," *Novel* (Winter 1986): 135.

27.     There is an interesting privileging of the "inner" in the image of the barometer, as if there were a shift in gender identity away from the visible to the invisible "inner" realm.

28.     Here, although I am in agreement with Deleuze that the search for lost time is the search for truth, I think that finding a limited truth is not always a source of joy, but is sometimes that which kills desire (15).

29.     As Jeffrey Mehlman says in a different context: "We too shall have come full circle: having begun with Marcel discovering himself as his mother (in Tante Léonie), we conclude with the author constituting himself as his own heir" (*Structural Study* 59).

30.     This is a notion discussed both by Bersani and Doubrovsky.

Furthermore, Bowie states: "the narrator becomes an incestuously desiring mother—a mother of the very kind that, as a child, he had most wished to have" (83). Shattuck, too, states: "His work had become a living being, making demands of its own . . . He knew he had given birth" (*Proust* 18).
31.     Jacques Petit discusses the rejected child in his *Essais de lectures des 'Diaboliques' de Barbey d'Aurevilly* (94–97).

## 8.     Voyeurism and the Recognition of Difference

1.     This gaze can also be female (her mother's gaze), but it is primarily male.
2.     Kurt Weinberg also sees this structure of doubling: "It would almost seem as though key episodes in *La Princesse de Clèves*, while evoking the abysmal depths of the heart, were constructed *en abîme*, as though to underscore the coincidence that, in heraldry, *coeur* and *abîme* are synonymous terms" (334).
3.     Lyons discusses the triangularity of the positions of these characters in "Speaking in Pictures, Speaking of Pictures: Problems of Representation in the Seventeenth Century" (176).
4.     Joan DeJean notes, in relation to the frequent absence of proper names in the novel, that "characters seem almost interchangeable" (891).
5.     This narcissistic aspect of the portrait scenes fits in nicely with John D. Lyons's observation linking narcissism with representation and with the intense preoccupation with visual perception in the seventeenth century: "It is highly appropriate that Alberti (two centuries before), the inventor of perspective, should designate Narcissus the inventor of painting, for it draws our attention to an image in which the subject is its own object" (167). Lyons also sees this structure in the painting which plays an important part in another Lafayette novel, *Zayde, histoire espagnole:* "The viewer within the image, the figure of the young woman, refuses to direct her gaze toward the figure of the patron who wishes to become the object of her vision" (172–173). In our reading of narcissistic male exhibitionism we are extending Naomi Schor's analysis of Nemours's male narcissism in "Portrait of a Gentleman." There Schor analyzes this scene of voyeurism by showing how Nemours's ultimate pleasure is in seeing the princess looking at his portrait and in her gaze at his (symbolic) male attributes, and how her refusal of Nemours is a refusal of male narcissism.
6.     This parallels Dalia Judovitz's argument, in "The Aesthetics of Implausibility: *La Princesse de Clèves,*" that "the novel attempts to delineate a new order or set of relations, that of representation, that reflects the

difference between signs and what they signify, between language and the world" (1038).

7.     In a fascinating suggestion, Patricia Fedkiw asserts that "To return to S. Thala is to return through a place of letters to the mother: S. Thala gives way to Thalassa, Greek for "the sea," which in French inscribes *la mer*, locus of the mother (la mère)" (83).

8.     "Duras uses this male narrator as a kind of front: first to present and explore the characteristics of traditional male narrative and then to dramatize the undoing of that very narrative, an undoing that is, in a sense, the risky unraveling of Duras's own past history as a writer" (Evans, *Masks* 125).

9.     In her excellent article on Duras, "Marguerite Duras's *Le Ravissement de Lol V. Stein*: A Woman's Long Search for Absence," Eva-Maria Schulz-Jander investigates this identity that "assumes a negative meaning—an absence more than a presence" (224).


## CONCLUSION. *The Comic Gaze*

1.     For an excellent overview of the history and legend of Lady Godiva see Joan C. Lancaster, and H. R. Ellis Davidson, *Godiva of Coventry*.

2.     Jacqueline Rose discusses this story very briefly in *Sexuality in the Field of Vision* (222–223).

3.     See Candace Lang's study of Stendhal and Proust in *Irony/Humor: Critical Paradigms*.

# Bibliography

Abraham, Karl. "Restrictions and Transformations of Scopophilia in Psycho-neurotics; With Remarks on Analogous Phenomena in Folk-Psychology." In *Selected Papers of Karl Abraham*, 169–234. London: Hogarth Press and the Institute of Psycho-analysis, 1973.

Allen, David. "A Psychoanalytic View." In *Exhibitionism: Description, Assessment, and Treatment*, 59–82. New York: Garland Press, 1980.

Appiah, Anthony. "The Uncompleted Argument: Du Bois and the Illusion of Race." In *"Race," Writing, and Difference*, ed. Henry Louis Gates, Jr. Chicago: University of Chicago Press, 1985.

Apter, Emily S. *Andre Gide and the Codes of Homotextuality*. Stanford French and Italian Studies, vol. 48. Saratoga, Calif.: Anma Libri, 1987.

Balzac, Honoré de. "L'Elixir de longue vie." Vol. 11 of *La Comédie humaine*. Paris: Pléiade, 1980. 473–524.

———. *La Fille aux yeux d'or*. Vol. 5 of *La Comédie humaine*. Paris: Pléiade, 1977.

———. *La Peau de chagrin*. Paris: Garnier Flammarion, 1971.

———. *La Peau de chagrin*. Paris: Garnier Frères, 1967.

———. *The Wild Ass's Skin*. Transl. Herbert J. Hunt. New York: Penguin, 1977.

Barbey d'Aurevilly. *Oeuvres complètes*. Paris: Pléiade, 1966.

Baudelaire, Charles. "Le Peintre de la vie moderne." In *Oeuvres Complètes*, 1152–1192. Paris: Pléiade, 1961.

Beasley, Faith. *Revising Memory: Women's Fiction and Memoirs in Seventeenth-Century France*. New Brunswick: Rutgers University Press, 1990.

Benjamin, Walter. *Charles Baudelaire: Lyric Poet in the Era of High Capitalism*. London: New Left Books, 1973.

Berger, John. *Ways of Seeing.* New York: Viking Press, 1972.

Bergstrom, Janet. "Enunciation and Sexual Difference." In *Feminism and Film Theory,* ed. Constance Penley, 159–185. New York: Routledge, 1988.

Bersani, Leo. *From Balzac to Beckett.* New York: Oxford University Press, 1970.

———. *Marcel Proust: The Fictions of Life and of Art.* New York: Oxford University Press, 1965.

Berthier, Philippe. *Barbey d'Aurevilly et l'imagination.* Genève: Droz, 1978.

———. "Barbey D'Aurevilly et Proust," *La Revue des Lettres Modernes* 260 (1971): 23–60.

Bowie, Malcolm. *Freud, Proust and Lacan: Theory as Fiction.* New York: Cambridge University Press, 1987.

Butor, Michel. *Répertoire.* Vol. 1. Paris: Editions de Minuit, 1982.


Campbell, Robert Jean. *Psychiatric Dictionary.* 5th ed. New York: Oxford University Press, 1981.

Caplan, Jay. *Framed Narratives: Diderot's Genealogy of the Beholder.* Theory and History of Literature, vol. 19. Minneapolis: University of Minnesota Press, 1985.

Chodorow, Nancy. *Feminism and Psychoanalytic Theory.* New Haven: Yale University Press, 1989.

Clément, Catherine. *Opera, or The Undoing of Woman.* Trans. Betsy Wing; foreword Susan McClary. Minneapolis: University of Minnesota Press, 1988.

Cook, Pam. "Approaching the Work of Dorothy Arzner." In *Feminism and Film Theory,* ed. Constance Penley, 46–56. New York: Routledge, 1988.

———. "Reflections on Eros," *Screen* 23, nos. 3–4 (Sept.-Oct. 1982): 127–131.

Cordelier, Jean. "Le Refus de la Princesse," *Dix-septième siècle* 108 (1975): 43–57.


Danger, Pierre. "La Castration dans *La Peau de chagrin,*" *L'Année balzacienne* 3 (1982): 227–246.

DeJean, Joan. "Lafayette's Ellipses: The Privileges of Anonymity," *PMLA* 99, no. 5 (October 1984): 884–902.

Deleuze, Gilles. *Proust and Signs.* Trans. Richard Howard. New York: Braziller, 1972.

Diderot, Denis. *La Religieuse.* Paris: Garnier Flammarion, 1968.

Doane, Mary Ann. "*Caught* and *Rebecca:* The Inscription of Femininity as Absence." In *Feminism and Film Theory,* ed. Constance Penley, 196–215. New York: Routledge, 1988.

———. *The Desire to Desire: The Woman's Film of the 1940's.* Bloomington: Indiana University Press, 1987.

———. "Film and the Masquerade: Theorising the Female Spectator," *Screen* 23, nos. 3–4 (Sept.-Oct. 1982): 74–87.

Doubrovsky, Serge. *Writing and Fantasy in Proust.* Trans. Carol Mastrangelo with Paul A. Bové. Lincoln: University of Nebraska Press, 1986.

Duras, Marguerite, and Michelle Porte. *Les Lieux de Marguerite Duras.* Paris: Minuit, 1977.

———. *Le Ravissement de Lol V. Stein.* Paris: Gallimard, 1964.

Evans, Martha Noel. "Hysteria and the Seduction of Theory." In *Seduction and Theory: Readings of Gender, Representation, and Rhetoric*, ed. Diane Hunter. Urbana: University of Illinois Press, 1989.

———. *Masks of Tradition: Women and the Politics of Writing in Twentieth-Century France*. Ithaca: Cornell University Press, 1987.

Fedkiw, Patricia. "Marguerite Duras: Feminine Field of Hysteria," *Enclitic* 6, no. 2 (Fall 1982): 78–86.

Felman, Shoshana. "Rereading Femininity." In *Yale French Studies* 62 (1981): 19–44.

Fenichel, Otto. "The Scopophilic Instinct and Identification." In *Collected Papers of Otto Fenichel*. First Series, 373–397. New York: W. W. Norton, 1953.

Fink, Beatrice. "Des mets et des mots de Suzanne." In *Diderot: Digression and Dispersion*, ed. Jack Undank and Herbert Josephs, 98–105. Lexington, Ky: French Forum, 1984.

Fletcher, John. *Alain Robbe-Grillet* New York: Methuen, 1983.

Fontenay, Elisabeth de. *Diderot: Reason and Resonance*. Trans. Jeffrey Mehlman. New York: George Braziller, 1982.

Freud, Sigmund. *Gesammelte Werke*. Vol. 5. London: Imago, 1942.

———. *Standard Edition of the Complete Psychological Works of Sigmund Freud*. London: Hogarth 1953–.

THE FOLLOWING VOLUMES WERE USED:

*Analysis of a Phobia in a Five-Year-Old Boy*. Vol. 10, 1–149. 1955.

" 'A Child Is Being Beaten': A Contribution to the Study of the Origin of Sexual Perversions." Vol 17, 175–204. 1955.

"Femininity." Vol. 22, 112–135. 1964

*Five Lectures on Psycho-analysis*. Vol. 11, 1–55. 1957.

"From the History of an Infantile Neurosis." Vol. 17, 1–122. 1955.

"Instincts and Their Vicissitudes." Vol 14, 109–140. 1957.

*Introductory Lectures on Psycho-Analysis*. Vol. 16. 1963.

*Jokes and Their Relation to the Unconscious*. Vol. 8. 1960.

*New Introductory Lectures*. Vol. 22, 5–182. 1964.

"Notes Upon a Case of Obsessional Neurosis." Vol. 10, 151–320. 1955.

"The Psycho-analytic View of Psychogenic Disturbance of Vision." Vol. 11, 209–218. 1957.

*Three Essays on the Theory of Sexuality*. Vol. 7, 123–245. 1953.

*Totem and Taboo*. Vol. 13, 1–162. 1955.

Gaillard, Françoise. "La Représentation comme mise en scène du voyeurisme," *Revue des sciences humaines* 154 (1974–1972): 267–282.

Gallop, Jane. *The Daughter's Seduction: Feminism and Psychoanalysis*. Ithaca: Cornell University Press, 1982.

———. *Reading Lacan*. Ithaca: Cornell University Press, 1985.

Gates, Henry Louis, Jr. "The 'Blackness of Blackness': A Critique of the Sign and the Signifying Monkey," *Critical Inquiry* 9 (June 1983): 685–723.

———. "Editor's Introduction: Writing 'Race' and the Difference It Makes." In

"Race," Writing, and Difference, ed. Henry Louis Gates, Jr., 1–20. Chicago: University of Chicago Press, 1985.

Gide, André. L'Immoraliste. Paris: Pléiade, 1958.

Gilman, Sander. Difference and Pathology: Stereotypes of Sexuality, Race, and Madness. Ithaca: Cornell University Press, 1985.

Goncourt, Edmond and Jules de. Manette Salomon. Paris: Union Générale d'Editions, 1979.

Grob, Charles S. "Single Case Study: Female Exhibitionism," The Journal of Nervous and Mental Disease: 173, no. 4 (April 1985): 253–256.

Heath, Stephen. The Nouveau Roman. Philadelphia: Temple University Press, 1972.

Herrmann, Claudine. Les Voleuses de langue. Paris: Edition des femmes, 1976.

Irigaray, Luce. Speculum of the Other Woman. Trans. Gillian C. Gill. Ithaca: Cornell University Press, 1985.

Jameson, Frederic. The Prisonhouse of Language. Princeton: Princeton University Press, 1972.

Johnston, Claire. "Dorothy Arzner: Critical Strategies." In Feminism and Film Theory, ed. Constance Penley, 36–45. New York: Routledge, 1988.

Josephs, Herbert. "Diderot's La Religieuse: Libertinism and the Dark Cave of the Soul," MLN, 91 (1976): 734–755.

Judovitz, Dalia. "The Aesthetics of Implausibility: La Princesse de Clèves," MLN 99 (Dec. 1984): 1035–1056.

Kaplan, E. Ann. Women and Film: Both Sides of the Camera. New York: Methuen, 1983.

———. Introduction to Women in Film Noir. London: British film Institute, 1978.

Kaplan, Louise J. Female Perversions: The Temptations of Emma Bovary. Garden City, New York: Doubleday, 1991.

Kappeler, Susanne. The Pornography of Representation. Minneapolis: University of Minnesota Press, 1986.

Kelly, Dorothy. Fictional Genders: Role and Representation in Nineteenth-Century French Narrative. Lincoln: University of Nebraska Press, 1989.

Kuhn, Annette. The Power of the Image: Essays on Representation and Sexuality. Boston: Routledge and Kegan Paul, 1985.

Lacan, Jacques. Ecrits. Paris: Seuil, 1970–1971.

Lafayette, Madame de. La Princesse de Clèves. Paris: Garnier-Flammarion, 1966.

Lancaster, Joan C., and H. R. Ellis Davidson. Godiva of Coventry. Coventry: Coventry Corporation, 1967.

Lane, Robert C. "Negative Voyeurism and Its Application to Psychoanalytic Practice," Current Issues in Psychoanalytic Practice 1, no. 3 (Fall 1984): 49–68.

Lang, Candace. Irony/Humor: Critical Paradigms. Baltimore: Johns Hopkins University Press, 1988.

Laplanche, J. and J.-B. Pontalis. "Fantasy and the Origin of Sexuality," *International Journal of Psychoanalysis* 49, no. 1 (1968): 1–18.
———. *The Language of Psychoanalysis.* Trans. Donald Nicholson-Smith. New York: W. W. Norton, 1973.
Lukacher, Ned. *Primal Scenes: Literature, Philosophy, Psychoanalysis.* Ithaca: Cornell University Press, 1986.
Lyons, John D. "Speaking in Pictures, Speaking of Pictures: Problems of Representation in the Seventeenth Century." In *Mimesis: From Mirror to Method, Augustine to Descartes,* 166–187. Hanover, N.H.: Dartmouth, 1982.

McDougall, Joyce. *Plaidoyer pour une certaine anormalité.* Paris: Gallimard, 1978.
McGrath, William J. *Freud's Discovery of Psychoanalysis.* Ithaca: Cornell University Press, 1986.
Maillet, Henri. *L'Immoraliste d'André Gide.* Paris: Hachette, 1972.
Marini, Marcelle. "Ricochets de lecture: La Fantasmatique des *Diaboliques*," *Littérature* 10 (May 1973): 3–19.
Masson, Jeffrey M. *Freud's Suppression of the Seduction Theory.* New York: Farrar, Strauss and Giroux, 1984.
Mayne, Judith. "The Woman at the Keyhole: Women's Cinema and Feminist Criticism." In *Re-vision: Essays in Feminist Film Criticism,* ed. Mary Ann Doane, Patricia Mellencamp, and Linda Williams, 49–66. Frederic, Md.: University Publications of America and The American Film Institute, 1984.
Mehlman, Jeffrey. *Cataract: A Study in Diderot.* Middletown, Conn.: Wesleyan University Press, 1979.
———. *A Structural Study of Autobiography.* Ithaca: Cornell University Press, 1974.
Merrill, Lisa. "Feminist Humor: Rebellious and Self-Affirming", *Women's Studies* 15 (1988): 271–280.
Miller, Nancy K. "Emphasis Added: Plots and Plausibilities in Women's Fiction," *PMLA* 96, no. 1 (Jan. 1981): 36–48.
Morrisette, Bruce. *The Novels of Robbe-Grillet.* Ithaca: Cornell University Press, 1975.
Mulvey, Laura. *Visual and Other Pleasures.* Bloomington: Indiana University Press, 1989.
Mylne, Vivienne. "What Suzanne Knew: Lesbianism and *La Religieuse*," *Studies on Voltaire and the Eighteenth Century,* 208 (1982): 167–173.

Neale, Steve. "Sexual Difference in Cinema—Issues of Fantasy, Narrative and the Look," *Oxford Literary Review* 8 (1986): 123–132.
Niess, Robert J. *Zola, Cézanne, and Manet: A Study of L'Oeuvre.* Ann Arbor: University of Michigan Press, 1968.
Nin, Anaïs. *Delta of Venus.* New York: Harcourt Brace Jovanovich 1977.
Nochlin, Linda. "The Imaginary Orient," *Art in America* (May 1983): 119–191.
———. *Women, Art, and Power and Other Essays.* New York: Harper and Row, 1988.
Nye, Robert A. *Crime, Madness, and Politics in Modern France.* Princeton: Princeton University Press, 1984.

Parker, Rozsika and Griselda Pollock. *Old Mistresses: Women, Art and Ideology.* New York: Pantheon Books, 1981.

Penley, Constance. *The Future of an Illusion: Film, Feminism, and Psychoanalysis.* Minneapolis: University of Minnesota Press, 1989.

Petit, Jacques. *Essais de lectures des 'Diaboliques' de Barbey d'Aurevilly.* Paris: Minard, 1974.

Pollock, Griselda. *Vision and Difference: Femininity, Feminism and Histories of Art.* New York: Routledge, 1988.

Proust, Marcel. *A la recherche du temps perdu.* Paris: Pléiade, 1954.

THE FOLLOWING NOVELS WERE USED:

*Le Côté de Guermantes.* Vol. 2, 9–597.

*Du Côté de chez Swann.* Vol. 1, 3–427.

*La Fugitive.* Vol. 3, 419–688.

*La Prisonnière.* Vol. 3, 9–415.

*Sodome et Gomorrhe.* Vol. 2, 601–1131.

*Le Temps retrouvé.* Vol 3, 689–1048.

Ricardou, Jean. *Pour une théorie du nouveau roman.* Paris: Seuil, 1971.

Robbe-Grillet, Alain. *Le Voyeur.* Paris: Minuit, 1955.

Rose, Jacqueline. "Paranoia and the Film System." In *Feminism and Film Theory,* ed. Constance Penley, 141–158. New York: Routledge, 1988.

———. *Sexuality in the Field of Vision.* London: Verso, 1986.

Rosolato, Guy. *Essais sur le symbolique.* Paris: Gallimard, 1964.

———. "Le Fétichisme dont se dérobe l'objet," *Nouvelle Revue de psychanalyse* 2 (Fall 1981): 31–39.

Ross, Kristin. "Albertine; or, The Limits of Representation," *Novel* (Winter 1986): 135–149.

Schor, Naomi. "Portrait of a Gentleman: Representing Men in (French) Women's Writing," *Representations* 20 (Fall 1987): 113–133.

Schulz-Jander, Eva-Maria. "Marguerite Duras's *Le Ravissement de Lol V. Stein:* A Woman's Long Search for Absence," *Symposium,* 40, no. 3 (Fall 1986): 223–233.

Shattuck, Roger. *Marcel Proust.* New York: Viking, 1974.

———. *Proust's Binoculars: A Study of Memory, Time, and Recognition in A la recherche du temps perdu.* Princeton: Princeton University Press, 1983.

Silverman, Kaja. *The Acoustic Mirror: The Female Voice in Psychoanalysis and Cinema.* Bloomington: Indiana University Press, 1988.

———*The Subject of Semiotics.* New York: Oxford University Press, 1983.

Sivert, Eileen Boyd. "Narration and Exhibitionism in *Le Rideau cramoisi,*" *Romanic Review* 70, no. 2 (1979): 146–158.

Stam, Robert, and Roberta Pearson. "Hitchcock's *Rear Window:* Reflexivity and the Critique of Voyeurism," *Enclitic* 7, no. 1 (1983): 136–145.

Stanton, Domna. "The Ideal of 'Repos' in Seventeenth-Century French Literature," *L'Esprit Créateur* 15, nos. 1–2 (Spring-Summer 1975): 79–104.

Stendhal. *La Chartreuse de Parme.* Paris: Gallimard, 1972.

Stoltzfus, Ben. *Alain Robbe-Grillet: The Body of the Text.* Rutherford, N.J.: Fairleigh Dickinson University Press, 1985.

Suter, Jacquelyn. "Feminine Discourse in *Christopher Strong.*" In *Feminism and Film Theory,* ed. Constance Penley, 89–103. New York: Routledge, 1988.

Weinberg, Kurt. "The Lady and the Unicorn, or M. de Nemours à Coulommiers: Enigma, Device, Blazon and Emblem in *La Princesse de Clèves,*" *Euphorion* 71, no. 4 (1977): 306–335.

Williams, Linda. "When the Woman Looks." In *Re-vision: Essays in Feminist Film Criticism,* ed. Mary Ann Doane, Patricia Mellencamp, and Linda Williams, 83–99. Frederic, Md.: University Publications of America and The American Film Institute, 1984.

Wollen, Peter. "Counter-Cinema and Sexual Difference." In New Museum of Contemporary Art, *Difference: On Representation and Sexuality,* 35–40. New York: New Museum of Contemporary Art, 1984.

Zola, Emile. *La Bête humaine.* Vol. 4 of *Les Rougon-Macquart.* Paris: Pléiade, 1966.

———. *L'Oeuvre.* Paris: Garnier-Flammarion, 1974.

# Index